2024

the Essene Book of Days

a personal journal—calendar—spiritual guide
which allows you to dissolve the barriers
to your own spiritual awareness gently
as you reconnect with the rhythms
of the natural order.

by Danaan Parry

the essene book of days 2024

To use this as your personal journal
is to call forth
the wisdom of the ancient Essene tradition,
as revealed in the Dead Sea Scrolls,
in the service of your own Spiritual Development.

Illustrated by Susan Hand
Cover Design by Diane Addesso

Sales of this journal help support the Earthstewards Network, a nonprofit organization founded by Danaan Parry.

Meditations and blessings used in this journal conform to the last revisions made by Danaan Parry in 1996. Astrological and other date information updated annually by Earthstewards Network Publications.

©2023 Estate of Danaan Parry
Earthstewards Network Publications
800-561-2909

All Rights Reserved
Printed on Recycled Paper

ISBN-13: 979-8397644655

table of contents

The Essenes & Me 7

The Apple Tree by Susan Hand 9

The Essenes 11

The Essene Book of Days 11

The Wheel of the Seasons 12

How to Use this Journal 13

Sample Page 15

The Solar and Lunar Cycles 16

Spiritual Practice 16

The Daily Physical Communions of the Essenes 18

My Goals for 2024 21

The Seasonal Meditations and Journal 22

    Imbolc .... February 1
    Spring Equinox .... March 19
    Beltane ....May 1
    Summer Solstice .... June 20
    Teltane .... August 1
    Autumn Equinox .... September 22
    Samhain .... November 1
    Winter Solstice .... December 21

Order Form 305, 369

More on the Essenes 405

Jesus and the Essenes 407

Bibliography 408

About Danaan Parry 409

The Earthstewards Network 410

To Contact Us 412

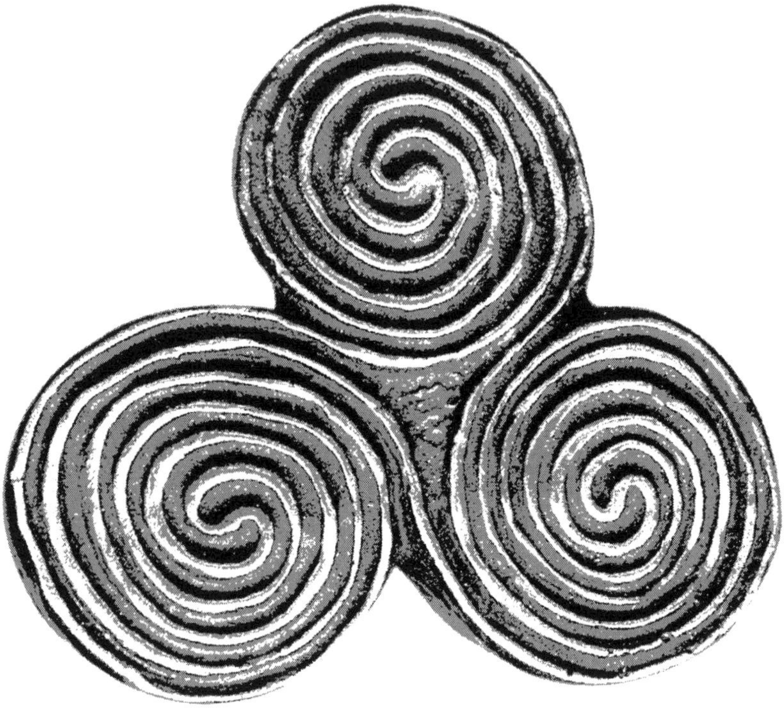

2024

january

S	M	T	W	T	F	S
	1	2	3	4	5	6
7	8	9	10	11	12	13
14	15	16	17	18	19	20
21	22	23	24	25	26	27
28	29	30	31			

february

S	M	T	W	T	F	S
				1	2	3
4	5	6	7	8	9	10
11	12	13	14	15	16	17
18	19	20	21	22	23	24
25	26	27	28	29		

march

S	M	T	W	T	F	S
					1	2
3	4	5	6	7	8	9
10	11	12	13	14	15	16
17	18	19	20	21	22	23
24	25	26	27	28	29	30
31						

april

S	M	T	W	T	F	S
	1	2	3	4	5	6
7	8	9	10	11	12	13
14	15	16	17	18	19	20
21	22	23	24	25	26	27
28	29	30				

may

S	M	T	W	T	F	S
			1	2	3	4
5	6	7	8	9	10	11
12	13	14	15	16	17	18
19	20	21	22	23	24	25
26	27	28	29	30	31	

june

S	M	T	W	T	F	S
						1
2	3	4	5	6	7	8
9	10	11	12	13	14	15
16	17	18	19	20	21	22
23	24	25	26	27	28	29
30						

july

S	M	T	W	T	F	S
	1	2	3	4	5	6
7	8	9	10	11	12	13
14	15	16	17	18	19	20
21	22	23	24	25	26	27
28	29	30	31			

august

S	M	T	W	T	F	S
				1	2	3
4	5	6	7	8	9	10
11	12	13	14	15	16	17
18	19	20	21	22	23	24
25	26	27	28	29	30	31

september

S	M	T	W	T	F	S
1	2	3	4	5	6	7
8	9	10	11	12	13	14
15	16	17	18	19	20	21
22	23	24	25	26	27	28
29	30					

october

S	M	T	W	T	F	S
		1	2	3	4	5
6	7	8	9	10	11	12
13	14	15	16	17	18	19
20	21	22	23	24	25	26
27	28	29	30	31		

november

S	M	T	W	T	F	S
					1	2
3	4	5	6	7	8	9
10	11	12	13	14	15	16
17	18	19	20	21	22	23
24	25	26	27	28	29	30

december

S	M	T	W	T	F	S
1	2	3	4	5	6	7
8	9	10	11	12	13	14
15	16	17	18	19	20	21
22	23	24	25	26	27	28
29	30	31				

Danaan Parry
1939-1996

the essenes and me

My *present* connection to the Essenes began with an "accidental" discovery in 1974. My friend Lila and I were at the Association for Research & Enlightenment (A.R.E.) in Virginia Beach, VA, which houses the library of research done on the life and "readings" of modern Christian mystic, Edgar Cayce. While pouring through the research on his ability to perform medical diagnoses on people while he was in a trance state, I began running into references to communities of white-robed spiritual seekers who lived in the deserts of the Holy Land around the time of Christ.

I remember my first encounter with these references to spiritual communities. It was in a reading/diagnosis for a middle-aged woman from Tennessee. In trance, Edgar Cayce said that her medical problem was only partially caused by dysfunction in her life today. He said that a good deal of it was residual from her life as an Essene in the community of Qumran, a hundred years before the birth of Jesus. He spoke of some conflict in that life that was still unresolved today, thereby leading to her imbalance. I found myself much more intrigued with Cayce's reference to the existence of this Essene community than to the medical diagnosis. I wondered who these people were and what they were doing in that barren land at that time? As I continued my studies of Cayce's readings, I came upon more references to these fascinating beings who walked out of major cities of the fertile crescent and gathered in communities in the most isolated parts of the desert. Cayce made vague reference to their common task, that of preparing the way for something very new and different. I was hooked.

I left the Cayce research and embarked upon a journey of discovery. I was almost addicted to the need to find out who the Essenes were, and why I felt such a deep kinship to these obscure people who I had never heard of. It turned out that not many other people had heard of them either, although it was supposed that they were the ones who wrote the "Dead Sea Scrolls" which had been found in caves near the ruins of an ancient spiritual center outside of Jericho, Palestine near the old Qumran water hole. As I digested the meager writings available on the Essene from biblical scholars, and read the more popular writers like Edmund Bordeaux Szekely, I felt a bond of knowing growing between me and those dedicated visionaries of 2000 years ago. I felt their message of love for one another and of the earth come alive again, needing to be shared in today's troubled times. I packed my bags and went to Qumran.

A Carmelite monastery sits on a hill overlooking another ancient community of the Essenes, and in that monastery is a deep well. The well has been there long before the monastery was built during the Crusades. I know that it is the well of my brother and sister Essenes. I drank from this well, I slept on the stones of the ancient community and felt their message, as alive and as pertinent today as it was 2000 years ago. I hope that this book conveys that message in a form that they would find acceptable.

It took me a few years to integrate the nonlinear learning I experienced at Qumran, but when it was ready to come out, it came out like a freight train. One of the most important places for me on earth is a meadow high-up on the north face of Mount Shasta in Northern California. For years, I have been making an annual spiritual retreat to the mountain, camping out in that same meadow. It is my "power spot." In 1979 I again went to this meadow, but there would be no meditating for me there that year. In the middle of the first night I awoke, grabbed my journal and started writing. Four days later I was *still* writing. I had used every page of my journal, and every square inch of every scrap of paper and paper bag I had with me. When those four days and nights were over, I was exhausted, covered with sweat and higher than a kite. I had the essence of the *Essene Book of Days* down on paper. Every daily meditation, every evening blessing, the interplay of daily and seasonal energies, I had them all. It took another year to bring the book to publication, but that was just the mechanics.

I did the first edition, *The Essene Book of Days for 1982*, entirely alone. My friend Lou Halligan did the artwork and I laid out the type and self-published it. It was a monumental task, and absolutely perfect. It felt like what an Essene would have done, to connect with the book and its essence at each level of reality.

As I look back on the years of integration of the Essene Way into my life, I see the effect they have had on me. My work in international conflict resolution looks very different than the simple lifestyle of the desert communities. But the seeds have been planted in me, and they bear fruit in the strangest ways. I am a preparer-of-the-way for something very new, as new and as needed as The Christ was needed 2000 years ago. And wherever I go, I meet my brothers and sisters who also quietly do their work of preparation. Perhaps you feel it too.

Each year I ask,"Should I change or update the Meditations?" And each year the message is given: "Leave them be; they were given." But most recently, I was told, "Prepare for the second cycle, the millennium." The seasonal flow of life-energy in this book has an important rhythm and consistency to it. It honors the part of us that is deeply rooted in the ebbs and flows of nature; the cycles of life, death and decay that lead to new birth. In our hectic lives, it is this connection to nature that gives us meaning, amidst the chaos that swirls around us. However . . . .

As we approached the year 2000, it seemed that we were being told to prepare for some important changes. The meditations now reflect these changes, so that we are ready for the challenge.

— *Danaan Parry, Bainbridge Island, 1996*

the apple tree

In preparing to illustrate *The Essene Book of Days,* I searched for a symbolic example of the solar and seasonal life of humankind. My long-time love, the apple tree, was my immediate choice for many reasons.

An ancient apple tree shaded the home where I grew up along the Beaverkill River in the Catskill Mountains of New York State. It was a standard-sized tree with three different grafts bearing three types of apples. Year after year the tree survived with its branches and trunk becoming more gnarled and twisted, but always more firmly rooted in the earth and our existence.

Its presence inspired my imagination. Its kindly branches embraced our very lives with its being. Bountiful pink and white blossoms heralded the promise of spring and, as our yearly life matured, so did the tree's fruits. In summer, often after a storm, our lawn would be peppered with small green apples that we loved to fling on sticks as far as we could to the other side of the river. As the seasons passed by our door yard the tree remained our beautiful guardian and spoke to us of change and productivity.

In caring for our own orchard, my husband Peter and I have accumulated a sizable amount of information concerning the culture and lore of the tree. From this hobby, I have formed a growing awareness of the tree's striking symbolism and of the many lovely myths concerning the apple tree. Most of the old tales contend with the idea of the tree's seasonal journey and its part in the beautiful and mysterious chain of life.

The apple tree is often found in the Greek myths. In one story Mother Earth, Rhea, gives the golden apple tree of eternal life to Hera when she marries Zeus. The tree is planted by Hera on an island of paradise at the edge of the world and is protected by Atlas's daughters, the Hesperides, and a dragon who never sleeps. They protected this symbol of life-everlasting and only allowed the gods to have access to its fruits. In this story, as in many others, the three golden apples of immortality gave representation to the passage of time, the necessity of love, and to the creative and procreative instincts.

Another tale relates the story of Pomona, the goddess of the art and science of fruit culture. She is said to have been so involved with the care of her orchards that she never noticed her admirers. Vertumnus, the god of the changing seasons, was the suitor who finally won her affection and married her. Together they were the guardians of the fruit trees.

In the old Welsh tales, Avalon ("aval" meaning apple) is described as a place of eternal happiness where there is no age, sickness, or death. The isle is ruled by the Celtic goddess of death, Morgan Le Fay and the three fates who ruled the earth, the sea, and the underworld. When King Arthur dies and leaves Camelot he is met by three virtuous women in black who carry him to Avalon where he will rest in the protection of the women and the apple trees until he is needed to return again to save the world.

It is for these reasons and also for my deep love for the apple tree at all times of the year, that I feel it is a delightful symbol of the coming of a new belief and a new life. It is a powerful example of tenacity and the ability to withstand wind, rain, cold, and heat, and all that may be encountered on the cyclical journey of seasonal life.

— *Susan B. Hand*

the essenes

Discovery of the Dead Sea Scrolls in 1947, in a series of caves near the Dead Sea, brought to new light the wisdom-teachings of the Essene communities that existed in the deserts of the Middle East well over 2000 years ago.

These spiritual communities were dedicated to preserving the ancient teachings and to preparing the way for the new age of Pisces, when Christ energy would flood the world. They lived in simple harmony with all of nature, following the spiritual wisdom of their inner voices, which the Buddhists call "living one's dharma." Their spiritual practices allowed them to absorb and channel the vibrations and healing powers of the plants, the sun, and the four elements of earth, air, fire, and water, for their own nourishment and for the healing of the earth itself. We have much to learn from these simple folk.

The Essene teachings tell us that John the Baptist was an Essene master, and that he and other Essene teachers trained the initiate Jesus in the ancient wisdom during that 20-year period of his life about which the Bible is silent. (More information on the Essenes is given at the end of this journal.)

the essene book of days

In this personal journal are presented many of the teachings of the Essenes which relate to our re-attunement to the natural cycles and rhythms of the earth and the cosmos. The teachings are given as daily readings which change according to the day of the week and the point on the seasonal wheel. Each reading/meditation involves a surrender of personality and an uplifting of personal vibration to align with the universal vibration. We find, as we proceed through the year, a heightened sense of identification with our higher Self and with the Plan of Light.

The evening Blessings attune us to the spiritual forces which will slowly guide our evolution toward higher consciousness, for ourselves and for our planet.

In addition to Essene teachings, this journal utilizes ancient Celtic wisdom relating to the pastoral and cosmic energies of the seasonal wheel for the northern hemisphere. These Celtic teachings are totally in harmony with the Essene teachings and serve as yet another illustration for the Oneness of the Spirit.

In accordance with ancient tradition, the solar year is divided into eight sub-seasons, as shown on the Wheel of the Seasons on the next page.

There are seven meditations for each sub-season, one for each day of the week. The repetition of these meditations allows the energies of that seasonal segment to become an integral part of your daily life.

The Wheel Of the Seasons

Summer Solstice

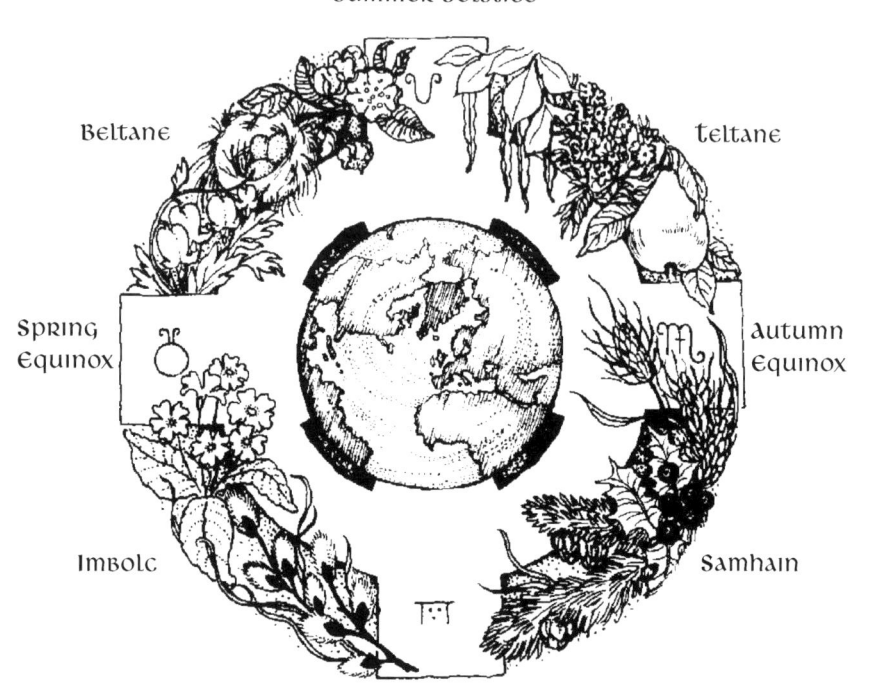

Beltane

Teltane

Spring Equinox

Autumn Equinox

Imbolc

Samhain

Winter Solstice

how to use this journal

For each day of the year, there is a full page. Each page contains the daily and seasonal information which indicates the quality of the earthly and cosmic vibrations affecting your environment and your physical, mental, and spiritual bodies that day. (This information applies only to the northern hemisphere. If you were to visit a friend in Argentina, for example, the information would be valid except that you would have to transpose all points on the wheel of the year, e.g. Winter Solstice would be Summer Solstice, Spring Equinox would become Fall Equinox, etc.)

deepening and opening

Deepenings and Openings are simple physical activities suggested for each day, in conjunction with the Morning Meditation. Use these to intensify your intuitive spiritual connection with every day of your life.

On every page there is an opportunity to develop that intense physical connection with your world that was the mark of Essene life.

The Essenes were committed to bringing their spiritual awareness into their daily lives — to make it real and meaningful and workable. If you take the small amount of time needed to practice the changing symbolic activities in each *deepening and opening*, you, too, will experience this blending of spirit and matter.

It will take months for the subtle intuitive awareness to permeate your body-mind. Do not intellectualize meanings into your actions of deepening and opening. Simply do the activities and allow your body and your inner wisdom to perform their magic in you. After this year of practice, then look back and observe the changes in your awareness.

morning meditation

It is suggested that the Morning Meditation be read aloud, if possible, immediately prior to entering a state of relaxed meditation, but meditation is not essential. Simply reading the Morning Meditation each day will work.

If you meditate with a group, the Morning Meditation is equally appropriate for sharing just prior to group silent meditation. It will create a high vibration with which the group may resonate during meditation.

Reading the Meditation aloud, even if you are alone, amplifies the penetrating effect of the vibration. (You might even try shouting it and watch the results!)

As you enter into your own meditation, simply allow the thought forms of what you have just read to float within you for a few moments and then let go of them and surrender to your meditation. If you do not meditate, then read the words again silently and dwell for a few moments on any area that catches your attention. And then let it go.

spiritual focus

Next, use the space in the middle of the page which begins "Today I will bring the spirit of (the quality of that day) to my (list day's activities)." Here is a wonderful opportunity for you to program your biocomputer, your brain, to include spiritual awareness as you go about your day. Each day suggests a spiritual focus from the Essene daily communions, and you can incorporate this focus into your daily activity. This raises the vibration of that activity to the higher vibration of spiritual service.

For example, on Fridays in January the focus is on what we would call Newness. The journal states, "Today I will bring the spirit of Newness to my . . .." You may wish to list some of the activities that you have in mind for the day that is unfolding before you. (See the sample page at the end of this section.) Then notice as "Newness" becomes infused into these daily activities. You do not have to "figure out" how to do it. You are working at a level of consciousness that transcends the intellect. Patience and faith and commitment are the tools for this job, not wracking your brain for answers.

feelings

This section of the page is for you to record any feelings, thoughts, traumas, dramas, joys, dreams — whatever feels appropriate in your day. Months from now, you will re-read these entries and be amazed at the unfolding of your journey. You are your own best teacher, so try to make some entry each day.

evening blessing

In the evening, read the Blessing. You may choose to use it as a blessing before your evening meal, or perhaps as an affirmation before going to sleep. Read it aloud.

The wisdom in the Blessing attunes us to the particular energies present during that evening and at that time of year and gives much grist for the "dream mill" that turns as we sleep.

claiming your "special days"

The upper corner of each page gives the day and date. There is a line under the moon at the bottom of each page for indicating special days for you. Some holidays are already indicated in this space. We suggest you use these spaces to write in those days which you feel are important to you. For example, you might indicate birthdays, important astrological transits, menstrual cycle, your conception day, any day to which you wish to bring special awareness.

seasonal focus
The seed stirs in the earth.

Friday, January 7, 2000

morning focus
The angel of Air

opening
Before reading meditation, take three very
deep breaths, exhaling fully so your lungs empty of air.

meditation *Feels great!*
There is a force in me,
Pushing, pushing,
Beginning its outbreath
After a long sleep.
Sacred darkness slowly yields
To newborn light.
As I move outward
From the s...
To s...
I sha... ...ife with all,
The in... ...Mother
That nu... ...me
Through the winter's night.

today I will bring the spirit of Newness to my _____
love relationships

feelings *It was so hard to sit still during this morning's meditation — but the deep breathing really helped a lot. I am so impatient — I want winter to be over! I ask for patience — to know that the growth is occurring in me! I can feel myself changing*

the blessing
I ask that the Light,
The Creative Force of the universe,
Breathe the cleansing outbreath of spirit
Into my heart and my deeds.
I rejoice in this time of promise,
Of new stirrings, of the rebirth of the lotus
Which will one day open fully to God.

Today is Caitlin's Birthday!

evening focus
Our Heavenly Father

15

solar and lunar cycles

At the top of each journal page is the symbol of the sun (see right). Within it is represented the relative amount of outward solar energy present on that day, taking Summer Solstice as 100%. This means the sun symbol will be completely white, with a small black dot in the center to remind us that in total yang is the seed of yin, and on the Winter Solstice in December the symbol will be completely black with a small white dot at the center. The sample shown here represents the Spring Equinox, when yin and yang are balanced.

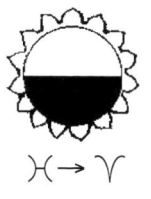

The symbol below the sun is the astrological sign in which the sun resides that day. The sign on this page shows that the sun is moving from Pisces to Aries, which would make this the symbol for Spring Equinox.

The symbol of the moon (shown left) can be found at the bottom of each journal page. This symbol shows the correct lunar phase for that day.

In this way, we make the progress of the solar and lunar cycles a part of our daily awareness, and we become more in tune with the rhythms of the world in which we live.

Aries	Taurus	Gemini	Cancer	Leo	Virgo
♈	♉	♊	♋	♌	♍

Libra	Scorpio	Sagittarius	Capricorn	Aquarius	Pisces
♎	♏	♐	♑	♒	♓

PLEASE NOTE: *All times and astrological notations in the* **Essene Book of Days** *correspond to Eastern Standard Time and Eastern Daylight Time. Please adjust for your time zone and daylight saving time.*

spiritual practice

There are very few remaining ways in which the environment that is most conducive to spiritual growth can be experienced in our modern world. One of these is through commitment to an ongoing spiritual practice. This means no more than the creation of a consistent time and space to devote to one's spirituality and the filling of that time with a repeated, concentrated regimen that allows the seeker to dwell totally in his or her spiritual nature. The key elements here are, in the words of Edgar Cayce, "patience, persistence, consistency."

If you feel that you are at the point in your own spiritual journey where you are ready to dive more deeply and to make the commitment that a spiritual practice requires, then you can use all the aspects of the *Essene Book of Days* as your spiritual practice.

As with all spiritual practices, the value, and also the difficulty, comes from transcending your moods, your ups and downs, your lower will. The practice helps you to develop your higher will, which permits you to maintain your commitment to yourself and your growth, regardless of the mood swings of your personality.

To utilize this book as a spiritual practice, daily meditation is required. Choose a time early in the day, a time that you know will be available to you each day. Your body will come to anticipate the consistency of your practice, and changing the time will be detrimental to your progress. This may require that you arise half an hour earlier than usual to assure a consistent time and quiet space for your meditation.

Read the Morning Meditation aloud each day, and then enter silent meditation for 10, 15, up to 30 minutes. After meditation, record your reflections and faithfully follow the suggestions in the section "How to Use this Journal." You may encounter a strong resistance welling up within you as you consistently maintain your daily practice. This is the classic "dark night of the soul" that the mystics have written about and wrestled with for ages. There will come a time when you will break through this ego resistance and begin to sense the clarity of spiritual vision that lies beyond the facade, the ego image of who you thought you were. The journey through resistance is an uphill climb for us all, and there has never been a more worthwhile endeavor. In fact, it is quite possibly the *only* endeavor.

As you develop your practice, you may decide to immerse yourself even more in the spirit of the ancient Essene way. For this, refer to the section on Daily Physical Communions of the Essenes which describes the methods used by the Essenes to bring a more physical dimension to each daily practice. Do not add this routine to your practice until you are sure you are ready to make the commitment to do it every day. This is a powerful vehicle for bodily transformation and not to be taken lightly. You will know if and when it is correct for you.

Consistency is important, however this journal is used. At the very least, read and take into yourself the Morning Meditation and Evening Blessing each day and write down something. The process is subtle, as is all of your own true spiritual growth. In the words given to the Essenes, "Be still and know that I Am God."

***

Scattered throughout this book are "teaching stories," modern stories located at specific points in the solar year. They do not pertain to the Essenes of 10 or 15 B.C., but to us, to our lives today. These are intended to bring the Essene teachings into a twentieth century framework so that the wisdom of the Essene stays fresh and relevant, challenging us to "love one another as *ourselves*."

the daily physical communions of the essenes

It was of the highest importance to the Essene communities that the world of the spirit would be integrated with the world of the flesh. They practiced not only mental but also physical attunement to the higher forces.

The following daily attunements are in keeping with this Essene practice. Combined with daily meditation, they can be used to connect intimately the world of the spirit, mind, and physical body that exist within your being.

saturday

The beginning of the Essene week is devoted to food consciousness. If possible, reserve this day for fasting. Take in only water, or perhaps some juice or herbal tea. If fasting is not possible every Saturday, consume as little food as is necessary and become highly conscious of the quality and the benefits of the food. Attune your body to the vibration of the liquid or food, so that you become nourished by its essence. In this way, water alone can become your food of life.

sunday

A day devoted to tending to the earth. In the spirit of regeneration, healing, and abundance, give as much time as possible to creative work in the garden. This garden may be your backyard garden, a communal farm, your rosebushes, or a small section of your city park that cries out for loving care. The focus is on your role as a steward of your planet, and on learning to absorb life energy from the plants and to give it back again.

monday

A day of silence. Change nothing in your daily routine with the exception of talking. Allow the world to deal with your silence, and be fully conscious of how you deal with it. Contemplate the many alternative ways of relating and communicating, and how the medium of speech at times dilutes the intensity of our relationships. Write in your journal about your experience.

tuesday

A day of simple contemplation of the joy of life, the fullness of your blessings. After morning meditation and breakfast, take an extended walk in a natural setting, silently. Avoid distractions, and focus on the colors, smells, and the state of nature at this point in the seasonal cycle. If a morning walk is not possible, any time of day or night will do. The focus is on creation of a silent, meditative walk through nature, becoming one with your surroundings. Write in your journal afterwards.

wednesday

Here the focus is on the sun, allowing its power and light to enter your body. Rise early and go to a place where you can observe sunrise. Begin your morning meditation as the first rays of the sun bathe your body. If possible, allow the sun's rays to nourish your naked body this day, even when the weather is cold.

thursday

A day of purification, of cleansing all the bodies of you. Carry the spirit of purification with you into the meditations. Arrange to bathe your body in a leisurely, contemplative atmosphere. Consider the connections between your own water, your blood, and the waters of life. Consider the sap in trees, the rivers, lakes, and oceans, the circulatory system of our Mother the Earth. Lengthy immersions in hot and cold tubs are of value, as is an occasional enema for internal cleansing (no more often than once a month, unless recommended for healing of a particular condition).

friday

The inbreath and outbreath of the universe is contemplated through long periods of controlled breathing. During meditation, alternately block the left and right nasal passages, taking ten breaths through each. Throughout the day, continually bring your awareness to your breath, taking long, deep inhalations frequently. Contemplate your Stillpoint, which occurs between exhalation and inhalation. It is the point where we "die" at each outbreath and are reborn with each inbreath. Write in your journal.

notes

my goals for 2024*

(6 month) Deepening   Between now and Summer Solstice (June 20),
                        I will deepen:

                        _____

                        _____

                        _____

                        _____

Opening   Between now and June 20, I will open up to:

                        _____

                        _____

                        _____

                        _____

(1 year) Deepening   Between now and Winter Solstice (December 21),
                        I will deepen:

                        _____

                        _____

                        _____

                        _____

Opening   Between now and December 21, I will open up to:

                        _____

                        _____

                        _____

                        _____

* Use this goal-setting as a gentle focus for yourself.
No guilt trips please, just awareness of your process.

Monday, January 1, 2024

seasonal focus
The seed stirs in the earth.

morning focus
The angel of Life

opening
Study your face in a mirror; what do you really see? Take this awareness to your meditation.

meditation
Slowly the balance shifts from inner creativity
To outer manifestation.
Slowly my core of inner strength streams outward
Along my nervous system,
Bringing health and vitality to the whole of my being.
The life in me prepares itself,
Strengthens itself for the moment in the cycle
When it will overflow its bounds,
Surging toward a oneness with all of life.

today I will bring the spirit of Honesty to my _____
_____

feelings_____
_____
_____
_____
_____
_____
_____
_____

evening focus
The angel of Peace

New Year's Day

the blessing
I evoke the forces of peace and harmony
And ask these forces
To prepare me as a channel
For their overlighting guidance.
My heart swells with thanksgiving
For a winter of inner preparation
Which will lead me to the first step
In becoming a channel for peace:
That of finding peace within my own being.

seasonal focus
The seed stirs in the earth.

morning focus
The angel of Joy

Tuesday, January 2, 2024

opening
Loosen all clothing. As you read,
cause your belly to hang out and relax.

meditation
Wherein lies the source of joy?
The inner peace of winter prepares me for the answer;
It shouts quietly to me,
"Do not seek happiness; seek rather
Your true nature, your true reason for being;
Seek your dharma.
Joy is the child of completeness,
Of living your dharma."
At this time of new, small beginnings,
I feel the clarity of vision growing in me,
And I am pregnant with joy.

today I will bring the spirit of Joy to my _____

feelings _____
_____
_____
_____
_____
_____

the blessing
The silent stirring of the new life in me
Fills me with an inner strength.
The strength is good;
And it comes from a place deep inside my being
That has only been reached
In the depth of ego-death.
This power I trust;
This is the power of love and compassion
The world cries out for.
The veil of illusion lifts slowly and reveals
The direction of my path.

evening focus
The angel of Power

Wednesday, January 3, 2024

seasonal focus
The seed stirs in the earth.

morning focus
The angel of the Sun

deepening
Focus on a candle flame before and after the reading.

meditation
The promise, the prophecy, is within me.
That which I have waited for is now present.
No longer need I fear.
Within me shines
The first glimmering of the Light,
And I am filled with the awareness
That the fulfilling of the prophecy
Is not a thing apart from me;
It *is* me.
As the first small rays of the sun
Return to my world,
I, too, return slowly to the world of form.
I humbly accept the mantle of that which I AM.
As I merge my light
With the light of all the beings of Light,
I surrender to my own divinity.

today I will bring the spirit of Courage to my _____

feelings _____

evening focus
The angel of Love

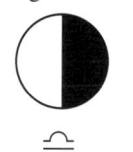

the blessing
Life, you are a profound expression of Love.
The gentle, quiet expansion
Of the winter-mother's love
Fills me with inner joy.
I bow before the purity of this love
Which nourishes without attachment.

seasonal focus
The seed stirs in the earth.

morning focus
The angel of Water

deepening
Hold water in your cupped hand as you read.
After, drink it as a sacred act.

meditation
As the clear winter water
Nourishes the seed within the earth,
I am nourished by new-found awareness
Of who I truly am.
This awareness has not yet fully matured,
And I rest content
In the arms of the unfolding universe,
Which will reveal all wisdom
In its time.
The Power of the unmanifest
Even now works within my spiritual heart,
And I am at peace.

today I will bring the spirit of Contentment to my

feelings _____

_____
_____
_____
_____

Thursday, January 4, 2024

the blessing
I call upon my own internal voice,
Which is ever linked with the universal voice
Of inner knowing.
I ask, as I slowly move
From winter's inner development
To the first stirrings of outer work,
That I be given the strength
To trust my own still small voice,
Whose guidance is never faulty.
For this blessing I give thanks.

evening focus
The angel of Wisdom

25

Friday, January 5, 2024

seasonal focus
The seed stirs in the earth.

morning focus
The angel of Air

opening
Before reading meditation, take three very deep breaths, exhaling fully so your lungs empty of air.

meditation
There is a force in me,
Pushing, pushing,
Beginning its outbreath
After a long sleep.
Sacred darkness slowly yields
To newborn light.
As I move outward
From the stillpoint of outer death
To share my new-found breath of life with all,
I shall never forget
The inbreath of the Mother
That nurtured me
Through the winter's night.

today I will bring the spirit of Newness to my _____

feelings _____
_____
_____
_____
_____
_____
_____

evening focus
Our Heavenly Father

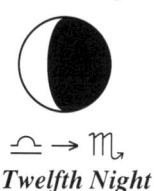

♎ → ♏
Twelfth Night

the blessing
I ask that the Light,
The Creative Force of the universe,
Breathe the cleansing outbreath of spirit
Into my heart and my deeds.
I rejoice in this time of promise,
Of new stirrings, of the rebirth of the lotus
Which will one day open fully to God.

From Age to Age

Around the time of the "twelfth night" after the infusion of Christ energy into our world, it is appropriate to ask about what is being born in ourselves.

Within many ancient spiritual traditions there exists the concept of an Age. It is always two thousand years in duration and always denotes a particular change process that is occurring during that period for the evolution of consciousness, for the good of all beings. Is it simply a coincidence that two thousand years ago, the Essenes were working in spiritual communities, preparing the way for something that was to change the course of human events forever? (One translation of Essene is "preparer of the Way.") And here we are today, in the birthing stage of a new millennium, feeling the urges to prepare ourselves for something very new, a new paradigm.

What were they preparing the way for two thousand years (one Age) ago? Their tradition tells of Missiayah, a term that comes from the even more ancient roots of the Melkezedekian theology. Today the Christian term Messiah is familiar to us and means Savior. But in its ancient meaning it was not a person, it was an energy. Missiayah was an energy field, a consciousness, that every two thousand years entered the earth plane. And if the earth was ready to receive this energy of expanded consciousness, then it would "alight" upon this plane and human consciousness would begin to expand so as to embrace it. And if the earth was not ready, it would come again. When? Why, two thousand years later of course.

The Essenes were, exactly one Age ago, helping to prepare our world for the coming of the Missiayah. They were, if you will, the "100th Monkey Effect" of that Age. They must have sensed that it does not require all beings to be preparing the way, but it does require a very focused, aware critical mass. The Essenes helped to bring in the energy of Missiayah which was missing and needed at that time in their world. What was the quality of that energy, that expanded consciousness, two thousand years ago? And what does it have to do with us today?

To understand this we must be aware that the spiritual traditions which speak of "Ages" also say that it takes the full two thousand years for the new, entering energy to be fully integrated on this material plane. In other words, what came in two thousand years ago is only now being consciously accepted in any broad manner. It has taken us the entire Age to "get it." What entered this plane at the beginning of what astrology calls the Piscean Age was Agape, brotherly and sisterly love. Love beyond ownership or possession, love of one human being for another simply because they are worthy of love and are a valued part of the same human family. That was the love-energy that was missing at that time, and it was this that Christ brought to our world, changing the course of human life forever.

As you may have noticed, we humans have been working on it for two thousand years now, and we still haven't quite got it. Our task is to "get it."

As the labor pains of the new birth, of the Aquarian Age, increase and quicken, there are those who are called from within to strengthen and share our love for all beings, beyond the differences that have divided us. We are just beginning to open to our sisters and brothers everywhere. Soon, we just might have developed that critical mass of love energy that is needed for the next infusion of Missiayah to alight this earth. Is this your life-purpose? Are we the Essenes of this new Age? It's worth considering.

And what will be the quality of this new infusion of love, of Missiayah? Two thousand years ago it brought the message "all men and women are your brothers and sisters; love one another." This time the message expands to, "You and I are not only brothers and sisters, we are One." Two thousand years ago the world could barely hear the wisdom of "love one another." It is something that we have been struggling with for almost 20 centuries. And now, as we, or at least a critical mass of "we," begin to open to that wisdom, we are preparing the way for the next teaching that tells us there really is no "other;" we are one. Two thousand years ago the Essenes helped to bring through the radical idea that we are all connected and must love one another as ourselves. Today, we are the preparers of the way for the intellect-boggling idea that the "other" is an illusion. You and I are one consciousness reflected in an infinite rainbow of seeming difference. Behind the illusion, we are One. Everyone. No one is excluded.

In this light our path becomes clear. As we embrace the wisdom of the preceding Age, we simultaneously prepare our world for the newness that awaits. We will learn to "love one another *as ourselves.*"

So it is now appropriate that you spend some moments reflecting on your life up to this point, what it has taught you about the coming tomorrows of your life, and what you might be "preparing for" in the new millennium.

Now that it is the year 2024, what does my intuitive sense of knowing tell me about what I have been and am *preparing for?*

I am preparing the way for:

_____

Now that the year 2024 is here, my life will have:

_____

My work in the world will be:

_____

seasonal focus
The seed stirs in the earth.

morning focus
Our Earthly Mother

deepening
Hold a seed in your hand as you read the meditation.

meditation
I am bathed in an ocean
Of love and guidance
As I begin my journey
Out from the center.
All the earth nourishes me
And I return this nourishment
As love.
As the wisdom of the Mother
Slowly urges me to new awareness,
I joyfully surrender
The safety of the womb
So as to experience my part
In the unfolding plan of Light.

today I will bring the spirit of Giving to my _____

feelings _____

Saturday, January 6, 2024

the blessing
As the long night slowly yields to day,
Even as the old millennium surrenders to the new,
I, too, surrender to my next step
Which carries me toward
My natural state of limitlessness.
The winter teaches me of inner abundance,
Inner completeness,
As I now prepare for the outer learning
That this new year brings.

evening focus
The angel of Eternal Life

Epiphany

Sunday, January 7, 2024

seasonal focus
The seed stirs in the earth.

morning focus
The angel of Earth

deepening
Hold earth, dirt, in your hand as you read. Feel it.

meditation
From the calm place
At my spiritual center
I have touched the wisdom
Of the earth in winter.
Regeneration streams
From the holy earth to me,
And I am full.
I now gather to me the lessons
Which will empower me
To channel this life-giving earth force
For the good of all beings.

today I will bring the spirit of Calmness to my _____

feelings _____

evening focus
The angel of Creative Work

the blessing
The winter's journey
To the source of inner creativity
Now turns and guides me slowly
Toward outward manifestation.
Depth will be fulfilled in expansion
As I contemplate
My dharmic path of service.
I give thanks for the Mother's gifts
Which have brought me to this.

seasonal focus
The seed stirs in the earth.

morning focus
The angel of Life

opening
Study your face in a mirror; what do you really see? Take this awareness to your meditation.

meditation
Slowly the balance shifts from inner creativity
To outer manifestation.
Slowly my core of inner strength streams outward
Along my nervous system,
Bringing health and vitality to the whole of my being.
The life in me prepares itself,
Strengthens itself for the moment in the cycle
When it will overflow its bounds,
Surging toward a oneness with all of life.

today I will bring the spirit of Honesty to my _____

feelings _____

Monday, January 8, 2024

the blessing
I evoke the forces of peace and harmony
And ask these forces
To prepare me as a channel
For their overlighting guidance.
My heart swells with thanksgiving
For a winter of inner preparation
Which will lead me to the first step
In becoming a channel for peace:
That of finding peace within my own being.

evening focus
The angel of Peace

Tuesday, January 9, 2024

seasonal focus
The seed stirs in the earth.

morning focus
The angel of Joy

opening
Loosen all clothing. As you read,
cause your belly to hang out and relax.

meditation
Wherein lies the source of joy?
The inner peace of winter prepares me for the answer;
It shouts quietly to me,
"Do not seek happiness; seek rather
Your true nature, your true reason for being;
Seek your dharma.
Joy is the child of completeness,
Of living your dharma."
At this time of new, small beginnings,
I feel the clarity of vision growing in me,
And I am pregnant with joy.

today I will bring the spirit of Joy to my _____
_____

feelings _____
_____
_____
_____
_____

evening focus
The angel of Power

the blessing
The silent stirring of the new life in me
Fills me with an inner strength.
The strength is good;
And it comes from a place deep inside my being
That has only been reached
In the depth of ego-death.
This power I trust;
This is the power of love and compassion
The world cries out for.
The veil of illusion lifts slowly and reveals
The direction of my path.

32

seasonal focus
The seed stirs in the earth.

morning focus
The angel of the Sun

deepening
Focus on a candle flame before and after the reading.

meditation
The promise, the prophecy, is within me.
That which I have waited for is now present.
No longer need I fear.
Within me shines
The first glimmering of the Light,
And I am filled with the awareness
That the fulfilling of the prophecy
Is not a thing apart from me;
It *is* me.
As the first small rays of the sun
Return to my world,
I, too, return slowly to the world of form.
I humbly accept the mantle of that which I AM.
As I merge my light
With the light of all the beings of Light,
I surrender to my own divinity.

today I will bring the spirit of Courage to my _____

feelings _____

Wednesday, January 10, 2024

the blessing
Life, you are a profound expression of Love.
The gentle, quiet expansion
Of the winter-mother's love
Fills me with inner joy.
I bow before the purity of this love
Which nourishes without attachment.

evening focus
The angel of Love

Thursday, January 11, 2024

seasonal focus
The seed stirs in the earth.

morning focus
The angel of Water

deepening
Hold water in your cupped hand as you read.
After, drink it as a sacred act.

meditation
As the clear winter water
Nourishes the seed within the earth,
I am nourished by new-found awareness
Of who I truly am.
This awareness has not yet fully matured,
And I rest content
In the arms of the unfolding universe,
Which will reveal all wisdom
In its time.
The Power of the unmanifest
Even now works within my spiritual heart,
And I am at peace.

today I will bring the spirit of Contentment to my

feelings _____

_____

_____

_____

_____

_____

evening focus
The angel of Wisdom

the blessing
I call upon my own internal voice,
Which is ever linked with the universal voice
Of inner knowing.
I ask, as I slowly move
From winter's inner development
To the first stirrings of outer work,
That I be given the strength
To trust my own still small voice,
Whose guidance is never faulty.
For this blessing I give thanks.

seasonal focus
The seed stirs in the earth.

morning focus
The angel of Air

Friday, January 12, 2024

opening
Before reading meditation, take three very deep breaths, exhaling fully so your lungs empty of air.

meditation
There is a force in me,
Pushing, pushing,
Beginning its outbreath
After a long sleep.
Sacred darkness slowly yields
To newborn light.
As I move outward
From the stillpoint of outer death
To share my new-found breath of life with all,
I shall never forget
The inbreath of the Mother
That nurtured me
Through the winter's night.

today I will bring the spirit of Newness to my _____

feelings _____

the blessing
I ask that the Light,
The Creative Force of the universe,
Breathe the cleansing outbreath of spirit
Into my heart and my deeds.
I rejoice in this time of promise,
Of new stirrings, of the rebirth of the lotus
Which will one day open fully to God.

evening focus
Our Heavenly Father

35

Saturday, January 13, 2024

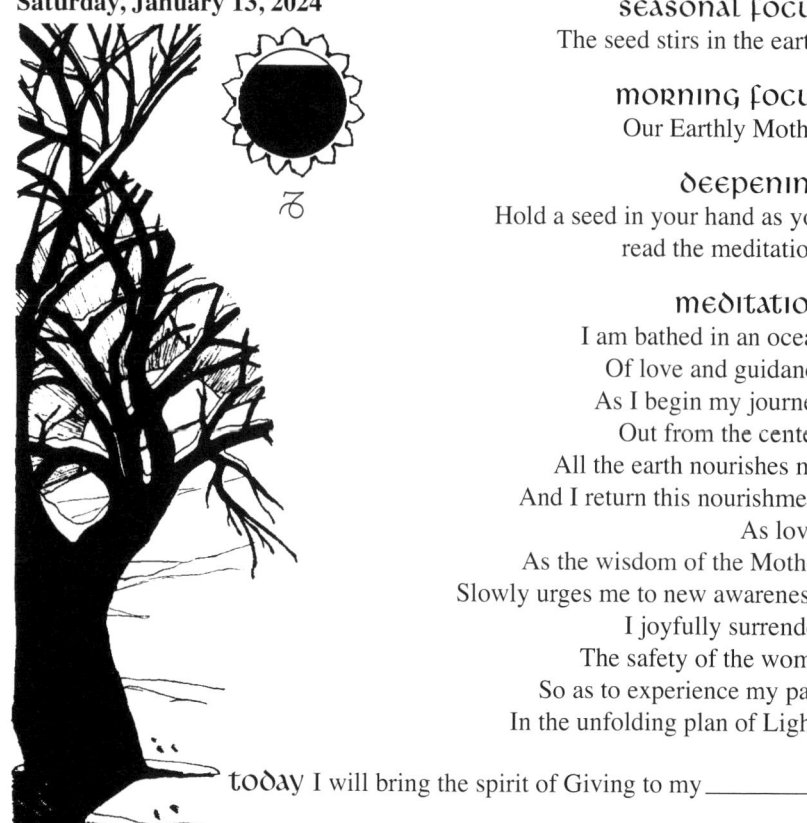

seasonal focus
The seed stirs in the earth.

morning focus
Our Earthly Mother

deepening
Hold a seed in your hand as you
read the meditation.

meditation
I am bathed in an ocean
Of love and guidance
As I begin my journey
Out from the center.
All the earth nourishes me
And I return this nourishment
As love.
As the wisdom of the Mother
Slowly urges me to new awareness,
I joyfully surrender
The safety of the womb
So as to experience my part
In the unfolding plan of Light.

today I will bring the spirit of Giving to my _____

feelings _____
_____
_____
_____
_____
_____

evening focus
The angel of Eternal Life

the blessing
As the long night slowly yields to day,
Even as the old millennium surrenders to the new,
I, too, surrender to my next step
Which carries me toward
My natural state of limitlessness.
The winter teaches me of inner abundance,
Inner completeness,
As I now prepare for the outer learning
That this new year brings.

Sunday, January 14, 2024

seasonal focus
The seed stirs in the earth.

morning focus
The angel of Earth

deepening
Hold earth, dirt, in your hand as you read.
Feel it.

meditation
From the calm place
At my spiritual center
I have touched the wisdom
Of the earth in winter.
Regeneration streams
From the holy earth to me,
And I am full.
I now gather to me the lessons
Which will empower me
To channel this life-giving earth force
For the good of all beings.

today I will bring the spirit of Calmness to my _____

feelings _____
_____
_____
_____
_____
_____
_____

the blessing
The winter's journey
To the source of inner creativity
Now turns and guides me slowly
Toward outward manifestation.
Depth will be fulfilled in expansion
As I contemplate
My dharmic path of service.
I give thanks for the Mother's gifts
Which have brought me to this.

evening focus
The angel of Creative Work

37

Monday, January 15, 2024

seasonal focus
The seed stirs in the earth.

morning focus
The angel of Life

opening
Study your face in a mirror; what do you really see? Take this awareness to your meditation.

meditation
Slowly the balance shifts from inner creativity
To outer manifestation.
Slowly my core of inner strength streams outward
Along my nervous system,
Bringing health and vitality to the whole of my being.
The life in me prepares itself,
Strengthens itself for the moment in the cycle
When it will overflow its bounds,
Surging toward a oneness with all of life.

today I will bring the spirit of Honesty to my _____

feelings _____
_____
_____
_____
_____
_____
_____
_____

evening focus
The angel of Peace

the blessing
I evoke the forces of peace and harmony
And ask these forces
To prepare me as a channel
For their overlighting guidance.
My heart swells with thanksgiving
For a winter of inner preparation
Which will lead me to the first step
In becoming a channel for peace:
That of finding peace within my own being.

seasonal focus
The seed stirs in the earth.

morning focus
The angel of Joy

Tuesday, January 16, 2024

opening
Loosen all clothing. As you read,
cause your belly to hang out and relax.

meditation
Wherein lies the source of joy?
The inner peace of winter prepares me for the answer;
It shouts quietly to me,
"Do not seek happiness; seek rather
Your true nature, your true reason for being;
Seek your dharma.
Joy is the child of completeness,
Of living your dharma."
At this time of new, small beginnings,
I feel the clarity of vision growing in me,
And I am pregnant with joy.

today I will bring the spirit of Joy to my _____
_____

feelings _____
_____
_____
_____
_____

the blessing
The silent stirring of the new life in me
Fills me with an inner strength.
The strength is good;
And it comes from a place deep inside my being
That has only been reached
In the depth of ego-death.
This power I trust;
This is the power of love and compassion
The world cries out for.
The veil of illusion lifts slowly and reveals
The direction of my path.

evening focus
The angel of Power

39

Wednesday, January 17, 2024

seasonal focus
The seed stirs in the earth.

morning focus
The angel of the Sun

deepening
Focus on a candle flame before and after the reading.

meditation
The promise, the prophecy, is within me.
That which I have waited for is now present.
No longer need I fear.
Within me shines
The first glimmering of the Light,
And I am filled with the awareness
That the fulfilling of the prophecy
Is not a thing apart from me;
It *is* me.
As the first small rays of the sun
Return to my world,
I, too, return slowly to the world of form.
I humbly accept the mantle of that which I AM.
As I merge my light
With the light of all the beings of Light,
I surrender to my own divinity.

today I will bring the spirit of Courage to my _____

feelings _____

evening focus
The angel of Love

the blessing
Life, you are a profound expression of Love.
The gentle, quiet expansion
Of the winter-mother's love
Fills me with inner joy.
I bow before the purity of this love
Which nourishes without attachment.

seasonal focus
The seed stirs in the earth.

morning focus
The angel of Water

deepening
Hold water in your cupped hand as you read.
After, drink it as a sacred act.

meditation
As the clear winter water
Nourishes the seed within the earth,
I am nourished by new-found awareness
Of who I truly am.
This awareness has not yet fully matured,
And I rest content
In the arms of the unfolding universe,
Which will reveal all wisdom
In its time.
The Power of the unmanifest
Even now works within my spiritual heart,
And I am at peace.

today I will bring the spirit of Contentment to my

feelings _____

_____
_____
_____
_____

Thursday, January 18, 2024

the blessing
I call upon my own internal voice,
Which is ever linked with the universal voice
Of inner knowing.
I ask, as I slowly move
From winter's inner development
To the first stirrings of outer work,
That I be given the strength
To trust my own still small voice,
Whose guidance is never faulty.
For this blessing I give thanks.

evening focus
The angel of Wisdom

♈ → ♉

Friday, January 19, 2024

seasonal focus
The seed stirs in the earth.

morning focus
The angel of Air

opening
Before reading meditation, take three very deep breaths, exhaling fully so your lungs empty of air.

meditation
There is a force in me,
Pushing, pushing,
Beginning its outbreath
After a long sleep.
Sacred darkness slowly yields
To newborn light.
As I move outward
From the stillpoint of outer death
To share my new-found breath of life with all,
I shall never forget
The inbreath of the Mother
That nurtured me
Through the winter's night.

today I will bring the spirit of Newness to my _____

feelings _____
_____
_____
_____
_____
_____
_____

evening focus
Our Heavenly Father

the blessing
I ask that the Light,
The Creative Force of the universe,
Breathe the cleansing outbreath of spirit
Into my heart and my deeds.
I rejoice in this time of promise,
Of new stirrings, of the rebirth of the lotus
Which will one day open fully to God.

seasonal focus
The seed stirs in the earth.

morning focus
Our Earthly Mother

deepening
Hold a seed in your hand as you read the meditation.

meditation
I am bathed in an ocean
Of love and guidance
As I begin my journey
Out from the center.
All the earth nourishes me
And I return this nourishment
As love.
As the wisdom of the Mother
Slowly urges me to new awareness,
I joyfully surrender
The safety of the womb
So as to experience my part
In the unfolding plan of Light.

today I will bring the spirit of Giving to my _____

feelings _____

_____

_____

_____

the blessing
As the long night slowly yields to day,
Even as the old millennium surrenders to the new,
I, too, surrender to my next step
Which carries me toward
My natural state of limitlessness.
The winter teaches me of inner abundance,
Inner completeness,
As I now prepare for the outer learning
That this new year brings.

Saturday, January 20, 2024

evening focus
The angel of Eternal Life

Sunday, January 21, 2024

seasonal focus
The seed stirs in the earth.

morning focus
The angel of Earth

deepening
Hold earth, dirt, in your hand as you read. Feel it.

meditation
From the calm place
At my spiritual center
I have touched the wisdom
Of the earth in winter.
Regeneration streams
From the holy earth to me,
And I am full.
I now gather to me the lessons
Which will empower me
To channel this life-giving earth force
For the good of all beings.

today I will bring the spirit of Calmness to my _____

feelings _____

_____

_____

_____

_____

_____

_____

evening focus
The angel of Creative Work

the blessing
The winter's journey
To the source of inner creativity
Now turns and guides me slowly
Toward outward manifestation.
Depth will be fulfilled in expansion
As I contemplate
My dharmic path of service.
I give thanks for the Mother's gifts
Which have brought me to this.

seasonal focus
The seed stirs in the earth.

morning focus
The angel of Life

opening
Study your face in a mirror; what do you really see? Take this awareness to your meditation.

meditation
Slowly the balance shifts from inner creativity
To outer manifestation.
Slowly my core of inner strength streams outward
Along my nervous system,
Bringing health and vitality to the whole of my being.
The life in me prepares itself,
Strengthens itself for the moment in the cycle
When it will overflow its bounds,
Surging toward a oneness with all of life.

today I will bring the spirit of Honesty to my _____

feelings _____

Monday, January 22, 2024

the blessing
I evoke the forces of peace and harmony
And ask these forces
To prepare me as a channel
For their overlighting guidance.
My heart swells with thanksgiving
For a winter of inner preparation
Which will lead me to the first step
In becoming a channel for peace:
That of finding peace within my own being.

evening focus
The angel of Peace

$\mathbb{II} \rightarrow \circledcirc$

Tuesday, January 23, 2024

seasonal focus
The seed stirs in the earth.

morning focus
The angel of Joy

opening
Loosen all clothing. As you read,
cause your belly to hang out and relax.

meditation
Wherein lies the source of joy?
The inner peace of winter prepares me for the answer;
It shouts quietly to me,
"Do not seek happiness; seek rather
Your true nature, your true reason for being;
Seek your dharma.
Joy is the child of completeness,
Of living your dharma."
At this time of new, small beginnings,
I feel the clarity of vision growing in me,
And I am pregnant with joy.

today I will bring the spirit of Joy to my _____
_____

feelings _____
_____
_____
_____
_____

evening focus
The angel of Power

the blessing
The silent stirring of the new life in me
Fills me with an inner strength.
The strength is good;
And it comes from a place deep inside my being
That has only been reached
In the depth of ego-death.
This power I trust;
This is the power of love and compassion
The world cries out for.
The veil of illusion lifts slowly and reveals
The direction of my path.

seasonal focus
The seed stirs in the earth.

morning focus
The angel of the Sun

deepening
Focus on a candle flame before and after the reading.

meditation
The promise, the prophecy, is within me.
That which I have waited for is now present.
No longer need I fear.
Within me shines
The first glimmering of the Light,
And I am filled with the awareness
That the fulfilling of the prophecy
Is not a thing apart from me;
It *is* me.
As the first small rays of the sun
Return to my world,
I, too, return slowly to the world of form.
I humbly accept the mantle of that which I AM.
As I merge my light
With the light of all the beings of Light,
I surrender to my own divinity.

today I will bring the spirit of Courage to my _____

feelings _____

_____
_____
_____
_____
_____

the blessing
Life, you are a profound expression of Love.
The gentle, quiet expansion
Of the winter-mother's love
Fills me with inner joy.
I bow before the purity of this love
Which nourishes without attachment.

evening focus
The angel of Love

Wednesday, January 24, 2024

Thursday, January 25, 2024

seasonal focus
The seed stirs in the earth.

morning focus
The angel of Water

deepening
Hold water in your cupped hand as you read.
After, drink it as a sacred act.

meditation
As the clear winter water
Nourishes the seed within the earth,
I am nourished by new-found awareness
Of who I truly am.
This awareness has not yet fully matured,
And I rest content
In the arms of the unfolding universe,
Which will reveal all wisdom
In its time.
The Power of the unmanifest
Even now works within my spiritual heart,
And I am at peace.

today I will bring the spirit of Contentment to my _____

feelings _____
_____
_____
_____
_____
_____

evening focus
The angel of Wisdom

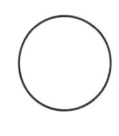

the blessing
I call upon my own internal voice,
Which is ever linked with the universal voice
Of inner knowing.
I ask, as I slowly move
From winter's inner development
To the first stirrings of outer work,
That I be given the strength
To trust my own still small voice,
Whose guidance is never faulty.
For this blessing I give thanks.

seasonal focus
The seed stirs in the earth.

Friday, January 26, 2024

morning focus
The angel of Air

opening
Before reading meditation, take three very deep breaths, exhaling fully so your lungs empty of air.

meditation
There is a force in me,
Pushing, pushing,
Beginning its outbreath
After a long sleep.
Sacred darkness slowly yields
To newborn light.
As I move outward
From the stillpoint of outer death
To share my new-found breath of life with all,
I shall never forget
The inbreath of the Mother
That nurtured me
Through the winter's night.

today I will bring the spirit of Newness to my _____

feelings _____

the blessing
I ask that the Light,
The Creative Force of the universe,
Breathe the cleansing outbreath of spirit
Into my heart and my deeds.
I rejoice in this time of promise,
Of new stirrings, of the rebirth of the lotus
Which will one day open fully to God.

evening focus
Our Heavenly Father

Saturday, January 27, 2024

seasonal focus
The seed stirs in the earth.

morning focus
Our Earthly Mother

deepening
Hold a seed in your hand as you
read the meditation.

meditation
I am bathed in an ocean
Of love and guidance
As I begin my journey
Out from the center.
All the earth nourishes me
And I return this nourishment
As love.
As the wisdom of the Mother
Slowly urges me to new awareness,
I joyfully surrender
The safety of the womb
So as to experience my part
In the unfolding plan of Light.

today I will bring the spirit of Giving to my _____

feelings _____
_____
_____
_____
_____

evening focus
The angel of Eternal Life

♌ → ♍

the blessing
As the long night slowly yields to day,
Even as the old millennium surrenders to the new,
I, too, surrender to my next step
Which carries me toward
My natural state of limitlessness.
The winter teaches me of inner abundance,
Inner completeness,
As I now prepare for the outer learning
That this new year brings.

seasonal focus
The seed stirs in the earth.

morning focus
The angel of Earth

deepening
Hold earth, dirt, in your hand as you read.
Feel it.

meditation
From the calm place
At my spiritual center
I have touched the wisdom
Of the earth in winter.
Regeneration streams
From the holy earth to me,
And I am full.
I now gather to me the lessons
Which will empower me
To channel this life-giving earth force
For the good of all beings.

today I will bring the spirit of Calmness to my _____

feelings _____
_____
_____
_____
_____
_____

the blessing
The winter's journey
To the source of inner creativity
Now turns and guides me slowly
Toward outward manifestation.
Depth will be fulfilled in expansion
As I contemplate
My dharmic path of service.
I give thanks for the Mother's gifts
Which have brought me to this.

evening focus
The angel of Creative Work

Sunday, January 28, 2024

51

Monday, January 29, 2024

seasonal focus
The seed stirs in the earth.

morning focus
The angel of Life

opening
Study your face in a mirror; what do you really see? Take this awareness to your meditation.

meditation
Slowly the balance shifts from inner creativity
To outer manifestation.
Slowly my core of inner strength streams outward
Along my nervous system,
Bringing health and vitality to the whole of my being.
The life in me prepares itself,
Strengthens itself for the moment in the cycle
When it will overflow its bounds,
Surging toward a oneness with all of life.

today I will bring the spirit of Honesty to my _____

_____

feelings_____

_____

_____

_____

_____

_____

_____

_____

evening focus
The angel of Peace

the blessing
I evoke the forces of peace and harmony
And ask these forces
To prepare me as a channel
For their overlighting guidance.
My heart swells with thanksgiving
For a winter of inner preparation
Which will lead me to the first step
In becoming a channel for peace:
That of finding peace within my own being.

seasonal focus
The seed stirs in the earth.

Tuesday, January 30, 2024

morning focus
The angel of Joy

opening
Loosen all clothing. As you read,
cause your belly to hang out and relax.

meditation
Wherein lies the source of joy?
The inner peace of winter prepares me for the answer;
It shouts quietly to me,
"Do not seek happiness; seek rather
Your true nature, your true reason for being;
Seek your dharma.
Joy is the child of completeness,
Of living your dharma."
At this time of new, small beginnings,
I feel the clarity of vision growing in me,
And I am pregnant with joy.

today I will bring the spirit of Joy to my _____

feelings _____

the blessing
The silent stirring of the new life in me
Fills me with an inner strength.
The strength is good;
And it comes from a place deep inside my being
That has only been reached
In the depth of ego-death.
This power I trust;
This is the power of love and compassion
The world cries out for.
The veil of illusion lifts slowly and reveals
The direction of my path.

evening focus
The angel of Power

Wednesday, January 31, 2024

seasonal focus
The seed stirs in the earth.

morning focus
The angel of the Sun

deepening
Focus on a candle flame before and after the reading.

meditation
The promise, the prophecy, is within me.
That which I have waited for is now present.
No longer need I fear.
Within me shines
The first glimmering of the Light,
And I am filled with the awareness
That the fulfilling of the prophecy
Is not a thing apart from me;
It *is* me.
As the first small rays of the sun
Return to my world,
I, too, return slowly to the world of form.
I humbly accept the mantle of that which I AM.
As I merge my light
With the light of all the beings of Light,
I surrender to my own divinity.

today I will bring the spirit of Courage to my _____

feelings _____

evening focus
The angel of Love

the blessing
Life, you are a profound expression of Love.
The gentle, quiet expansion
Of the winter-mother's love
Fills me with inner joy.
I bow before the purity of this love
Which nourishes without attachment.

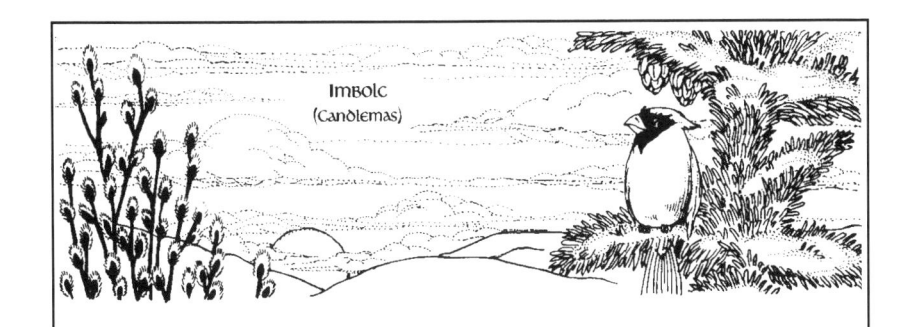

IMBOLC
(Candlemas)

Early February is the traditional time for the celebration of Imbolc, the festival of the washing of the earth's face. In ancient Britain, it was known as Oimelc, and later Brigantia, the day of Brigit. She is the Celtic goddess of the maidens, and she rules over the movement outward from winter to springtime. On the eve of Imbolc, the old Woman goddess of winter, the Cailleach, drinks from the sacred well and is transformed into the virgin Brigit.

This transformation is occurring in each of us, as we experience the shift from an inner contemplative focus toward an outer focus of conscious manifestation. The time is approaching when we will gather together all of the inner peace and love and wholeness that has quietly permeated our beings during the long regeneration of winter, and we will find that it becomes available for us to use in our daily lives. As we share this wholeness with others, it becomes even more available to us.

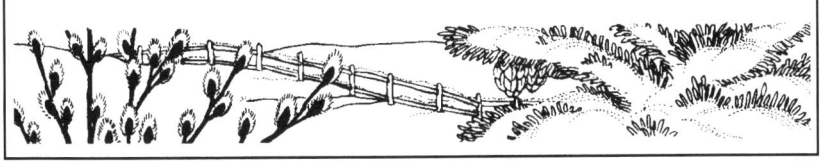

Thursday, February 1, 2024

seasonal focus
Brooks run free and buds appear.

morning focus
The angel of Water

deepening
Having caught rainwater in a bowl,
sprinkle it on your face before the reading.

meditation
About me flow the waters of nourishment;
Within me flows the water of nourishment.
My bloodstream is aglow with the impulse of life
As I challenge the dark places in my being,
As I expand beyond the security of the womb,
As I move past my own definitions.
And surrounding this, engulfing me,
Is the cosmic ocean of Love and Light
From whence I truly came.

today I will bring the spirit of Oneness to my _____
_____

feelings _____
_____
_____
_____
_____
_____

At Imbolc, seeds break through the frozen earth and buds appear.

evening focus
The angel of Wisdom

the blessing
I pause to honor
The overlighting stream of wisdom
That guides each living thing on its journey home.
That journey is my journey;
That home is my home;
And that wisdom is as alive in me
As it is in the highest of beings.
As I grow in spiritual maturity,
I see that this wisdom is always available
To the extent that I have prepared myself
To receive it.

Friday, February 2, 2024

seasonal focus
Brooks run free and buds appear.

morning focus
The angel of Air

opening
Before reading, place hands over heart.
Three deep breaths, pausing after each exhale.
Choose to breathe again.

meditation
The earth, long my home
Through the dark of winter,
Has yielded to the morning breath of air.
The Plan now urges me to outbreathe,
To expand to meet my destiny.
Why am I here?
For what have I returned this time?
And the air breathes its laughing answer past me.
"You are life.
You are the all in the process of becoming One.
Experience yourself."

today I will bring the spirit of Laughter to my _____

feelings _____

the blessing
What is this that gently forces me
From the still safe place of inaction?
What force compels me to abandon my comfort
Of well-worn despair?
Our Heavenly Father does not work from without,
But from within my own heart.
As the Law manifests itself through Love,
I stand in humble awe of the part of God that I AM.

evening focus
Our Heavenly Father

Saturday, February 3, 2024

seasonal focus
Brooks run free and buds appear.

morning focus
Our Earthly Mother

deepening
Hold a sprouted seed in your palm as you read.
(Alfalfa, mung bean, any will do.)

meditation
The path of the spirit calls to me to grow,
And grow I will.
But the journey home will take me far from my roots
Before I can once again return to the source.
Mother, at this time of new outer growth,
Fill my being with your love.
While my roots still are young,
Teach me to use Mind as servant,
Never as master.

today I will bring the spirit of Planetary Stewardship to my
_____

feelings _____
_____
_____
_____
_____
_____
_____
_____

evening focus
The angel of Eternal Life

the blessing
At this time of newness,
Of moving faster into the unknown,
Let me never forget that while I am new,
I am also old.
There is an ancient part of me
That will provide the source of knowing
As my newness wanders forth
To seek its true identity.
I am new. I am ancient.
I AM.

seasonal focus
Brooks run free and buds appear.

Sunday, February 4, 2024

morning focus
The angel of Earth

deepening
Hold a handful of your local dirt as you read.
Explore its makeup.

meditation
There is a part of me
That is rooted firmly in the earth.
It is to this grounded, solid me
That I now deeply bow.
For without this,
There could be no expansion,
No life-giving nourishment
Coursing to my tender new leaves,
No strong stem to reach toward the sun.
The earth is my home for this incarnation,
And I am blessed.

today I will bring the spirit of Fullness to my _____

feelings _____

the blessing
There is a sacredness which infuses my life
As I realize that my own growth is my work.
I am the canvas
I am the artist
I am the paint.
I ask that the artist be ever guided by the Artist,
And that as I grow, I come to know the perfection
Of the unfinished masterpiece
That is Life.

evening focus
The angel of Creative Work

Monday, February 5, 2024

seasonal focus
Brooks run free and buds appear.

morning focus
The angel of Life

opening
Meditate while touching a house plant.
Exchange energy with this being.

meditation
And now the life-force in me,
As in all beings,
Cries out to know itself
Apart from the Mother.
My life,
The uniqueness of that which I am,
Calls to me to experience,
For it is only in the full freedom
Of my own experiencing
That I gain the wisdom of my connectedness
With all that is.
For I am the one
And I am also the many.

today I will bring the spirit of Uniqueness to my____
_____
feelings_____
_____

_____
_____
_____
_____
_____

evening focus
The angel of Peace

the blessing
As I experience the new life in me
Bursting its bounds,
I ask to be made more clearly aware
Of my part in the Plan,
That I may prepare myself
To become the fullest expression and channel
For peace.

Tuesday, February 6, 2024

seasonal focus
Brooks run free and buds appear.

morning focus
The angel of Joy

opening
Hold the image in your mind of someone
who loves you. (A photo to gaze on is good, too.)

meditation
How strong in me is my need to grow
To expand
To meet the promise of the coming spring.
There is a joy in me that carries me onward
From this physical being
To the awareness of the cosmic ocean of Love
In which I dwell.
May I be blessed
To share this joy with all beings,
In whatever way I can.

today I will bring the spirit of Growth to my _____

feelings _____

the blessing
There is a Power at work in the world
Which assists each living thing
To rise above its prison
Of desire and attachment,
And to soar in the freedom of God's love.
I place myself in the path of this Power
And surrender to the divine Will
That charts the course of the path.
It is this Power that allows me to grow.

evening focus
The angel of Power

♐ → ♑

Wednesday, February 7, 2024

seasonal focus
Brooks run free and buds appear.

morning focus
The angel of the Sun

opening
Focus intensely on a candle flame,
until you sense a merging of you and the flame.

meditation
As the force of new life wells up in me,
I hear the far call
Of my ancient spiritual father, the sun.
This is a time for reaching upward,
A time for growing toward the sky
As I still draw nourishment
From my mother the earth.
I am the link;
I am the channel between the sun and the earth.
I am the life.

today I will bring the spirit of Connectedness to my ____

feelings _____

evening focus
The angel of Love

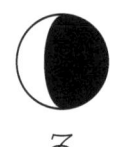

the blessing
Mother, you are love in me, overflowing,
And I bless you as I grow.
Father, you are love in me, guiding me,
And I bless you as I strive to know
My true nature.
Soon my buds will open,
And my own young channel of love
Will be available for you to use to heal the earth.

Thursday, February 8, 2024

seasonal focus
Brooks run free and buds appear.

morning focus
The angel of Water

deepening
Having caught rainwater in a bowl,
sprinkle it on your face before the reading.

meditation
About me flow the waters of nourishment;
Within me flows the water of nourishment.
My bloodstream is aglow with the impulse of life
As I challenge the dark places in my being,
As I expand beyond the security of the womb,
As I move past my own definitions.
And surrounding this, engulfing me,
Is the cosmic ocean of Love and Light
From whence I truly came.

today I will bring the spirit of Oneness to my _____

feelings _____

the blessing
I pause to honor
The overlighting stream of wisdom
That guides each living thing on its journey home.
That journey is my journey;
That home is my home;
And that wisdom is as alive in me
As it is in the highest of beings.
As I grow in spiritual maturity,
I see that this wisdom is always available
To the extent that I have prepared myself
To receive it.

evening focus
The angel of Wisdom

Friday, February 9, 2024

seasonal focus
Brooks run free and buds appear.

morning focus
The angel of Air

opening
Before reading, place hands over heart.
Three deep breaths, pausing after each exhale.
Choose to breathe again.

meditation
The earth, long my home
Through the dark of winter,
Has yielded to the morning breath of air.
The Plan now urges me to outbreathe,
To expand to meet my destiny.
Why am I here?
For what have I returned this time?
And the air breathes its laughing answer past me.
"You are life.
You are the all in the process of becoming One.
Experience yourself."

today I will bring the spirit of Laughter to my _____

feelings _____

_____

_____

_____

_____

_____

evening focus
Our Heavenly Father

the blessing
What is this that gently forces me
From the still safe place of inaction?
What force compels me to abandon my comfort
Of well-worn despair?
Our Heavenly Father does not work from without,
But from within my own heart.
As the Law manifests itself through Love,
I stand in humble awe of the part of God that I AM.

Saturday, February 10, 2024

seasonal focus
Brooks run free and buds appear.

morning focus
Our Earthly Mother

deepening
Hold a sprouted seed in your palm as you read.
(Alfalfa, mung bean, any will do.)

meditation
The path of the spirit calls to me to grow,
And grow I will.
But the journey home will take me far from my roots
Before I can once again return to the source.
Mother, at this time of new outer growth,
Fill my being with your love.
While my roots still are young,
Teach me to use Mind as servant,
Never as master.

today I will bring the spirit of Planetary Stewardship to my _____

feelings _____
_____
_____
_____
_____
_____
_____

the blessing
At this time of newness,
Of moving faster into the unknown,
Let me never forget that while I am new,
I am also old.
There is an ancient part of me
That will provide the source of knowing
As my newness wanders forth
To seek its true identity.
I am new. I am ancient.
I AM.

evening focus
The angel of Eternal Life

Sunday, February 11, 2024

seasonal focus
Brooks run free and buds appear.

morning focus
The angel of Earth

deepening
Hold a handful of your local dirt as you read.
Explore its makeup.

meditation
There is a part of me
That is rooted firmly in the earth.
It is to this grounded, solid me
That I now deeply bow.
For without this,
There could be no expansion,
No life-giving nourishment
Coursing to my tender new leaves,
No strong stem to reach toward the sun.
The earth is my home for this incarnation,
And I am blessed.

today I will bring the spirit of Fullness to my _____

feelings _____

_____

_____

_____

_____

_____

_____

_____

evening focus
The angel of Creative Work

the blessing
There is a sacredness which infuses my life
As I realize that my own growth is my work.
I am the canvas
I am the artist
I am the paint.
I ask that the artist be ever guided by the Artist,
And that as I grow, I come to know the perfection
Of the unfinished masterpiece
That is Life.

seasonal focus
Brooks run free and buds appear.

Monday, February 12, 2024

morning focus
The angel of Life

opening
Meditate while touching a house plant.
Exchange energy with this being.

meditation
And now the life-force in me,
As in all beings,
Cries out to know itself
Apart from the Mother.
My life,
The uniqueness of that which I am,
Calls to me to experience,
For it is only in the full freedom
Of my own experiencing
That I gain the wisdom of my connectedness
With all that is.
For I am the one
And I am also the many.

today I will bring the spirit of Uniqueness to my _____

feelings _____

the blessing
As I experience the new life in me
Bursting its bounds,
I ask to be made more clearly aware
Of my part in the Plan,
That I may prepare myself
To become the fullest expression and channel
For peace.

evening focus
The angel of Peace

♓ → ♈

Tuesday, February 13, 2024

seasonal focus
Brooks run free and buds appear.

morning focus
The angel of Joy

opening
Hold the image in your mind of someone who loves you. (A photo to gaze on is good, too.)

meditation
How strong in me is my need to grow
To expand
To meet the promise of the coming spring.
There is a joy in me that carries me onward
From this physical being
To the awareness of the cosmic ocean of Love
In which I dwell.
May I be blessed
To share this joy with all beings,
In whatever way I can.

today I will bring the spirit of Growth to my _____

feelings _____

evening focus
The angel of Power

the blessing
There is a Power at work in the world
Which assists each living thing
To rise above its prison
Of desire and attachment,
And to soar in the freedom of God's love.
I place myself in the path of this Power
And surrender to the divine Will
That charts the course of the path.
It is this Power that allows me to grow.

Wednesday, February 14, 2024

seasonal focus
Brooks run free and buds appear.

morning focus
The angel of the Sun

opening
Focus intensely on a candle flame,
until you sense a merging of you and the flame.

meditation
As the force of new life wells up in me,
I hear the far call
Of my ancient spiritual father, the sun.
This is a time for reaching upward,
A time for growing toward the sky
As I still draw nourishment
From my mother the earth.
I am the link;
I am the channel between the sun and the earth.
I am the life.

today I will bring the spirit of Connectedness to my _____

feelings _____

the blessing
Mother, you are love in me, overflowing,
And I bless you as I grow.
Father, you are love in me, guiding me,
And I bless you as I strive to know
My true nature.
Soon my buds will open,
And my own young channel of love
Will be available for you to use to heal the earth.

evening focus
The angel of Love

♈ → ♉

Ash Wednesday
St. Valentine's Day

69

Thursday, February 15, 2024

seasonal focus
Brooks run free and buds appear.

morning focus
The angel of Water

deepening
Having caught rainwater in a bowl,
sprinkle it on your face before the reading.

meditation
About me flow the waters of nourishment;
Within me flows the water of nourishment.
My bloodstream is aglow with the impulse of life
As I challenge the dark places in my being,
As I expand beyond the security of the womb,
As I move past my own definitions.
And surrounding this, engulfing me,
Is the cosmic ocean of Love and Light
From whence I truly came.

today I will bring the spirit of Oneness to my _____
_____

feelings _____
_____
_____
_____
_____
_____
_____

evening focus
The angel of Wisdom

the blessing
I pause to honor
The overlighting stream of wisdom
That guides each living thing on its journey home.
That journey is my journey;
That home is my home;
And that wisdom is as alive in me
As it is in the highest of beings.
As I grow in spiritual maturity,
I see that this wisdom is always available
To the extent that I have prepared myself
To receive it.

seasonal focus
Brooks run free and buds appear.

Friday, February 16, 2024

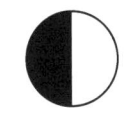

morning focus
The angel of Air

opening
Before reading, place hands over heart.
Three deep breaths, pausing after each exhale.
Choose to breathe again.

meditation
The earth, long my home
Through the dark of winter,
Has yielded to the morning breath of air.
The Plan now urges me to outbreathe,
To expand to meet my destiny.
Why am I here?
For what have I returned this time?
And the air breathes its laughing answer past me.
"You are life.
You are the all in the process of becoming One.
Experience yourself."

today I will bring the spirit of Laughter to my _____
_____

feelings _____
_____
_____
_____
_____
_____
_____

the blessing
What is this that gently forces me
From the still safe place of inaction?
What force compels me to abandon my comfort
Of well-worn despair?
Our Heavenly Father does not work from without,
But from within my own heart.
As the Law manifests itself through Love,
I stand in humble awe of the part of God that I AM.

evening focus
Our Heavenly Father

♉ → ♊

71

Saturday, February 17, 2024

seasonal focus
Brooks run free and buds appear.

morning focus
Our Earthly Mother

deepening
Hold a sprouted seed in your palm as you read.
(Alfalfa, mung bean, any will do.)

meditation
The path of the spirit calls to me to grow,
And grow I will.
But the journey home will take me far from my roots
Before I can once again return to the source.
Mother, at this time of new outer growth,
Fill my being with your love.
While my roots still are young,
Teach me to use Mind as servant,
Never as master.

today I will bring the spirit of Planetary Stewardship to my
_____

feelings _____
_____
_____
_____
_____
_____
_____
_____

evening focus
The angel of Eternal Life

the blessing
At this time of newness,
Of moving faster into the unknown,
Let me never forget that while I am new,
I am also old.
There is an ancient part of me
That will provide the source of knowing
As my newness wanders forth
To seek its true identity.
I am new. I am ancient.
I AM.

seasonal focus
Brooks run free and buds appear.

morning focus
The angel of Earth

deepening
Hold a handful of your local dirt as you read.
Explore its makeup.

meditation
There is a part of me
That is rooted firmly in the earth.
It is to this grounded, solid me
That I now deeply bow.
For without this,
There could be no expansion,
No life-giving nourishment
Coursing to my tender new leaves,
No strong stem to reach toward the sun.
The earth is my home for this incarnation,
And I am blessed.

today I will bring the spirit of Fullness to my _____

feelings _____

the blessing
There is a sacredness which infuses my life
As I realize that my own growth is my work.
I am the canvas
I am the artist
I am the paint.
I ask that the artist be ever guided by the Artist,
And that as I grow, I come to know the perfection
Of the unfinished masterpiece
That is Life.

evening focus
The angel of Creative Work

Sunday, February 18, 2024

Monday, February 19, 2024

seasonal focus
Brooks run free and buds appear.

morning focus
The angel of Life

opening
Meditate while touching a house plant.
Exchange energy with this being.

meditation
And now the life-force in me,
As in all beings,
Cries out to know itself
Apart from the Mother.
My life,
The uniqueness of that which I am,
Calls to me to experience,
For it is only in the full freedom
Of my own experiencing
That I gain the wisdom of my connectedness
With all that is.
For I am the one
And I am also the many.

today I will bring the spirit of Uniqueness to my ____
_____
feelings _____
_____
_____
_____
_____
_____
_____
_____

evening focus
The angel of Peace

the blessing
As I experience the new life in me
Bursting its bounds,
I ask to be made more clearly aware
Of my part in the Plan,
That I may prepare myself
To become the fullest expression and channel
For peace.

Tuesday, February 20, 2024

seasonal focus
Brooks run free and buds appear.

morning focus
The angel of Joy

opening
Hold the image in your mind of someone
who loves you. (A photo to gaze on is good, too.)

meditation
How strong in me is my need to grow
To expand
To meet the promise of the coming spring.
There is a joy in me that carries me onward
From this physical being
To the awareness of the cosmic ocean of Love
In which I dwell.
May I be blessed
To share this joy with all beings,
In whatever way I can.

today I will bring the spirit of Growth to my _____

feelings _____

the blessing
There is a Power at work in the world
Which assists each living thing
To rise above its prison
Of desire and attachment,
And to soar in the freedom of God's love.
I place myself in the path of this Power
And surrender to the divine Will
That charts the course of the path.
It is this Power that allows me to grow.

evening focus
The angel of Power

Wednesday, February 21, 2024

seasonal focus
Brooks run free and buds appear.

morning focus
The angel of the Sun

opening
Focus intensely on a candle flame,
until you sense a merging of you and the flame.

meditation
As the force of new life wells up in me,
I hear the far call
Of my ancient spiritual father, the sun.
This is a time for reaching upward,
A time for growing toward the sky
As I still draw nourishment
From my mother the earth.
I am the link;
I am the channel between the sun and the earth.
I am the life.

today I will bring the spirit of Connectedness to my _____

feelings _____

evening focus
The angel of Love

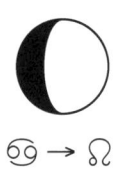

the blessing
Mother, you are love in me, overflowing,
And I bless you as I grow.
Father, you are love in me, guiding me,
And I bless you as I strive to know
My true nature.
Soon my buds will open,
And my own young channel of love
Will be available for you to use to heal the earth.

seasonal focus
Brooks run free and buds appear.

Thursday, February 22, 2024

morning focus
The angel of Water

deepening
Having caught rainwater in a bowl,
sprinkle it on your face before the reading.

meditation
About me flow the waters of nourishment;
Within me flows the water of nourishment.
My bloodstream is aglow with the impulse of life
As I challenge the dark places in my being,
As I expand beyond the security of the womb,
As I move past my own definitions.
And surrounding this, engulfing me,
Is the cosmic ocean of Love and Light
From whence I truly came.

today I will bring the spirit of Oneness to my _____

feelings _____

_____

_____

_____

_____

_____

_____

_____

the blessing
I pause to honor
The overlighting stream of wisdom
That guides each living thing on its journey home.
That journey is my journey;
That home is my home;
And that wisdom is as alive in me
As it is in the highest of beings.
As I grow in spiritual maturity,
I see that this wisdom is always available
To the extent that I have prepared myself
To receive it.

evening focus
The angel of Wisdom

Friday, February 23, 2024

seasonal focus
Brooks run free and buds appear.

morning focus
The angel of Air

opening
Before reading, place hands over heart.
Three deep breaths, pausing after each exhale.
Choose to breathe again.

meditation
The earth, long my home
Through the dark of winter,
Has yielded to the morning breath of air.
The Plan now urges me to outbreathe,
To expand to meet my destiny.
Why am I here?
For what have I returned this time?
And the air breathes its laughing answer past me.
"You are life.
You are the all in the process of becoming One.
Experience yourself."

today I will bring the spirit of Laughter to my _____

feelings _____

evening focus
Our Heavenly Father

the blessing
What is this that gently forces me
From the still safe place of inaction?
What force compels me to abandon my comfort
Of well-worn despair?
Our Heavenly Father does not work from without,
But from within my own heart.
As the Law manifests itself through Love,
I stand in humble awe of the part of God that I AM.

Saturday, February 24, 2024

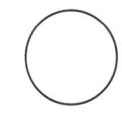

seasonal focus
Brooks run free and buds appear.

morning focus
Our Earthly Mother

deepening
Hold a sprouted seed in your palm as you read.
(Alfalfa, mung bean, any will do.)

meditation
The path of the spirit calls to me to grow,
And grow I will.
But the journey home will take me far from my roots
Before I can once again return to the source.
Mother, at this time of new outer growth,
Fill my being with your love.
While my roots still are young,
Teach me to use Mind as servant,
Never as master.

today I will bring the spirit of Planetary Stewardship to my _____

feelings _____
_____
_____
_____
_____
_____
_____

the blessing
At this time of newness,
Of moving faster into the unknown,
Let me never forget that while I am new,
I am also old.
There is an ancient part of me
That will provide the source of knowing
As my newness wanders forth
To seek its true identity.
I am new. I am ancient.
I AM.

evening focus
The angel of Eternal Life

Sunday, February 25, 2024

seasonal focus
Brooks run free and buds appear.

morning focus
The angel of Earth

deepening
Hold a handful of your local dirt as you read.
Explore its makeup.

meditation
There is a part of me
That is rooted firmly in the earth.
It is to this grounded, solid me
That I now deeply bow.
For without this,
There could be no expansion,
No life-giving nourishment
Coursing to my tender new leaves,
No strong stem to reach toward the sun.
The earth is my home for this incarnation,
And I am blessed.

today I will bring the spirit of Fullness to my _____

feelings_____

_____

_____

_____

_____

_____

_____

evening focus
The angel of Creative Work

the blessing
There is a sacredness which infuses my life
As I realize that my own growth is my work.
I am the canvas
I am the artist
I am the paint.
I ask that the artist be ever guided by the Artist,
And that as I grow, I come to know the perfection
Of the unfinished masterpiece
That is Life.

seasonal focus
Brooks run free and buds appear.

Monday, February 26, 2024

morning focus
The angel of Life

opening
Meditate while touching a house plant.
Exchange energy with this being.

meditation
And now the life-force in me,
As in all beings,
Cries out to know itself
Apart from the Mother.
My life,
The uniqueness of that which I am,
Calls to me to experience,
For it is only in the full freedom
Of my own experiencing
That I gain the wisdom of my connectedness
With all that is.
For I am the one
And I am also the many.

today I will bring the spirit of Uniqueness to my _____

feelings _____

the blessing
As I experience the new life in me
Bursting its bounds,
I ask to be made more clearly aware
Of my part in the Plan,
That I may prepare myself
To become the fullest expression and channel
For peace.

evening focus
The angel of Peace

Tuesday, February 27, 2024

seasonal focus
Brooks run free and buds appear.

morning focus
The angel of Joy

opening
Hold the image in your mind of someone who loves you. (A photo to gaze on is good, too.)

meditation
How strong in me is my need to grow
To expand
To meet the promise of the coming spring.
There is a joy in me that carries me onward
From this physical being
To the awareness of the cosmic ocean of Love
In which I dwell.
May I be blessed
To share this joy with all beings,
In whatever way I can.

today I will bring the spirit of Growth to my _____
_____

feelings_____
_____
_____
_____
_____
_____
_____

evening focus
The angel of Power

the blessing
There is a Power at work in the world
Which assists each living thing
To rise above its prison
Of desire and attachment,
And to soar in the freedom of God's love.
I place myself in the path of this Power
And surrender to the divine Will
That charts the course of the path.
It is this Power that allows me to grow.

seasonal focus
Brooks run free and buds appear.

Wednesday, February 28, 2024

morning focus
The angel of the Sun

opening
Focus intensely on a candle flame,
until you sense a merging of you and the flame.

meditation
As the force of new life wells up in me,
I hear the far call
Of my ancient spiritual father, the sun.
This is a time for reaching upward,
A time for growing toward the sky
As I still draw nourishment
From my mother the earth.
I am the link;
I am the channel between the sun and the earth.
I am the life.

today I will bring the spirit of Connectedness to my _____

feelings _____

the blessing
Mother, you are love in me, overflowing,
And I bless you as I grow.
Father, you are love in me, guiding me,
And I bless you as I strive to know
My true nature.
Soon my buds will open,
And my own young channel of love
Will be available for you to use to heal the earth.

evening focus
The angel of Love

Thursday, February 29, 2024

seasonal focus
Brooks run free and buds appear.

morning focus
The angel of Water

deepening
Having caught rainwater in a bowl,
sprinkle it on your face before the reading.

meditation
About me flow the waters of nourishment;
Within me flows the water of nourishment.
My bloodstream is aglow with the impulse of life
As I challenge the dark places in my being,
As I expand beyond the security of the womb,
As I move past my own definitions.
And surrounding this, engulfing me,
Is the cosmic ocean of Love and Light
From whence I truly came.

today I will bring the spirit of Oneness to my _____

feelings _____

evening focus
The angel of Wisdom

the blessing
I pause to honor
The overlighting stream of wisdom
That guides each living thing on its journey home.
That journey is my journey;
That home is my home;
And that wisdom is as alive in me
As it is in the highest of beings.
As I grow in spiritual maturity,
I see that this wisdom is always available
To the extent that I have prepared myself
To receive it.

seasonal focus
Brooks run free and buds appear.

Friday, March 1, 2024

morning focus
The angel of Air

opening
Before reading, place hands over heart.
Three deep breaths, pausing after each exhale.
Choose to breathe again.

meditation
The earth, long my home
Through the dark of winter,
Has yielded to the morning breath of air.
The Plan now urges me to outbreathe,
To expand to meet my destiny.
Why am I here?
For what have I returned this time?
And the air breathes its laughing answer past me.
"You are life.
You are the all in the process of becoming One.
Experience yourself."

today I will bring the spirit of Laughter to my _____

feelings _____

the blessing
What is this that gently forces me
From the still safe place of inaction?
What force compels me to abandon my comfort
Of well-worn despair?
Our Heavenly Father does not work from without,
But from within my own heart.
As the Law manifests itself through Love,
I stand in humble awe of the part of God that I AM.

evening focus
Our Heavenly Father

Saturday, March 2, 2024

seasonal focus
Brooks run free and buds appear.

morning focus
Our Earthly Mother

deepening
Hold a sprouted seed in your palm as you read.
(Alfalfa, mung bean, any will do.)

meditation
The path of the spirit calls to me to grow,
And grow I will.
But the journey home will take me far from my roots
Before I can once again return to the source.
Mother, at this time of new outer growth,
Fill my being with your love.
While my roots still are young,
Teach me to use Mind as servant,
Never as master.

today I will bring the spirit of Planetary Stewardship to my
_____

feelings _____
_____
_____
_____
_____
_____
_____

evening focus
The angel of Eternal Life

the blessing
At this time of newness,
Of moving faster into the unknown,
Let me never forget that while I am new,
I am also old.
There is an ancient part of me
That will provide the source of knowing
As my newness wanders forth
To seek its true identity.
I am new. I am ancient.
I AM.

Sunday, March 3, 2024

seasonal focus
Brooks run free and buds appear.

morning focus
The angel of Earth

deepening
Hold a handful of your local dirt as you read.
Explore its makeup.

meditation
There is a part of me
That is rooted firmly in the earth.
It is to this grounded, solid me
That I now deeply bow.
For without this,
There could be no expansion,
No life-giving nourishment
Coursing to my tender new leaves,
No strong stem to reach toward the sun.
The earth is my home for this incarnation,
And I am blessed.

today I will bring the spirit of Fullness to my _____

_____

feelings _____

_____
_____
_____
_____
_____
_____

the blessing
There is a sacredness which infuses my life
As I realize that my own growth is my work.
I am the canvas
I am the artist
I am the paint.
I ask that the artist be ever guided by the Artist,
And that as I grow, I come to know the perfection
Of the unfinished masterpiece
That is Life.

evening focus
The angel of Creative Work

Monday, March 4, 2024

seasonal focus
Brooks run free and buds appear.

morning focus
The angel of Life

opening
Meditate while touching a house plant.
Exchange energy with this being.

meditation
And now the life-force in me,
As in all beings,
Cries out to know itself
Apart from the Mother.
My life,
The uniqueness of that which I am,
Calls to me to experience,
For it is only in the full freedom
Of my own experiencing
That I gain the wisdom of my connectedness
With all that is.
For I am the one
And I am also the many.

today I will bring the spirit of Uniqueness to my ____

feelings ____

___
___
___
___
___

evening focus
The angel of Peace

the blessing
As I experience the new life in me
Bursting its bounds,
I ask to be made more clearly aware
Of my part in the Plan,
That I may prepare myself
To become the fullest expression and channel
For peace.

seasonal focus
Brooks run free and buds appear.

Tuesday, March 5, 2024

morning focus
The angel of Joy

opening
Hold the image in your mind of someone
who loves you. (A photo to gaze on is good, too.)

meditation
How strong in me is my need to grow
To expand
To meet the promise of the coming spring.
There is a joy in me that carries me onward
From this physical being
To the awareness of the cosmic ocean of Love
In which I dwell.
May I be blessed
To share this joy with all beings,
In whatever way I can.

today I will bring the spirit of Growth to my _____

feelings _____

the blessing
There is a Power at work in the world
Which assists each living thing
To rise above its prison
Of desire and attachment,
And to soar in the freedom of God's love.
I place myself in the path of this Power
And surrender to the divine Will
That charts the course of the path.
It is this Power that allows me to grow.

evening focus
The angel of Power

Wednesday, March 6, 2024

seasonal focus
Brooks run free and buds appear.

morning focus
The angel of the Sun

opening
Focus intensely on a candle flame,
until you sense a merging of you and the flame.

meditation
As the force of new life wells up in me,
I hear the far call
Of my ancient spiritual father, the sun.
This is a time for reaching upward,
A time for growing toward the sky
As I still draw nourishment
From my mother the earth.
I am the link;
I am the channel between the sun and the earth.
I am the life.

today I will bring the spirit of Connectedness to my ____
_____

feelings _____
_____
_____
_____
_____
_____
_____
_____

evening focus
The angel of Love

the blessing
Mother, you are love in me, overflowing,
And I bless you as I grow.
Father, you are love in me, guiding me,
And I bless you as I strive to know
My true nature.
Soon my buds will open,
And my own young channel of love
Will be available for you to use to heal the earth.

seasonal focus
Brooks run free and buds appear.

Thursday, March 7, 2024

morning focus
The angel of Water

deepening
Having caught rainwater in a bowl,
sprinkle it on your face before the reading.

meditation
About me flow the waters of nourishment;
Within me flows the water of nourishment.
My bloodstream is aglow with the impulse of life
As I challenge the dark places in my being,
As I expand beyond the security of the womb,
As I move past my own definitions.
And surrounding this, engulfing me,
Is the cosmic ocean of Love and Light
From whence I truly came.

today I will bring the spirit of Oneness to my _____

feelings _____

the blessing
I pause to honor
The overlighting stream of wisdom
That guides each living thing on its journey home.
That journey is my journey;
That home is my home;
And that wisdom is as alive in me
As it is in the highest of beings.
As I grow in spiritual maturity,
I see that this wisdom is always available
To the extent that I have prepared myself
To receive it.

evening focus
The angel of Wisdom

91

Friday, March 8, 2024

seasonal focus
Brooks run free and buds appear.

morning focus
The angel of Air

opening
Before reading, place hands over heart.
Three deep breaths, pausing after each exhale.
Choose to breathe again.

meditation
The earth, long my home
Through the dark of winter,
Has yielded to the morning breath of air.
The Plan now urges me to outbreathe,
To expand to meet my destiny.
Why am I here?
For what have I returned this time?
And the air breathes its laughing answer past me.
"You are life.
You are the all in the process of becoming One.
Experience yourself."

today I will bring the spirit of Laughter to my _____
_____

feelings_____
_____
_____

_____
_____
_____
_____

evening focus
Our Heavenly Father

the blessing
What is this that gently forces me
From the still safe place of inaction?
What force compels me to abandon my comfort
Of well-worn despair?
Our Heavenly Father does not work from without,
But from within my own heart.
As the Law manifests itself through Love,
I stand in humble awe of the part of God that I AM.

Saturday, March 9, 2024

seasonal focus
Brooks run free and buds appear.

morning focus
Our Earthly Mother

deepening
Hold a sprouted seed in your palm as you read.
(Alfalfa, mung bean, any will do.)

meditation
The path of the spirit calls to me to grow,
And grow I will.
But the journey home will take me far from my roots
Before I can once again return to the source.
Mother, at this time of new outer growth,
Fill my being with your love.
While my roots still are young,
Teach me to use Mind as servant,
Never as master.

today I will bring the spirit of Planetary Stewardship to my
_____

feelings _____
_____
_____
_____
_____
_____
_____

the blessing
At this time of newness,
Of moving faster into the unknown,
Let me never forget that while I am new,
I am also old.
There is an ancient part of me
That will provide the source of knowing
As my newness wanders forth
To seek its true identity.
I am new. I am ancient.
I AM.

evening focus
The angel of Eternal Life

Sunday, March 10, 2024

seasonal focus
Brooks run free and buds appear.

morning focus
The angel of Earth

deepening
Hold a handful of your local dirt as you read.
Explore its makeup.

meditation
There is a part of me
That is rooted firmly in the earth.
It is to this grounded, solid me
That I now deeply bow.
For without this,
There could be no expansion,
No life-giving nourishment
Coursing to my tender new leaves,
No strong stem to reach toward the sun.
The earth is my home for this incarnation,
And I am blessed.

today I will bring the spirit of Fullness to my _____

feelings _____

_____

_____

_____

_____

_____

evening focus
The angel of Creative Work

the blessing
There is a sacredness which infuses my life
As I realize that my own growth is my work.
I am the canvas
I am the artist
I am the paint.
I ask that the artist be ever guided by the Artist,
And that as I grow, I come to know the perfection
Of the unfinished masterpiece
That is Life.

seasonal focus
Brooks run free and buds appear.

Monday, March 11, 2024

morning focus
The angel of Life

opening
Meditate while touching a house plant.
Exchange energy with this being.

meditation
And now the life-force in me,
As in all beings,
Cries out to know itself
Apart from the Mother.
My life,
The uniqueness of that which I am,
Calls to me to experience,
For it is only in the full freedom
Of my own experiencing
That I gain the wisdom of my connectedness
With all that is.
For I am the one
And I am also the many.

today I will bring the spirit of Uniqueness to my _____

feelings _____

the blessing
As I experience the new life in me
Bursting its bounds,
I ask to be made more clearly aware
Of my part in the Plan,
That I may prepare myself
To become the fullest expression and channel
For peace.

evening focus
The angel of Peace

Tuesday, March 12, 2024

seasonal focus
Brooks run free and buds appear.

morning focus
The angel of Joy

opening
Hold the image in your mind of someone who loves you. (A photo to gaze on is good, too.)

meditation
How strong in me is my need to grow
To expand
To meet the promise of the coming spring.
There is a joy in me that carries me onward
From this physical being
To the awareness of the cosmic ocean of Love
In which I dwell.
May I be blessed
To share this joy with all beings,
In whatever way I can.

today I will bring the spirit of Growth to my _____

feelings _____

evening focus
The angel of Power

the blessing
There is a Power at work in the world
Which assists each living thing
To rise above its prison
Of desire and attachment,
And to soar in the freedom of God's love.
I place myself in the path of this Power
And surrender to the divine Will
That charts the course of the path.
It is this Power that allows me to grow.

seasonal focus
Brooks run free and buds appear.

Wednesday, March 13, 2024

morning focus
The angel of the Sun

opening
Focus intensely on a candle flame,
until you sense a merging of you and the flame.

meditation
As the force of new life wells up in me,
I hear the far call
Of my ancient spiritual father, the sun.
This is a time for reaching upward,
A time for growing toward the sky
As I still draw nourishment
From my mother the earth.
I am the link;
I am the channel between the sun and the earth.
I am the life.

today I will bring the spirit of Connectedness to my _____
_____

feelings _____
_____
_____
_____
_____
_____
_____
_____
_____

the blessing
Mother, you are love in me, overflowing,
And I bless you as I grow.
Father, you are love in me, guiding me,
And I bless you as I strive to know
My true nature.
Soon my buds will open,
And my own young channel of love
Will be available for you to use to heal the earth.

evening focus
The angel of Love

Thursday, March 14, 2024

seasonal focus
Brooks run free and buds appear.

morning focus
The angel of Water

deepening
Having caught rainwater in a bowl,
sprinkle it on your face before the reading.

meditation
About me flow the waters of nourishment;
Within me flows the water of nourishment.
My bloodstream is aglow with the impulse of life
As I challenge the dark places in my being,
As I expand beyond the security of the womb,
As I move past my own definitions.
And surrounding this, engulfing me,
Is the cosmic ocean of Love and Light
From whence I truly came.

today I will bring the spirit of Oneness to my _____

feelings _____

evening focus
The angel of Wisdom

the blessing
I pause to honor
The overlighting stream of wisdom
That guides each living thing on its journey home.
That journey is my journey;
That home is my home;
And that wisdom is as alive in me
As it is in the highest of beings.
As I grow in spiritual maturity,
I see that this wisdom is always available
To the extent that I have prepared myself
To receive it.

seasonal focus
Brooks run free and buds appear.

Friday, March 15, 2024

morning focus
The angel of Air

opening
Before reading, place hands over heart.
Three deep breaths, pausing after each exhale.
Choose to breathe again.

meditation
The earth, long my home
Through the dark of winter,
Has yielded to the morning breath of air.
The Plan now urges me to outbreathe,
To expand to meet my destiny.
Why am I here?
For what have I returned this time?
And the air breathes its laughing answer past me.
"You are life.
You are the all in the process of becoming One.
Experience yourself."

today I will bring the spirit of Laughter to my _____
_____

feelings _____
_____
_____
_____
_____
_____

the blessing
What is this that gently forces me
From the still safe place of inaction?
What force compels me to abandon my comfort
Of well-worn despair?
Our Heavenly Father does not work from without,
But from within my own heart.
As the Law manifests itself through Love,
I stand in humble awe of the part of God that I AM.

evening focus
Our Heavenly Father

Saturday, March 16, 2024

seasonal focus
Brooks run free and buds appear.

morning focus
Our Earthly Mother

deepening
Hold a sprouted seed in your palm as you read.
(Alfalfa, mung bean, any will do.)

meditation
The path of the spirit calls to me to grow,
And grow I will.
But the journey home will take me far from my roots
Before I can once again return to the source.
Mother, at this time of new outer growth,
Fill my being with your love.
While my roots still are young,
Teach me to use Mind as servant,
Never as master.

today I will bring the spirit of Planetary Stewardship to my
_____

feelings _____
_____
_____
_____
_____
_____
_____

evening focus
The angel of Eternal Life

the blessing
At this time of newness,
Of moving faster into the unknown,
Let me never forget that while I am new,
I am also old.
There is an ancient part of me
That will provide the source of knowing
As my newness wanders forth
To seek its true identity.
I am new. I am ancient.
I AM.

seasonal focus
Brooks run free and buds appear.

Sunday, March 17, 2024

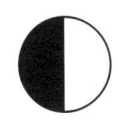

morning focus
The angel of Earth

deepening
Hold a handful of your local dirt as you read.
Explore its makeup.

meditation
There is a part of me
That is rooted firmly in the earth.
It is to this grounded, solid me
That I now deeply bow.
For without this,
There could be no expansion,
No life-giving nourishment
Coursing to my tender new leaves,
No strong stem to reach toward the sun.
The earth is my home for this incarnation,
And I am blessed.

today I will bring the spirit of Fullness to my _____

feelings _____

the blessing
There is a sacredness which infuses my life
As I realize that my own growth is my work.
I am the canvas
I am the artist
I am the paint.
I ask that the artist be ever guided by the Artist,
And that as I grow, I come to know the perfection
Of the unfinished masterpiece
That is Life.

evening focus
The angel of Creative Work

St. Patrick's Day

Monday, March 18, 2024

seasonal focus
Brooks run free and buds appear.

morning focus
The angel of Life

opening
Meditate while touching a house plant.
Exchange energy with this being.

meditation
And now the life-force in me,
As in all beings,
Cries out to know itself
Apart from the Mother.
My life,
The uniqueness of that which I am,
Calls to me to experience,
For it is only in the full freedom
Of my own experiencing
That I gain the wisdom of my connectedness
With all that is.
For I am the one
And I am also the many.

today I will bring the spirit of Uniqueness to my ___

feelings ___

___
___
___
___
___

evening focus
The angel of Peace

the blessing
As I experience the new life in me
Bursting its bounds,
I ask to be made more clearly aware
Of my part in the Plan,
That I may prepare myself
To become the fullest expression and channel
For peace.

SPRING EQUINOX

We are at the point in the yearly cycle when balance exists between light and dark. The day of Spring Equinox has equal times of daylight and darkness.

As the Sun moves from Pisces to Aries, it will cross the earth's celestial equator, and momentary balance of day and night is achieved. Thereafter, the hours of light will predominate and the hours of dark will fade into the background.

The Equinox then, is a time for us to examine our own balance. Does a balance exist between our poles of yin and yang, or are we prisoners of images of how we "should" behave? As we move toward our outer nature (the light), do we honor our inner nature (the dark)?

It was Carl Jung who reminded us that without the darkness we could not see the light of the candle flame.

Tuesday, March 19, 2024

seasonal focus
Buds unfold to early flowers.

morning focus
The angel of Joy

opening
Hold the image in your mind
of someone whom you love.

meditation
I am conscious of nature's outward thrust
In this season of the flowers,
And my heart is filled with joy.
The colors of my world,
The colors of my being,
The excitement of my life,
All these are the love of God
Shining upon my spirit.
There is no more that I need,
For I am complete.

today I will bring the spirit of Excitement to my _____
_____

feelings _____
_____
_____
_____
_____
_____
_____
_____

At Spring Equinox, the flowers announce the promise of fruit.

evening focus
The angel of Power

the blessing
The joyful thrust of all of life,
Reaching for the sun,
Reminds me of the power that is mine
In the service of the Light.
May I remember always
That I am the server,
And that God is the Power.

seasonal focus
Buds unfold to early flowers.

Wednesday, March 20, 2024

morning focus
The angel of the Sun

opening
Meditate on a candle flame. After, pinch out the flame, walk outdoors and be still for a few minutes.

meditation
The cells within my being
Respond to the call of
My spiritual father,
The sun.
As I grow,
As I expand to fill the outer limits
Of my potential,
I am nourished by the warmth
Of our ancient star
And I have all that I could ever need
To guide me safely home.

today I will bring the spirit of Completeness to my _____

feelings _____

the blessing
Who could not see,
Who could not feel,
The expression of divine Love
That fills the world this day?
As my buds softly open
Into rainbow flowers,
I return this Love
In every way I can.

evening focus
The angel of Love

Thursday, March 21, 2024

seasonal focus
Buds unfold to early flowers.

morning focus
The angel of Water

deepening
Hold water in your favorite bowl
as you read. After, give water to your plants.

meditation
In my upward movement
Toward the perfect flower
That I truly am,
What feeds my inner being
But the waters of the earth,
Given by the Father to the Mother
And given back again?
Waters of the Spirit,
Waters of the earth,
Fill me fully with your life
And make me whole.

today I will bring the spirit of Perfection to my _____

feelings _____

evening focus
The angel of Wisdom

the blessing
There is a knowing in this universe
That opens flowers in their time,
That gives me strength to grow.
The wisdom of this primal source
Is always mine to tap,
For I am one with all,
And all is mine to know.

Friday, March 22, 2024

seasonal focus
Buds unfold to early flowers.

morning focus
The angel of Air

opening
Hands over heart, then arms out to sides
as you inhale, opening lungs fully (five times).
Hands back to heart on each exhalation.

meditation
Within the quiet of this morning
Stirs the constant movement
Of my breath.
The inbreath of my life-force
Draws the world to me.
And as the outbreath streams from me
I share my life with others.
So goes the process of my growth,
Inbreath, outbreath,
Giving, receiving,
And all is One.

today I will bring the spirit of Sharing to my _____

feelings _____

the blessing
Before you I stand, humble, yet assured,
A reflection of your own radiance and perfection
As I grow.
I am my own gift to you,
My spiritual Father.
I am the promise of the new,
And I am ever mindful
Of the reason for my life.

evening focus
Our Heavenly Father

♌ → ♍

107

Saturday, March 23, 2024

seasonal focus
Buds unfold to early flowers.

morning focus
Our Earthly Mother

deepening
Hold a flower bud as you meditate.
Appreciate it and yourself.

meditation
Mother, in this season of the flowers
I bow to you in humble awe.
The brilliant colors of my blossoms
Are growing now,
Soon to be fruit.
I feel the need to give to you
For all that you have given to me,
And though the moment is not yet right,
One day my fruit will yield its seed
To your sweet earth.

today I will bring the spirit of Humility to my _____

feelings _____

evening focus
The angel of Eternal Life

the blessing
In the joyful outbreath
Of this season of my growth,
It is difficult to remember
The cycles of my life.
But remember I will,
For it is the rhythm of my living/dying
That gives the meaning to my journey,
And it is the surrender of yesterday's fruit
That allows the new seed to grow
To flower.

seasonal focus
Buds unfold to early flowers

morning focus
The angel of Earth

deepening
Hold a handful of moist, decaying, living earth as you meditate.

meditation
My petals spread upward to the sun,
My roots dig deeply in the earth.
Outward streams my love
To touch all life,
Inward streams the love
Life shares with me.
Let me open fully to it all,
For love and life and growth
Come in many colors
And sing many different songs.

today I will bring the spirit of Openness to my _____

feelings _____

Sunday, March 24, 2024

the blessing
The season's work comes clear to me,
Amidst my outward growth.
To love it all,
The bitter and the sweet,
For each is drawn to me,
Bringing lessons
To aid my journey home.
How blessed is the student,
How wise the teacher.
And are they not the same?

evening focus
The angel of Creative Work

♍ → ♎

Palm Sunday

109

Monday, March 25, 2024

seasonal focus
Buds unfold to early flowers.

morning focus
The angel of Life

opening
Meditate while touching a living plant,
bush, tree or pet. Exchange love with this being.

meditation
My life is guided onward
Toward the Light.
All about me are the signs of growth,
The signs of new life
Bursting from containment.
I, too, feel this primal urge
To cast off limitation
And open my petals to the sun.
No longer must I wait.
I share my life with those I love.

today I will bring the spirit of Freedom to my _____

feelings _____

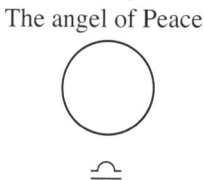

evening focus
The angel of Peace

the blessing
Beauty surrounds me, beauty all around me.
Quiet beauty of the new flowers of springtime
Within me, the peaceful beauty of my being
Reflects the richness of my life.
And I am blessed.

Tuesday, March 26, 2024

seasonal focus
Buds unfold to early flowers.

morning focus
The angel of Joy

opening
Hold the image in your mind
of someone whom you love.

meditation
I am conscious of nature's outward thrust
In this season of the flowers,
And my heart is filled with joy.
The colors of my world,
The colors of my being,
The excitement of my life,
All these are the love of God
Shining upon my spirit.
There is no more that I need,
For I am complete.

today I will bring the spirit of Excitement to my _____
_____

feelings _____
_____
_____
_____
_____
_____
_____
_____
_____

the blessing
The joyful thrust of all of life,
Reaching for the sun,
Reminds me of the power that is mine
In the service of the Light.
May I remember always
That I am the server,
And that God is the Power.

evening focus
The angel of Power

Wednesday, March 27, 2024

seasonal focus
Buds unfurl to early flowers.

morning focus
The angel of the Sun

opening
Meditate on a candle flame. After, pinch out the flame, walk outdoors and be still for a few minutes.

meditation
The cells within my being
Respond to the call of
My spiritual father,
The sun.
As I grow,
As I expand to fill the outer limits
Of my potential,
I am nourished by the warmth
Of our ancient star
And I have all that I could ever need
To guide me safely home.

today I will bring the spirit of Completeness to my
_____

feelings_____
_____
_____
_____
_____
_____
_____

evening focus
The angel of Love

♎ → ♏

the blessing
Who could not see,
Who could not feel,
The expression of divine Love
That fills the world this day?
As my buds softly open
Into rainbow flowers,
I return this Love
In every way I can.

Thursday, March 28, 2024

seasonal focus
Buds unfold to early flowers.

morning focus
The angel of Water

deepening
Hold water in your favorite bowl as you read.
After, give water to your plants.

meditation
In my upward movement
Toward the perfect flower
That I truly am,
What feeds my inner being
But the waters of the earth,
Given by the Father to the Mother
And given back again?
Waters of the Spirit,
Waters of the earth,
Fill me fully with your life
And make me whole.

today I will bring the spirit of Perfection to my _____

feelings _____

the blessing
There is a knowing in this universe
That opens flowers in their time,
That gives me strength to grow.
The wisdom of this primal source
Is always mine to tap,
For I am one with all,
And all is mine to know.

evening focus
The angel of Wisdom

Friday, March 29, 2024

seasonal focus
Buds unfold to early flowers.

morning focus
The angel of Air

opening
Hands over heart, then arms out to sides
as you inhale, opening lungs fully (five times).
Hands back to heart on each exhalation.

meditation
Within the quiet of this morning
Stirs the constant movement
Of my breath.
The inbreath of my life-force
Draws the world to me.
And as the outbreath streams from me
I share my life with others.
So goes the process of my growth,
Inbreath, outbreath,
Giving, receiving,
And all is One.

today I will bring the spirit of Sharing to my _____

feelings _____
_____
_____
_____

_____
_____
_____
_____

evening focus
Our Heavenly Father

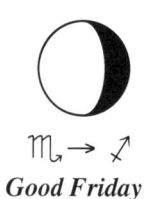

Good Friday

the blessing
Before you I stand, humble, yet assured,
A reflection of your own radiance and perfection
As I grow.
I am my own gift to you,
My spiritual Father.
I am the promise of the new,
And I am ever mindful
Of the reason for my life.

Saturday, March 30, 2024

seasonal focus
Buds unfold to early flowers.

morning focus
Our Earthly Mother

deepening
Hold a flower bud as you meditate.
Appreciate it and yourself.

meditation
Mother, in this season of the flowers
I bow to you in humble awe.
The brilliant colors of my blossoms
Are growing now,
Soon to be fruit.
I feel the need to give to you
For all that you have given to me,
And though the moment is not yet right,
One day my fruit will yield its seed
To your sweet earth.

today I will bring the spirit of Humility to my _____

feelings _____

the blessing
In the joyful outbreath
Of this season of my growth,
It is difficult to remember
The cycles of my life.
But remember I will,
For it is the rhythm of my living/dying
That gives the meaning to my journey,
And it is the surrender of yesterday's fruit
That allows the new seed to grow
To flower.

evening focus
The angel of Eternal Life

Sunday, March 31, 2024

seasonal focus
Buds unfold to early flowers.

morning focus
The angel of Earth

deepening
Hold a handful of moist, decaying, living earth as you meditate.

meditation
My petals spread upward to the sun,
My roots dig deeply in the earth.
Outward streams my love
To touch all life,
Inward streams the love
Life shares with me.
Let me open fully to it all,
For love and life and growth
Come in many colors
And sing many different songs.

today I will bring the spirit of Openness to my _____

feelings _____

_____
_____
_____
_____
_____

_____
_____
_____

evening focus
The angel of Creative Work

Easter Sunday

the blessing
The season's work comes clear to me,
Amidst my outward growth.
To love it all,
The bitter and the sweet,
For each is drawn to me,
Bringing lessons
To aid my journey home.
How blessed is the student,
How wise the teacher.
And are they not the same?

116

Monday, April 1, 2024

seasonal focus
Buds unfold to early flowers.

morning focus
The angel of Life

opening
Meditate while touching a living plant,
bush, tree or pet. Exchange love with this being.

meditation
My life is guided onward
Toward the Light.
All about me are the signs of growth,
The signs of new life
Bursting from containment.
I, too, feel this primal urge
To cast off limitation
And open my petals to the sun.
No longer must I wait.
I share my life with those I love.

today I will bring the spirit of Freedom to my _____
_____

feelings _____
_____
_____
_____
_____
_____
_____
_____

the blessing
Beauty surrounds me, beauty all around me.
Quiet beauty of the new flowers of springtime
Within me, the peaceful beauty of my being
Reflects the richness of my life.
And I am blessed.

evening focus
The angel of Peace

117

Tuesday, April 2, 2024

seasonal focus
Buds unfold to early flowers.

morning focus
The angel of Joy

opening
Hold the image in your mind
of someone whom you love.

meditation
I am conscious of nature's outward thrust
In this season of the flowers,
And my heart is filled with joy.
The colors of my world,
The colors of my being,
The excitement of my life,
All these are the love of God
Shining upon my spirit.
There is no more that I need,
For I am complete.

today I will bring the spirit of Excitement to my _____
_____

feelings _____
_____
_____
_____
_____
_____
_____
_____

evening focus
The angel of Power

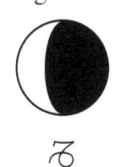

the blessing
The joyful thrust of all of life,
Reaching for the sun,
Reminds me of the power that is mine
In the service of the Light.
May I remember always
That I am the server,
And that God is the Power.

Wednesday, April 3, 2024

seasonal focus
Buds unfold to early flowers.

morning focus
The angel of the Sun

opening
Meditate on a candle flame. After, pinch out the flame, walk outdoors and be still for a few minutes.

meditation
The cells within my being
Respond to the call of
My spiritual father,
The sun.
As I grow,
As I expand to fill the outer limits
Of my potential,
I am nourished by the warmth
Of our ancient star
And I have all that I could ever need
To guide me safely home.

today I will bring the spirit of Completeness to my _____

feelings _____

the blessing
Who could not see,
Who could not feel,
The expression of divine Love
That fills the world this day?
As my buds softly open
Into rainbow flowers,
I return this Love
In every way I can.

evening focus
The angel of Love

119

Thursday, April 4, 2024

seasonal focus
Buds unfold to early flowers.

morning focus
The angel of Water

deepening
Hold water in your favorite bowl
as you read. After, give water to your plants.

meditation
In my upward movement
Toward the perfect flower
That I truly am,
What feeds my inner being
But the waters of the earth,
Given by the Father to the Mother
And given back again?
Waters of the Spirit,
Waters of the earth,
Fill me fully with your life
And make me whole.

today I will bring the spirit of Perfection to my _____

feelings _____

evening focus
The angel of Wisdom

the blessing
There is a knowing in this universe
That opens flowers in their time,
That gives me strength to grow.
The wisdom of this primal source
Is always mine to tap,
For I am one with all,
And all is mine to know.

seasonal focus
Buds unfold to early flowers.

Friday, April 5, 2024

morning focus
The angel of Air

opening
Hands over heart, then arms out to sides
as you inhale, opening lungs fully (five times).
Hands back to heart on each exhalation.

meditation
Within the quiet of this morning
Stirs the constant movement
Of my breath.
The inbreath of my life-force
Draws the world to me.
And as the outbreath streams from me
I share my life with others.
So goes the process of my growth,
Inbreath, outbreath,
Giving, receiving,
And all is One.

today I will bring the spirit of Sharing to my _____

feelings _____
_____
_____
_____
_____
_____
_____

the blessing
Before you I stand, humble, yet assured,
A reflection of your own radiance and perfection
As I grow.
I am my own gift to you,
My spiritual Father.
I am the promise of the new,
And I am ever mindful
Of the reason for my life.

evening focus
Our Heavenly Father

≈≈≈ → ⟩(

Saturday, April 6, 2024

seasonal focus
Buds unfold to early flowers.

morning focus
Our Earthly Mother

deepening
Hold a flower bud as you meditate.
Appreciate it and yourself.

meditation
Mother, in this season of the flowers
I bow to you in humble awe.
The brilliant colors of my blossoms
Are growing now,
Soon to be fruit.
I feel the need to give to you
For all that you have given to me,
And though the moment is not yet right,
One day my fruit will yield its seed
To your sweet earth.

today I will bring the spirit of Humility to my _____

feelings _____

evening focus
The angel of Eternal Life

the blessing
In the joyful outbreath
Of this season of my growth,
It is difficult to remember
The cycles of my life.
But remember I will,
For it is the rhythm of my living/dying
That gives the meaning to my journey,
And it is the surrender of yesterday's fruit
That allows the new seed to grow
To flower.

seasonal focus
Buds unfold to early flowers

morning focus
The angel of Earth

deepening
Hold a handful of moist, decaying, living earth as you meditate.

meditation
My petals spread upward to the sun,
My roots dig deeply in the earth.
Outward streams my love
To touch all life,
Inward streams the love
Life shares with me.
Let me open fully to it all,
For love and life and growth
Come in many colors
And sing many different songs.

today I will bring the spirit of Openness to my _____

feelings _____

the blessing
The season's work comes clear to me,
Amidst my outward growth.
To love it all,
The bitter and the sweet,
For each is drawn to me,
Bringing lessons
To aid my journey home.
How blessed is the student,
How wise the teacher.
And are they not the same?

Sunday, April 7, 2024

evening focus
The angel of Creative Work

Monday, April 8, 2024

seasonal focus
Buds unfold to early flowers.

morning focus
The angel of Life

opening
Meditate while touching a living plant,
bush, tree or pet. Exchange love with this being.

meditation
My life is guided onward
Toward the Light.
All about me are the signs of growth,
The signs of new life
Bursting from containment.
I, too, feel this primal urge
To cast off limitation
And open my petals to the sun.
No longer must I wait.
I share my life with those I love.

today I will bring the spirit of Freedom to my _____
_____

feelings_____
_____
_____
_____
_____
_____
_____
_____
_____
_____

evening focus
The angel of Peace

the blessing
Beauty surrounds me, beauty all around me.
Quiet beauty of the new flowers of springtime
Within me, the peaceful beauty of my being
Reflects the richness of my life.
And I am blessed.

Tuesday, April 9, 2024

seasonal focus
Buds unfold to early flowers.

morning focus
The angel of Joy

opening
Hold the image in your mind
of someone whom you love.

meditation
I am conscious of nature's outward thrust
In this season of the flowers,
And my heart is filled with joy.
The colors of my world,
The colors of my being,
The excitement of my life,
All these are the love of God
Shining upon my spirit.
There is no more that I need,
For I am complete.

today I will bring the spirit of Excitement to my _____
_____

feelings _____
_____
_____
_____
_____
_____
_____
_____

the blessing
The joyful thrust of all of life,
Reaching for the sun,
Reminds me of the power that is mine
In the service of the Light.
May I remember always
That I am the server,
And that God is the Power.

evening focus
The angel of Power

Wednesday, April 10, 2024

seasonal focus
Buds unfurl to early flowers.

morning focus
The angel of the Sun

opening
Meditate on a candle flame. After, pinch out the flame, walk outdoors and be still for a few minutes.

meditation
The cells within my being
Respond to the call of
My spiritual father,
The sun.
As I grow,
As I expand to fill the outer limits
Of my potential,
I am nourished by the warmth
Of our ancient star
And I have all that I could ever need
To guide me safely home.

today I will bring the spirit of Completeness to my
_____

feelings_____
_____
_____
_____
_____
_____
_____
_____

evening focus
The angel of Love

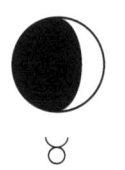

the blessing
Who could not see,
Who could not feel,
The expression of divine Love
That fills the world this day?
As my buds softly open
Into rainbow flowers,
I return this Love
In every way I can.

Thursday, April 11, 2024

seasonal focus
Buds unfold to early flowers.

morning focus
The angel of Water

deepening
Hold water in your favorite bowl as you read.
After, give water to your plants.

meditation
In my upward movement
Toward the perfect flower
That I truly am,
What feeds my inner being
But the waters of the earth,
Given by the Father to the Mother
And given back again?
Waters of the Spirit,
Waters of the earth,
Fill me fully with your life
And make me whole.

today I will bring the spirit of Perfection to my _____
_____

feelings _____
_____
_____
_____
_____
_____
_____
_____

the blessing
There is a knowing in this universe
That opens flowers in their time,
That gives me strength to grow.
The wisdom of this primal source
Is always mine to tap,
For I am one with all,
And all is mine to know.

evening focus
The angel of Wisdom

♉ → ♊

Friday, April 12, 2024

seasonal focus
Buds unfold to early flowers.

morning focus
The angel of Air

opening
Hands over heart, then arms out to sides
as you inhale, opening lungs fully (five times).
Hands back to heart on each exhalation.

meditation
Within the quiet of this morning
Stirs the constant movement
Of my breath.
The inbreath of my life-force
Draws the world to me.
And as the outbreath streams from me
I share my life with others.
So goes the process of my growth,
Inbreath, outbreath,
Giving, receiving,
And all is One.

today I will bring the spirit of Sharing to my _____

feelings _____

evening focus
Our Heavenly Father

the blessing
Before you I stand, humble, yet assured,
A reflection of your own radiance and perfection
As I grow.
I am my own gift to you,
My spiritual Father.
I am the promise of the new,
And I am ever mindful
Of the reason for my life.

seasonal focus
Buds unfold to early flowers.

morning focus
Our Earthly Mother

deepening
Hold a flower bud as you meditate.
Appreciate it and yourself.

meditation
Mother, in this season of the flowers
I bow to you in humble awe.
The brilliant colors of my blossoms
Are growing now,
Soon to be fruit.
I feel the need to give to you
For all that you have given to me,
And though the moment is not yet right,
One day my fruit will yield its seed
To your sweet earth.

today I will bring the spirit of Humility to my _____
_____

feelings _____
_____
_____
_____
_____
_____
_____

Saturday, April 13, 2024

the blessing
In the joyful outbreath
Of this season of my growth,
It is difficult to remember
The cycles of my life.
But remember I will,
For it is the rhythm of my living/dying
That gives the meaning to my journey,
And it is the surrender of yesterday's fruit
That allows the new seed to grow
To flower.

evening focus
The angel of Eternal Life

Sunday, April 14, 2024

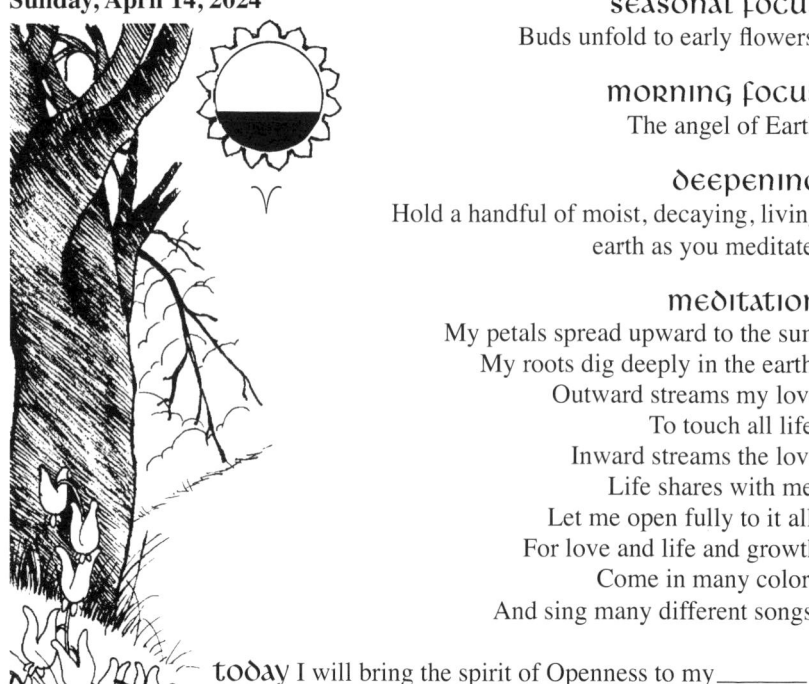

seasonal focus
Buds unfold to early flowers.

morning focus
The angel of Earth

deepening
Hold a handful of moist, decaying, living
earth as you meditate.

meditation
My petals spread upward to the sun,
My roots dig deeply in the earth.
Outward streams my love
To touch all life,
Inward streams the love
Life shares with me.
Let me open fully to it all,
For love and life and growth
Come in many colors
And sing many different songs.

today I will bring the spirit of Openness to my _____

feelings _____

_____

_____

_____

_____

_____

_____

_____

evening focus
The angel of Creative Work

the blessing
The season's work comes clear to me,
Amidst my outward growth.
To love it all,
The bitter and the sweet,
For each is drawn to me,
Bringing lessons
To aid my journey home.
How blessed is the student,
How wise the teacher.
And are they not the same?

Monday, April 15, 2024

seasonal focus
Buds unfold to early flowers.

morning focus
The angel of Life

opening
Meditate while touching a living plant,
bush, tree or pet. Exchange love with this being.

meditation
My life is guided onward
Toward the Light.
All about me are the signs of growth,
The signs of new life
Bursting from containment.
I, too, feel this primal urge
To cast off limitation
And open my petals to the sun.
No longer must I wait.
I share my life with those I love.

today I will bring the spirit of Freedom to my _____
_____

feelings _____
_____
_____
_____
_____
_____
_____
_____
_____

the blessing
Beauty surrounds me, beauty all around me.
Quiet beauty of the new flowers of springtime
Within me, the peaceful beauty of my being
Reflects the richness of my life.
And I am blessed.

evening focus
The angel of Peace

Tuesday, April 16, 2024

seasonal focus
Buds unfold to early flowers.

morning focus
The angel of Joy

opening
Hold the image in your mind
of someone whom you love.

meditation
I am conscious of nature's outward thrust
In this season of the flowers,
And my heart is filled with joy.
The colors of my world,
The colors of my being,
The excitement of my life,
All these are the love of God
Shining upon my spirit.
There is no more that I need,
For I am complete.

today I will bring the spirit of Excitement to my _____

feelings _____

evening focus
The angel of Power

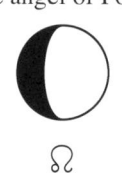

the blessing
The joyful thrust of all of life,
Reaching for the sun,
Reminds me of the power that is mine
In the service of the Light.
May I remember always
That I am the server,
And that God is the Power.

seasonal focus
Buds unfold to early flowers.

Wednesday, April 17, 2024

morning focus
The angel of the Sun

opening
Meditate on a candle flame. After, pinch out the flame, walk outdoors and be still for a few minutes.

meditation
The cells within my being
Respond to the call of
My spiritual father,
The sun.
As I grow,
As I expand to fill the outer limits
Of my potential,
I am nourished by the warmth
Of our ancient star
And I have all that I could ever need
To guide me safely home.

today I will bring the spirit of Completeness to my _____

feelings _____
_____
_____
_____
_____
_____
_____
_____

the blessing
Who could not see,
Who could not feel,
The expression of divine Love
That fills the world this day?
As my buds softly open
Into rainbow flowers,
I return this Love
In every way I can.

evening focus
The angel of Love

Thursday, April 18, 2024

seasonal focus
Buds unfold to early flowers.

morning focus
The angel of Water

deepening
Hold water in your favorite bowl
as you read. After, give water to your plants.

meditation
In my upward movement
Toward the perfect flower
That I truly am,
What feeds my inner being
But the waters of the earth,
Given by the Father to the Mother
And given back again?
Waters of the Spirit,
Waters of the earth,
Fill me fully with your life
And make me whole.

today I will bring the spirit of Perfection to my ____
_____

feelings _____
_____
_____
_____
_____
_____
_____
_____

evening focus
The angel of Wisdom

the blessing
There is a knowing in this universe
That opens flowers in their time,
That gives me strength to grow.
The wisdom of this primal source
Is always mine to tap,
For I am one with all,
And all is mine to know.

seasonal focus
Buds unfold to early flowers.

Friday, April 19, 2024

morning focus
The angel of Air

opening
Hands over heart, then arms out to sides
as you inhale, opening lungs fully (five times).
Hands back to heart on each exhalation.

meditation
Within the quiet of this morning
Stirs the constant movement
Of my breath.
The inbreath of my life-force
Draws the world to me.
And as the outbreath streams from me
I share my life with others.
So goes the process of my growth,
Inbreath, outbreath,
Giving, receiving,
And all is One.

today I will bring the spirit of Sharing to my _____

feelings _____

the blessing
Before you I stand, humble, yet assured,
A reflection of your own radiance and perfection
As I grow.
I am my own gift to you,
My spiritual Father.
I am the promise of the new,
And I am ever mindful
Of the reason for my life.

evening focus
Our Heavenly Father

Saturday, April 20, 2024

seasonal focus
Buds unfold to early flowers.

morning focus
Our Earthly Mother

deepening
Hold a flower bud as you meditate.
Appreciate it and yourself.

meditation
Mother, in this season of the flowers
I bow to you in humble awe.
The brilliant colors of my blossoms
Are growing now,
Soon to be fruit.
I feel the need to give to you
For all that you have given to me,
And though the moment is not yet right,
One day my fruit will yield its seed
To your sweet earth.

today I will bring the spirit of Humility to my _____

feelings _____

evening focus
The angel of Eternal Life

the blessing
In the joyful outbreath
Of this season of my growth,
It is difficult to remember
The cycles of my life.
But remember I will,
For it is the rhythm of my living/dying
That gives the meaning to my journey,
And it is the surrender of yesterday's fruit
That allows the new seed to grow
To flower.

seasonal focus
Buds unfold to early flowers.

Sunday, April 21, 2024

morning focus
The angel of Earth

deepening
Hold a handful of moist, decaying, living earth as you meditate.

meditation
My petals spread upward to the sun,
My roots dig deeply in the earth.
Outward streams my love
To touch all life,
Inward streams the love
Life shares with me.
Let me open fully to it all,
For love and life and growth
Come in many colors
And sing many different songs.

today I will bring the spirit of Openness to my _____

feelings _____

the blessing
The season's work comes clear to me,
Amidst my outward growth.
To love it all,
The bitter and the sweet,
For each is drawn to me,
Bringing lessons
To aid my journey home.
How blessed is the student,
How wise the teacher.
And are they not the same?

evening focus
The angel of Creative Work

Monday, April 22, 2024

seasonal focus
Buds unfold to early flowers.

morning focus
The angel of Life

opening
Meditate while touching a living plant,
bush, tree or pet. Exchange love with this being.

meditation
My life is guided onward
Toward the Light.
All about me are the signs of growth,
The signs of new life
Bursting from containment.
I, too, feel this primal urge
To cast off limitation
And open my petals to the sun.
No longer must I wait.
I share my life with those I love.

today I will bring the spirit of Freedom to my _____
_____

feelings_____
_____
_____
_____
_____
_____
_____
_____
_____

evening focus
The angel of Peace

Passover begins

the blessing
Beauty surrounds me, beauty all around me.
Quiet beauty of the new flowers of springtime
Within me, the peaceful beauty of my being
Reflects the richness of my life.
And I am blessed.

138

seasonal focus
Buds unfold to early flowers.

Tuesday, April 23, 2024

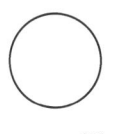

morning focus
The angel of Joy

opening
Hold the image in your mind
of someone whom you love.

meditation
I am conscious of nature's outward thrust
In this season of the flowers,
And my heart is filled with joy.
The colors of my world,
The colors of my being,
The excitement of my life,
All these are the love of God
Shining upon my spirit.
There is no more that I need,
For I am complete.

today I will bring the spirit of Excitement to my _____

feelings _____

the blessing
The joyful thrust of all of life,
Reaching for the sun,
Reminds me of the power that is mine
In the service of the Light.
May I remember always
That I am the server,
And that God is the Power.

evening focus
The angel of Power

Wednesday, April 24, 2024

seasonal focus
Buds unfurl to early flowers.

morning focus
The angel of the Sun

opening
Meditate on a candle flame. After, pinch out the flame, walk outdoors and be still for a few minutes.

meditation
The cells within my being
Respond to the call of
My spiritual father,
The sun.
As I grow,
As I expand to fill the outer limits
Of my potential,
I am nourished by the warmth
Of our ancient star
And I have all that I could ever need
To guide me safely home.

today I will bring the spirit of Completeness to my _____

feelings _____

_____

_____

_____

_____

_____

_____

evening focus
The angel of Love

the blessing
Who could not see,
Who could not feel,
The expression of divine Love
That fills the world this day?
As my buds softly open
Into rainbow flowers,
I return this Love
In every way I can.

Thursday, April 25, 2024

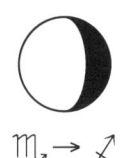

seasonal focus
Buds unfold to early flowers.

morning focus
The angel of Water

deepening
Hold water in your favorite bowl as you read.
After, give water to your plants.

meditation
In my upward movement
Toward the perfect flower
That I truly am,
What feeds my inner being
But the waters of the earth,
Given by the Father to the Mother
And given back again?
Waters of the Spirit,
Waters of the earth,
Fill me fully with your life
And make me whole.

today I will bring the spirit of Perfection to my _____

feelings _____
_____
_____
_____
_____
_____
_____
_____

the blessing
There is a knowing in this universe
That opens flowers in their time,
That gives me strength to grow.
The wisdom of this primal source
Is always mine to tap,
For I am one with all,
And all is mine to know.

evening focus
The angel of Wisdom

Friday, April 26, 2024

seasonal focus
Buds unfold to early flowers.

morning focus
The angel of Air

opening
Hands over heart, then arms out to sides
as you inhale, opening lungs fully (five times).
Hands back to heart on each exhalation.

meditation
Within the quiet of this morning
Stirs the constant movement
Of my breath.
The inbreath of my life-force
Draws the world to me.
And as the outbreath streams from me
I share my life with others.
So goes the process of my growth,
Inbreath, outbreath,
Giving, receiving,
And all is One.

today I will bring the spirit of Sharing to my _____

feelings _____

evening focus
Our Heavenly Father

the blessing
Before you I stand, humble, yet assured,
A reflection of your own radiance and perfection
As I grow.
I am my own gift to you,
My spiritual Father.
I am the promise of the new,
And I am ever mindful
Of the reason for my life.

seasonal focus
Buds unfold to early flowers.

morning focus
Our Earthly Mother

deepening
Hold a flower bud as you meditate.
Appreciate it and yourself.

meditation
Mother, in this season of the flowers
I bow to you in humble awe.
The brilliant colors of my blossoms
Are growing now,
Soon to be fruit.
I feel the need to give to you
For all that you have given to me,
And though the moment is not yet right,
One day my fruit will yield its seed
To your sweet earth.

today I will bring the spirit of Humility to my _____

feelings _____

Saturday, April 27, 2024

the blessing
In the joyful outbreath
Of this season of my growth,
It is difficult to remember
The cycles of my life.
But remember I will,
For it is the rhythm of my living/dying
That gives the meaning to my journey,
And it is the surrender of yesterday's fruit
That allows the new seed to grow
To flower.

evening focus
The angel of Eternal Life

Sunday, April 28, 2024

seasonal focus
Buds unfold to early flowers.

morning focus
The angel of Earth

deepening
Hold a handful of moist, decaying, living earth as you meditate.

meditation
My petals spread upward to the sun,
My roots dig deeply in the earth.
Outward streams my love
To touch all life,
Inward streams the love
Life shares with me.
Let me open fully to it all,
For love and life and growth
Come in many colors
And sing many different songs.

today I will bring the spirit of Openness to my _____

feelings _____

evening focus
The angel of Creative Work

the blessing
The season's work comes clear to me,
Amidst my outward growth.
To love it all,
The bitter and the sweet,
For each is drawn to me,
Bringing lessons
To aid my journey home.
How blessed is the student,
How wise the teacher.
And are they not the same?

seasonal focus
Buds unfold to early flowers.

Monday, April 29, 2024

morning focus
The angel of Life

opening
Meditate while touching a living plant,
bush, tree or pet. Exchange love with this being.

meditation
My life is guided onward
Toward the Light.
All about me are the signs of growth,
The signs of new life
Bursting from containment.
I, too, feel this primal urge
To cast off limitation
And open my petals to the sun.
No longer must I wait.
I share my life with those I love.

today I will bring the spirit of Freedom to my _____

feelings _____

the blessing
Beauty surrounds me, beauty all around me.
Quiet beauty of the new flowers of springtime
Within me, the peaceful beauty of my being
Reflects the richness of my life.
And I am blessed.

evening focus
The angel of Peace

Tuesday, April 30, 2024

seasonal focus
Buds unfold to early flowers.

morning focus
The angel of Joy

opening
Hold the image in your mind
of someone whom you love.

meditation
I am conscious of nature's outward thrust
In this season of the flowers,
And my heart is filled with joy.
The colors of my world,
The colors of my being,
The excitement of my life,
All these are the love of God
Shining upon my spirit.
There is no more that I need,
For I am complete.

today I will bring the spirit of Excitement to my _____

feelings _____

evening focus
The angel of Power

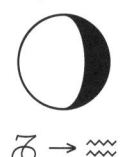

the blessing
The joyful thrust of all of life,
Reaching for the sun,
Reminds me of the power that is mine
In the service of the Light.
May I remember always
That I am the server,
And that God is the Power.

Beltane

The first day of May has been celebrated for thousands of years as the point of fertility, as a time when nature blatantly displays its beauty to bring about the conception of new life. In Celtic tradition, it is known as Beltane, or Bealten, the magic of flowers.

The virgin aspect of the Earth Mother now grows into the aspect of a young woman on her journey to the fullness of summer. And as with each of us, the focus is now on the acceptance of our adult role and owning of our fullness. We are here upon this earth for a purpose, and a major aspect of this is to be of authentic service, to share our light and our love genuinely as we grow in consciousness.

This is a time of doing, of making love manifest on the physical plane, and of drawing down the Light in very real ways to guide and strengthen us all.

Wednesday, May 1, 2024

seasonal focus
Flowers announce the promise of fruit.

morning focus
The angel of the Sun

opening
Read the meditation and the blessing outside.
Be still and notice. . .

meditation
I enter into the season of the sun,
And the Sun within me responds in kind.
My heart tells me
To build my castles high
With love and clarity.
My soul tells me
To bring the Plan to earth.
My mind tells me
To bring perfection to my work.
There is much to do and I am equal to the task.

today I will bring the spirit of Clarity to my _____

_____

feelings_____

_____

_____

_____

_____

At Beltane, the sun begins to ripen the fruits of the coming summer.

evening focus
The angel of Love

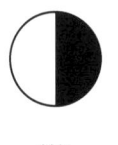

the blessing
Many are the ways to share
The mystery that is me,
And the greatest of these is Love.
To love one another, truly,
Without expectation of gain,
Is to transform the world.
I am learning to move
Beyond possession and manipulation
And into the awareness of lovingness,
Where I need ask for naught
And simply share my love.

Thursday, May 2, 2024

seasonal focus
Flowers announce the promise of fruit.

morning focus
The angel of Water

deepening
Hold water in your bowl as you read.
Sometime this day, share it
(tea with a friend; sprinkle a loved one?).

meditation
A wave of the ocean glides over the sea
And crashes upon the shore.
My body dances over the meadow
And joyfully leaps in the air.
Is the wave not still one with the ocean?
Am I not one with All?
Can I separate myself from my Source
When that wellspring flows deep within me
And not on some distant mountain?

today I will bring the spirit of my Divine Nature to my _____

feelings _____
_____
_____
_____
_____
_____
_____
_____

the blessing
This is the season of searching outside me,
To discover the teachers who Know.
But deep within me I must remember
"When the Student is ready,
The Teacher appears."
When I ask the right questions
Answers always are there
For my teachers are everywhere.

evening focus
The angel of Wisdom

Friday, May 3, 2024

seasonal focus
Flowers announce the promise of fruit.

morning focus
The angel of Air

opening
Before reading,
extend arms out to sides and behind,
stretching upper torso, expanding chest.
Five deep breaths.

meditation
I can feel it, almost see it;
There is electricity in the air
Which urges life to live.
"Fully live," it calls to me,
"Fully know your Self,
Accept the challenge of your life,
Experience it all."
"I am the Word," God said,
"All this and more are you."
"I am the Word," I say to God,
"I accept your task for me."

today I will bring the spirit of Service to my _____
_____

feelings _____
_____
_____
_____
_____

evening focus
Our Heavenly Father

the blessing
It is I who asks
For your blessing, Father,
No longer in whimpered tones.
I have grown throughout the seasons
And stand now tall and sure.
I am sensing
Who I truly am,
And I stand to meet that test.
I am your Word within this life,
This lifetime
Know I this.

seasonal focus
Flowers announce the promise of fruit.

Saturday, May 4, 2024

morning focus
Our Earthly Mother

deepening
Hold a piece of local fruit which is ripe
in this season. Make it part of your next meal.

meditation
I feel the presence
Of our Earthly Mother within me,
And that presence is illuminated
By the warm rays of the Father of us all.
All about me are the gifts
Of the Mother's ripening fruits,
And I know that in my own way
I am ripening too.

today I will bring the spirit of Authenticity to my _____

feelings _____

the blessing
Even as my fruits ripen,
As my gifts become manifest,
As I mature in openness and love,
I remember that I have walked this path before,
And will again.
For the fruits of now
Contain the seeds of tomorrow,
And my seeds of bygone seasons
Have brought this day's joy to me.
My seeds, my fruits will come and go,
And I will carry on.

evening focus
The angel of Eternal Life

151

Sunday, May 5, 2024

seasonal focus
Flowers announce the promise of fruit.

morning focus
The angel of Earth

deepening
Hold a handful of moist, decaying,
living earth as you meditate.

meditation
What is the source
From whence gushes the frenzied growth
All about me?
What overlighting presence
Guides the living things of earth
Toward the zenith of their life?
I, as one of these living things,
Marvel at the perfection of our unfolding.
Blessed am I to be a part of the Plan.

today I will bring the spirit of Wholeness to my _____

feelings_____

evening focus
The angel of Creative Work

the blessing
My heart tells me
That the time of compromise
Has passed.
Now, the work I do
Must nourish me
And heal the earth
And free our common spirit.

Monday, May 6, 2024

seasonal focus
Flowers announce the promise of fruit.

morning focus
The angel of Life

opening
Meditate while touching a living plant,
bush, tree or pet. Exchange love with this being.

meditation
From the point from which all Life flows,
It flows to me.
My part is to accept this life consciously
As a manifestation of God on earth.
It is I
Who bring Light and Love into this existence.
No angelic being can do it for me.
Yes, heartily do I accept
This responsibility!
Yes, gladly do I accept
The God in me!

today I will bring the spirit of Responsibility to my
_____

feelings _____
_____
_____
_____
_____
_____
_____

the blessing
Throughout me there is movement;
There is growth
Streaming to the outer bounds of my potential,
And I feel full and overflowing.
Yet at my center, at the very core of me,
There is a quiet place
From which my guidance comes.
Let me learn to seek this center
Often.

evening focus
The angel of Peace

♈ → ♉

Tuesday, May 7, 2024

seasonal focus
Flowers announce the promise of fruit.

morning focus
The angel of Joy

opening
Imagine someone whom you dislike.
Enfold that person's image in your *love*,
without forcing yourself to like them.

meditation
From each moment
I draw life.
From each living being
I draw love.
From the earth and the sun
I draw nourishment.
From each I receive
And to each I joyfully give,
For the web that connects each to me
Weaves its tapestry throughout my being,
Uniting me with all.
Separateness
Is an illusion.

today I will bring the spirit of Joy to my _____
_____

feelings_____
_____
_____
_____
_____

evening focus
The angel of Power

the blessing
As our sun
Daily shares more and more of its power with me,
I stand in awe of the power
That also lies within me.
I take upon myself the yoke of responsibility for my power,
And direct that power
In the service of positive, liberating evolution
For myself and all beings.
So be it.

seasonal focus
Flowers announce the promise of fruit.

Wednesday, May 8, 2024

morning focus
The angel of the Sun

opening
Read the meditation and the blessing outside.
Be still and notice. . .

meditation
I enter into the season of the sun,
And the Sun within me responds in kind.
My heart tells me
To build my castles high with love and clarity.
My soul tells me
To bring the Plan to earth.
My mind tells me
To bring perfection to my work.
There is much to do and I am equal to the task.

today I will bring the spirit of Clarity to my _____
_____

feelings _____
_____
_____
_____
_____
_____
_____

the blessing
Many are the ways to share
The mystery that is me,
And the greatest of these is Love.
To love one another, truly,
Without expectation of gain,
Is to transform the world.
I am learning to move
Beyond possession and manipulation
And into the awareness of lovingness,
Where I need ask for naught
And simply share my love.

evening focus
The angel of Love

155

Thursday, May 9, 2024

seasonal focus
Flowers announce the promise of fruit.

morning focus
The angel of Water

deepening
Hold water in your bowl as you read.
Sometime this day, share it
(tea with a friend; sprinkle a loved one?).

meditation
A wave of the ocean glides over the sea
And crashes upon the shore.
My body dances over the meadow
And joyfully leaps in the air.
Is the wave not still one with the ocean?
Am I not one with All?
Can I separate myself from my Source
When that wellspring flows deep within me
And not on some distant mountain?

today I will bring the spirit of my Divine Nature to my
_____

feelings _____
_____
_____
_____
_____
_____
_____

evening focus
The angel of Wisdom

the blessing
This is the season of searching outside me,
To discover the teachers who Know.
But deep within me I must remember
"When the Student is ready,
The Teacher appears."
When I ask the right questions
Answers always are there
For my teachers are everywhere.

seasonal focus
Flowers announce the promise of fruit.

Friday, May 10, 2024

morning focus
The angel of Air

opening
Before reading,
extend arms out to sides and behind,
stretching upper torso, expanding chest.
Five deep breaths.

meditation
I can feel it, almost see it;
There is electricity in the air
Which urges life to live.
"Fully live," it calls to me,
"Fully know your Self,
Accept the challenge of your life,
Experience it all."
"I am the Word," God said,
"All this and more are you."
"I am the Word," I say to God,
"I accept your task for me."

today I will bring the spirit of Service to my _____

feelings _____
_____
_____
_____
_____
_____

the blessing
It is I who asks
For your blessing, Father,
No longer in whimpered tones.
I have grown throughout the seasons
And stand now tall and sure.
I am sensing who I truly am,
And I stand to meet that test.
I am your Word within this life,
This lifetime
Know I this.

evening focus
Our Heavenly Father

♊ → ♋

Saturday, May 11, 2024

seasonal focus
Flowers announce the promise of fruit.

morning focus
Our Earthly Mother

deepening
Hold a piece of local fruit which is ripe in this season. Make it part of your next meal.

meditation
I feel the presence
Of our Earthly Mother within me,
And that presence is illuminated
By the warm rays of the Father of us all.
All about me are the gifts
Of the Mother's ripening fruits,
And I know that in my own way
I am ripening too.

today I will bring the spirit of Authenticity to my _____

feelings _____

evening focus
The angel of Eternal Life

the blessing
Even as my fruits ripen,
As my gifts become manifest,
As I mature in openness and love,
I remember that I have walked this path before,
And will again.
For the fruits of now
Contain the seeds of tomorrow,
And my seeds of bygone seasons
Have brought this day's joy to me.
My seeds, my fruits will come and go,
And I will carry on.

Sunday, May 12, 2024

seasonal focus
Flowers announce the promise of fruit.

morning focus
The angel of Earth

deepening
Hold a handful of moist, decaying,
living earth as you meditate.

meditation
What is the source
From whence gushes the frenzied growth
All about me?
What overlighting presence
Guides the living things of earth
Toward the zenith of their life?
I, as one of these living things,
Marvel at the perfection of our unfolding.
Blessed am I to be a part of the Plan.

today I will bring the spirit of Wholeness to my _____

feelings _____

the blessing
My heart tells me
That the time of compromise
Has passed.
Now, the work I do
Must nourish me
And heal the earth
And free our common spirit.

evening focus
The angel of Creative Work

Mother's Day

Monday, May 13, 2024

seasonal focus
Flowers announce the promise of fruit.

morning focus
The angel of Life

opening
Meditate while touching a living plant,
bush, tree or pet. Exchange love with this being.

meditation
From the point from which all Life flows,
It flows to me.
My part is to accept this life consciously
As a manifestation of God on earth.
It is I
Who bring Light and Love into this existence.
No angelic being can do it for me.
Yes, heartily do I accept
This responsibility!
Yes, gladly do I accept
The God in me!

today I will bring the spirit of Responsibility to my
_____

feelings _____

_____
_____
_____
_____
_____
_____

evening focus
The angel of Peace

♋ → ♌

the blessing
Throughout me there is movement;
There is growth
Streaming to the outer bounds of my potential,
And I feel full and overflowing.
Yet at my center, at the very core of me,
There is a quiet place
From which my guidance comes.
Let me learn to seek this center
Often.

Tuesday, May 14, 2024

seasonal focus
Flowers announce the promise of fruit.

morning focus
The angel of Joy

opening
Imagine someone whom you dislike.
Enfold that person's image in your *love*,
without forcing yourself to like them.

meditation
From each moment
I draw life.
From each living being
I draw love.
From the earth and the sun
I draw nourishment.
From each I receive
And to each I joyfully give,
For the web that connects each to me
Weaves its tapestry throughout my being,
Uniting me with all.
Separateness
Is an illusion.

today I will bring the spirit of Joy to my _____

feelings _____

the blessing
As our sun
Daily shares more and more of its power with me,
I stand in awe of the power
That also lies within me.
I take upon myself the yoke of responsibility for my power,
And direct that power
In the service of positive, liberating evolution
For myself and all beings.
So be it.

evening focus
The angel of Power

Wednesday, May 15, 2024

seasonal focus
Flowers announce the promise of fruit.

morning focus
The angel of the Sun

opening
Read the meditation and the blessing outside.
Be still and notice. . .

meditation
I enter into the season of the sun,
And the Sun within me responds in kind.
My heart tells me
To build my castles high
With love and clarity.
My soul tells me
To bring the Plan to earth.
My mind tells me
To bring perfection to my work.
There is much to do and I am equal to the task.

today I will bring the spirit of Clarity to my _____
_____

feelings_____
_____
_____
_____
_____
_____
_____

evening focus
The angel of Love

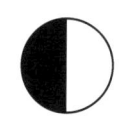

the blessing
Many are the ways to share
The mystery that is me,
And the greatest of these is Love.
To love one another, truly,
Without expectation of gain,
Is to transform the world.
I am learning to move
Beyond possession and manipulation
And into the awareness of lovingness,
Where I need ask for naught
And simply share my love.

seasonal focus
Flowers announce the promise of fruit.

Thursday, May 16, 2024

morning focus
The angel of Water

deepening
Hold water in your bowl as you read.
Sometime this day, share it
(tea with a friend; sprinkle a loved one?).

meditation
A wave of the ocean glides over the sea
And crashes upon the shore.
My body dances over the meadow
And joyfully leaps in the air.
Is the wave not still one with the ocean?
Am I not one with All?
Can I separate myself from my Source
When that wellspring flows deep within me
And not on some distant mountain?

today I will bring the spirit of my Divine Nature to my _____

feelings _____

the blessing
This is the season of searching outside me,
To discover the teachers who Know.
But deep within me I must remember
"When the Student is ready,
The Teacher appears."
When I ask the right questions
Answers always are there
For my teachers are everywhere.

evening focus
The angel of Wisdom

Friday, May 17, 2024

seasonal focus
Flowers announce the promise of fruit.

morning focus
The angel of Air

opening
Before reading,
extend arms out to sides and behind,
stretching upper torso, expanding chest.
Five deep breaths.

meditation
I can feel it, almost see it;
There is electricity in the air
Which urges life to live.
"Fully live," it calls to me,
"Fully know your Self,
Accept the challenge of your life,
Experience it all."
"I am the Word," God said,
"All this and more are you."
"I am the Word," I say to God,
"I accept your task for me."

today I will bring the spirit of Service to my _____
_____

feelings _____
_____
_____
_____
_____

evening focus
Our Heavenly Father

the blessing
It is I who asks
For your blessing, Father,
No longer in whimpered tones.
I have grown throughout the seasons
And stand now tall and sure.
I am sensing
Who I truly am,
And I stand to meet that test.
I am your Word within this life,
This lifetime
Know I this.

seasonal focus
Flowers announce the promise of fruit.

Saturday, May 18, 2024

morning focus
Our Earthly Mother

deepening
Hold a piece of local fruit which is ripe
in this season. Make it part of your next meal.

meditation
I feel the presence
Of our Earthly Mother within me,
And that presence is illuminated
By the warm rays of the Father of us all.
All about me are the gifts
Of the Mother's ripening fruits,
And I know that in my own way
I am ripening too.

today I will bring the spirit of Authenticity to my _____

feelings _____
_____
_____
_____
_____
_____

the blessing
Even as my fruits ripen,
As my gifts become manifest,
As I mature in openness and love,
I remember that I have walked this path before,
And will again.
For the fruits of now
Contain the seeds of tomorrow,
And my seeds of bygone seasons
Have brought this day's joy to me.
My seeds, my fruits will come and go,
And I will carry on.

evening focus
The angel of Eternal Life

♍ → ♎

Sunday, May 19, 2024

seasonal focus
Flowers announce the promise of fruit.

morning focus
The angel of Earth

deepening
Hold a handful of moist, decaying, living earth as you meditate.

meditation
What is the source
From whence gushes the frenzied growth
All about me?
What overlighting presence
Guides the living things of earth
Toward the zenith of their life?
I, as one of these living things,
Marvel at the perfection of our unfolding.
Blessed am I to be a part of the Plan.

today I will bring the spirit of Wholeness to my _____

feelings_____

evening focus
The angel of Creative Work

the blessing
My heart tells me
That the time of compromise
Has passed.
Now, the work I do
Must nourish me
And heal the earth
And free our common spirit.

seasonal focus
Flowers announce the promise of fruit.

Monday, May 20, 2024

morning focus
The angel of Life

opening
Meditate while touching a living plant,
bush, tree or pet. Exchange love with this being.

meditation
From the point from which all Life flows,
It flows to me.
My part is to accept this life consciously
As a manifestation of God on earth.
It is I
Who bring Light and Love into this existence.
No angelic being can do it for me.
Yes, heartily do I accept
This responsibility!
Yes, gladly do I accept
The God in me!

today I will bring the spirit of Responsibility to my
_____

feelings _____
_____
_____
_____
_____

_____
_____
_____

the blessing
Throughout me there is movement;
There is growth
Streaming to the outer bounds of my potential,
And I feel full and overflowing.
Yet at my center, at the very core of me,
There is a quiet place
From which my guidance comes.
Let me learn to seek this center
Often.

evening focus
The angel of Peace

167

Tuesday, May 21, 2024

seasonal focus
Flowers announce the promise of fruit.

morning focus
The angel of Joy

opening
Imagine someone whom you dislike.
Enfold that person's image in your *love*,
without forcing yourself to like them.

meditation
From each moment
I draw life.
From each living being
I draw love.
From the earth and the sun
I draw nourishment.
From each I receive
And to each I joyfully give,
For the web that connects each to me
Weaves its tapestry throughout my being,
Uniting me with all.
Separateness
Is an illusion.

today I will bring the spirit of Joy to my _____

feelings _____

evening focus
The angel of Power

the blessing
As our sun
Daily shares more and more of its power with me,
I stand in awe of the power
That also lies within me.
I take upon myself the yoke of responsibility for my power,
And direct that power
In the service of positive, liberating evolution
For myself and all beings.
So be it.

seasonal focus
Flowers announce the promise of fruit.

Wednesday, May 22, 2024

morning focus
The angel of the Sun

opening
Read the meditation and the blessing outside.
Be still and notice. . .

meditation
I enter into the season of the sun,
And the Sun within me responds in kind.
My heart tells me
To build my castles high with love and clarity.
My soul tells me
To bring the Plan to earth.
My mind tells me
To bring perfection to my work.
There is much to do and I am equal to the task.

today I will bring the spirit of Clarity to my _____

feelings _____

the blessing
Many are the ways to share
The mystery that is me,
And the greatest of these is Love.
To love one another, truly,
Without expectation of gain,
Is to transform the world.
I am learning to move
Beyond possession and manipulation
And into the awareness of lovingness,
Where I need ask for naught
And simply share my love.

evening focus
The angel of Love

169

Thursday, May 23, 2024

seasonal focus
Flowers announce the promise of fruit.

morning focus
The angel of Water

deepening
Hold water in your bowl as you read.
Sometime this day, share it
(tea with a friend; sprinkle a loved one?).

meditation
A wave of the ocean glides over the sea
And crashes upon the shore.
My body dances over the meadow
And joyfully leaps in the air.
Is the wave not still one with the ocean?
Am I not one with All?
Can I separate myself from my Source
When that wellspring flows deep within me
And not on some distant mountain?

today I will bring the spirit of my Divine Nature to my

_____

feelings _____

_____

_____

_____

_____

_____

_____

evening focus
The angel of Wisdom

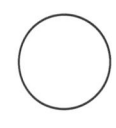

the blessing
This is the season of searching outside me,
To discover the teachers who Know.
But deep within me I must remember
"When the Student is ready,
The Teacher appears."
When I ask the right questions
Answers always are there
For my teachers are everywhere.

seasonal focus
Flowers announce the promise of fruit.

Friday, May 24, 2024

morning focus
The angel of Air

opening
Before reading,
extend arms out to sides and behind,
stretching upper torso, expanding chest.
Five deep breaths.

meditation
I can feel it, almost see it;
There is electricity in the air
Which urges life to live.
"Fully live," it calls to me,
"Fully know your Self,
Accept the challenge of your life,
Experience it all."
"I am the Word," God said,
"All this and more are you."
"I am the Word," I say to God,
"I accept your task for me."

today I will bring the spirit of Service to my _____
_____

feelings _____
_____
_____
_____
_____

the blessing
It is I who asks
For your blessing, Father,
No longer in whimpered tones.
I have grown throughout the seasons
And stand now tall and sure.
I am sensing who I truly am,
And I stand to meet that test.
I am your Word within this life,
This lifetime
Know I this.

evening focus
Our Heavenly Father

Saturday, May 25, 2024

seasonal focus
Flowers announce the promise of fruit.

morning focus
Our Earthly Mother

deepening
Hold a piece of local fruit which is ripe
in this season. Make it part of your next meal.

meditation
I feel the presence
Of our Earthly Mother within me,
And that presence is illuminated
By the warm rays of the Father of us all.
All about me are the gifts
Of the Mother's ripening fruits,
And I know that in my own way
I am ripening too.

today I will bring the spirit of Authenticity to my _____

feelings _____

---

evening focus
The angel of Eternal Life

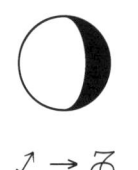

the blessing
Even as my fruits ripen,
As my gifts become manifest,
As I mature in openness and love,
I remember that I have walked this path before,
And will again.
For the fruits of now
Contain the seeds of tomorrow,
And my seeds of bygone seasons
Have brought this day's joy to me.
My seeds, my fruits will come and go,
And I will carry on.

seasonal focus
Flowers announce the promise of fruit.

Sunday, May 26, 2024

morning focus
The angel of Earth

deepening
Hold a handful of moist, decaying,
living earth as you meditate.

meditation
What is the source
From whence gushes the frenzied growth
All about me?
What overlighting presence
Guides the living things of earth
Toward the zenith of their life?
I, as one of these living things,
Marvel at the perfection of our unfolding.
Blessed am I to be a part of the Plan.

today I will bring the spirit of Wholeness to my _____

feelings _____

the blessing
My heart tells me
That the time of compromise
Has passed.
Now, the work I do
Must nourish me
And heal the earth
And free our common spirit.

evening focus
The angel of Creative Work

Monday, May 27, 2024

seasonal focus
Flowers announce the promise of fruit.

morning focus
The angel of Life

opening
Meditate while touching a living plant,
bush, tree or pet. Exchange love with this being.

meditation
From the point from which all Life flows,
It flows to me.
My part is to accept this life consciously
As a manifestation of God on earth.
It is I
Who bring Light and Love into this existence.
No angelic being can do it for me.
Yes, heartily do I accept
This responsibility!
Yes, gladly do I accept
The God in me!

today I will bring the spirit of Responsibility to my
_____

feelings_____
_____
_____
_____
_____
_____
_____
_____

evening focus
The angel of Peace

the blessing
Throughout me there is movement;
There is growth
Streaming to the outer bounds of my potential,
And I feel full and overflowing.
Yet at my center, at the very core of me,
There is a quiet place
From which my guidance comes.
Let me learn to seek this center
Often.

seasonal focus
Flowers announce the promise of fruit.

Tuesday, May 28, 2024

morning focus
The angel of Joy

opening
Imagine someone whom you dislike.
Enfold that person's image in your *love*,
without forcing yourself to like them.

meditation
From each moment
I draw life.
From each living being
I draw love.
From the earth and the sun
I draw nourishment.
From each I receive
And to each I joyfully give,
For the web that connects each to me
Weaves its tapestry throughout my being,
Uniting me with all.
Separateness
Is an illusion.

today I will bring the spirit of Joy to my _____

feelings _____

the blessing
As our sun
Daily shares more and more of its power with me,
I stand in awe of the power
That also lies within me.
I take upon myself the yoke of responsibility for my power,
And direct that power
In the service of positive, liberating evolution
For myself and all beings.
So be it.

evening focus
The angel of Power

Wednesday, May 29, 2024

seasonal focus
Flowers announce the promise of fruit.

morning focus
The angel of the Sun

opening
Read the meditation and the blessing outside.
Be still and notice. . .

meditation
I enter into the season of the sun,
And the Sun within me responds in kind.
My heart tells me
To build my castles high
With love and clarity.
My soul tells me
To bring the Plan to earth.
My mind tells me
To bring perfection to my work.
There is much to do and I am equal to the task.

today I will bring the spirit of Clarity to my _____

feelings _____

_____
_____
_____
_____
_____

evening focus
The angel of Love

the blessing
Many are the ways to share
The mystery that is me,
And the greatest of these is Love.
To love one another, truly,
Without expectation of gain,
Is to transform the world.
I am learning to move
Beyond possession and manipulation
And into the awareness of lovingness,
Where I need ask for naught
And simply share my love.

Thursday, May 30, 2024

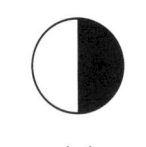

seasonal focus
Flowers announce the promise of fruit.

morning focus
The angel of Water

deepening
Hold water in your bowl as you read.
Sometime this day, share it
(tea with a friend; sprinkle a loved one?).

meditation
A wave of the ocean glides over the sea
And crashes upon the shore.
My body dances over the meadow
And joyfully leaps in the air.
Is the wave not still one with the ocean?
Am I not one with All?
Can I separate myself from my Source
When that wellspring flows deep within me
And not on some distant mountain?

today I will bring the spirit of my Divine Nature to my
_____

feelings _____
_____
_____
_____
_____
_____
_____
_____

the blessing
This is the season of searching outside me,
To discover the teachers who Know.
But deep within me I must remember
"When the Student is ready,
The Teacher appears."
When I ask the right questions
Answers always are there
For my teachers are everywhere.

evening focus
The angel of Wisdom

Friday, May 31, 2024

seasonal focus
Flowers announce the promise of fruit.

morning focus
The angel of Air

opening
Before reading,
extend arms out to sides and behind,
stretching upper torso, expanding chest.
Five deep breaths.

meditation
I can feel it, almost see it;
There is electricity in the air
Which urges life to live.
"Fully live," it calls to me,
"Fully know your Self,
Accept the challenge of your life,
Experience it all."
"I am the Word," God said,
"All this and more are you."
"I am the Word," I say to God,
"I accept your task for me."

today I will bring the spirit of Service to my _____
_____

feelings _____
_____
_____
_____
_____

evening focus
Our Heavenly Father

the blessing
It is I who asks
For your blessing, Father,
No longer in whimpered tones.
I have grown throughout the seasons
And stand now tall and sure.
I am sensing
Who I truly am,
And I stand to meet that test.
I am your Word within this life,
This lifetime
Know I this.

seasonal focus
Flowers announce the promise of fruit.

Saturday, June 1, 2024

morning focus
Our Earthly Mother

deepening
Hold a piece of local fruit which is ripe
in this season. Make it part of your next meal.

meditation
I feel the presence
Of our Earthly Mother within me,
And that presence is illuminated
By the warm rays of the Father of us all.
All about me are the gifts
Of the Mother's ripening fruits,
And I know that in my own way
I am ripening too.

today I will bring the spirit of Authenticity to my _____

_____

feelings _____

_____
_____
_____
_____
_____

_____

the blessing
Even as my fruits ripen,
As my gifts become manifest,
As I mature in openness and love,
I remember that I have walked this path before,
And will again.
For the fruits of now
Contain the seeds of tomorrow,
And my seeds of bygone seasons
Have brought this day's joy to me.
My seeds, my fruits will come and go,
And I will carry on.

evening focus
The angel of Eternal Life

Sunday, June 2, 2024

seasonal focus
Flowers announce the promise of fruit.

morning focus
The angel of Earth

deepening
Hold a handful of moist, decaying,
living earth as you meditate.

meditation
What is the source
From whence gushes the frenzied growth
All about me?
What overlighting presence
Guides the living things of earth
Toward the zenith of their life?
I, as one of these living things,
Marvel at the perfection of our unfolding.
Blessed am I to be a part of the Plan.

today I will bring the spirit of Wholeness to my _____

feelings _____

evening focus
The angel of Creative Work

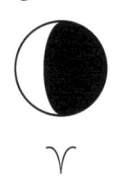

the blessing
My heart tells me
That the time of compromise
Has passed.
Now, the work I do
Must nourish me
And heal the earth
And free our common spirit.

seasonal focus
Flowers announce the promise of fruit.

Monday, June 3, 2024

morning focus
The angel of Life

opening
Meditate while touching a living plant,
bush, tree or pet. Exchange love with this being.

meditation
From the point from which all Life flows,
It flows to me.
My part is to accept this life consciously
As a manifestation of God on earth.
It is I
Who bring Light and Love into this existence.
No angelic being can do it for me.
Yes, heartily do I accept
This responsibility!
Yes, gladly do I accept
The God in me!

today I will bring the spirit of Responsibility to my _____

feelings _____

the blessing
Throughout me there is movement;
There is growth
Streaming to the outer bounds of my potential,
And I feel full and overflowing.
Yet at my center, at the very core of me,
There is a quiet place
From which my guidance comes.
Let me learn to seek this center
Often.

evening focus
The angel of Peace

Tuesday, June 4, 2024

seasonal focus
Flowers announce the promise of fruit.

morning focus
The angel of Joy

opening
Imagine someone whom you dislike.
Enfold that person's image in your *love*,
without forcing yourself to like them.

meditation
From each moment
I draw life.
From each living being
I draw love.
From the earth and the sun
I draw nourishment.
From each I receive
And to each I joyfully give,
For the web that connects each to me
Weaves its tapestry throughout my being,
Uniting me with all.
Separateness
Is an illusion.

today I will bring the spirit of Joy to my _____

feelings _____

evening focus
The angel of Power

the blessing
As our sun
Daily shares more and more of its power with me,
I stand in awe of the power
That also lies within me.
I take upon myself the yoke of responsibility for my power,
And direct that power
In the service of positive, liberating evolution
For myself and all beings.
So be it.

seasonal focus
Flowers announce the promise of fruit.

Wednesday, June 5, 2024

morning focus
The angel of the Sun

opening
Read the meditation and the blessing outside.
Be still and notice...

meditation
I enter into the season of the sun,
And the Sun within me responds in kind.
My heart tells me
To build my castles high with love and clarity.
My soul tells me
To bring the Plan to earth.
My mind tells me
To bring perfection to my work.
There is much to do and I am equal to the task.

today I will bring the spirit of Clarity to my _____
_____

feelings _____
_____
_____
_____
_____
_____
_____
_____

the blessing
Many are the ways to share
The mystery that is me,
And the greatest of these is Love.
To love one another, truly,
Without expectation of gain,
Is to transform the world.
I am learning to move
Beyond possession and manipulation
And into the awareness of lovingness,
Where I need ask for naught
And simply share my love.

evening focus
The angel of Love

$\beta \rightarrow \text{II}$

183

Thursday, June 6, 2024

seasonal focus
Flowers announce the promise of fruit.

morning focus
The angel of Water

deepening
Hold water in your bowl as you read.
Sometime this day, share it
(tea with a friend; sprinkle a loved one?).

meditation
A wave of the ocean glides over the sea
And crashes upon the shore.
My body dances over the meadow
And joyfully leaps in the air.
Is the wave not still one with the ocean?
Am I not one with All?
Can I separate myself from my Source
When that wellspring flows deep within me
And not on some distant mountain?

today I will bring the spirit of my Divine Nature to my
_____

feelings _____
_____
_____
_____
_____
_____
_____
_____

evening focus
The angel of Wisdom

the blessing
This is the season of searching outside me,
To discover the teachers who Know.
But deep within me I must remember
"When the Student is ready,
The Teacher appears."
When I ask the right questions
Answers always are there
For my teachers are everywhere.

seasonal focus
Flowers announce the promise of fruit.

Friday, June 7, 2024

morning focus
The angel of Air

opening
Before reading,
extend arms out to sides and behind,
stretching upper torso, expanding chest.
Five deep breaths.

meditation
I can feel it, almost see it;
There is electricity in the air
Which urges life to live.
"Fully live," it calls to me,
"Fully know your Self,
Accept the challenge of your life,
Experience it all."
"I am the Word," God said,
"All this and more are you."
"I am the Word," I say to God,
"I accept your task for me."

today I will bring the spirit of Service to my _____

feelings _____

the blessing
It is I who asks
For your blessing, Father,
No longer in whimpered tones.
I have grown throughout the seasons
And stand now tall and sure.
I am sensing who I truly am,
And I stand to meet that test.
I am your Word within this life,
This lifetime
Know I this.

evening focus
Our Heavenly Father

Saturday, June 8, 2024

seasonal focus
Flowers announce the promise of fruit.

morning focus
Our Earthly Mother

deepening
Hold a piece of local fruit which is ripe in this season. Make it part of your next meal.

meditation
I feel the presence
Of our Earthly Mother within me,
And that presence is illuminated
By the warm rays of the Father of us all.
All about me are the gifts
Of the Mother's ripening fruits,
And I know that in my own way
I am ripening too.

today I will bring the spirit of Authenticity to my _____

_____

feelings_____

_____

_____

_____

_____

_____

evening focus
The angel of Eternal Life

the blessing
Even as my fruits ripen,
As my gifts become manifest,
As I mature in openness and love,
I remember that I have walked this path before,
And will again.
For the fruits of now
Contain the seeds of tomorrow,
And my seeds of bygone seasons
Have brought this day's joy to me.
My seeds, my fruits will come and go,
And I will carry on.

Sunday, June 9, 2024

seasonal focus
Flowers announce the promise of fruit.

morning focus
The angel of Earth

deepening
Hold a handful of moist, decaying,
living earth as you meditate.

meditation
What is the source
From whence gushes the frenzied growth
All about me?
What overlighting presence
Guides the living things of earth
Toward the zenith of their life?
I, as one of these living things,
Marvel at the perfection of our unfolding.
Blessed am I to be a part of the Plan.

today I will bring the spirit of Wholeness to my _____

feelings _____

the blessing
My heart tells me
That the time of compromise
Has passed.
Now, the work I do
Must nourish me
And heal the earth
And free our common spirit.

evening focus
The angel of Creative Work

Monday, June 10, 2024

seasonal focus
Flowers announce the promise of fruit.

morning focus
The angel of Life

opening
Meditate while touching a living plant,
bush, tree or pet. Exchange love with this being.

meditation
From the point from which all Life flows,
It flows to me.
My part is to accept this life consciously
As a manifestation of God on earth.
It is I
Who bring Light and Love into this existence.
No angelic being can do it for me.
Yes, heartily do I accept
This responsibility!
Yes, gladly do I accept
The God in me!

today I will bring the spirit of Responsibility to my

feelings _____

_____

_____

_____

_____

_____

_____

evening focus
The angel of Peace

the blessing
Throughout me there is movement;
There is growth
Streaming to the outer bounds of my potential,
And I feel full and overflowing.
Yet at my center, at the very core of me,
There is a quiet place
From which my guidance comes.
Let me learn to seek this center
Often.

seasonal focus
Flowers announce the promise of fruit.

Tuesday, June 11, 2024

morning focus
The angel of Joy

opening
Imagine someone whom you dislike.
Enfold that person's image in your *love*,
without forcing yourself to like them.

meditation
From each moment
I draw life.
From each living being
I draw love.
From the earth and the sun
I draw nourishment.
From each I receive
And to each I joyfully give,
For the web that connects each to me
Weaves its tapestry throughout my being,
Uniting me with all.
Separateness
Is an illusion.

today I will bring the spirit of Joy to my _____

feelings _____

the blessing
As our sun
Daily shares more and more of its power with me,
I stand in awe of the power
That also lies within me.
I take upon myself the yoke of responsibility for my power,
And direct that power
In the service of positive, liberating evolution
For myself and all beings.
So be it.

evening focus
The angel of Power

Wednesday, June 12, 2024

seasonal focus
Flowers announce the promise of fruit.

morning focus
The angel of the Sun

opening
Read the meditation and the blessing outside.
Be still and notice. . .

meditation
I enter into the season of the sun,
And the Sun within me responds in kind.
My heart tells me
To build my castles high
With love and clarity.
My soul tells me
To bring the Plan to earth.
My mind tells me
To bring perfection to my work.
There is much to do and I am equal to the task.

today I will bring the spirit of Clarity to my _____

feelings_____
_____
_____
_____
_____
_____

evening focus
The angel of Love

the blessing
Many are the ways to share
The mystery that is me,
And the greatest of these is Love.
To love one another, truly,
Without expectation of gain,
Is to transform the world.
I am learning to move
Beyond possession and manipulation
And into the awareness of lovingness,
Where I need ask for naught
And simply share my love.

seasonal focus
Flowers announce the promise of fruit.

Thursday, June 13, 2024

morning focus
The angel of Water

deepening
Hold water in your bowl as you read.
Sometime this day, share it
(tea with a friend; sprinkle a loved one?).

meditation
A wave of the ocean glides over the sea
And crashes upon the shore.
My body dances over the meadow
And joyfully leaps in the air.
Is the wave not still one with the ocean?
Am I not one with All?
Can I separate myself from my Source
When that wellspring flows deep within me
And not on some distant mountain?

today I will bring the spirit of my Divine Nature to my _____

feelings _____

the blessing
This is the season of searching outside me,
To discover the teachers who Know.
But deep within me I must remember
"When the Student is ready,
The Teacher appears."
When I ask the right questions
Answers always are there
For my teachers are everywhere.

evening focus
The angel of Wisdom

Friday, June 14, 2024

seasonal focus
Flowers announce the promise of fruit.

morning focus
The angel of Air

opening
Before reading,
extend arms out to sides and behind,
stretching upper torso, expanding chest.
Five deep breaths.

meditation
I can feel it, almost see it;
There is electricity in the air
Which urges life to live.
"Fully live," it calls to me,
"Fully know your Self,
Accept the challenge of your life,
Experience it all."
"I am the Word," God said,
"All this and more are you."
"I am the Word," I say to God,
"I accept your task for me."

today I will bring the spirit of Service to my_____
_____

feelings _____
_____
_____
_____

evening focus
Our Heavenly Father

♍ → ♎

the blessing
It is I who asks
For your blessing, Father,
No longer in whimpered tones.
I have grown throughout the seasons
And stand now tall and sure.
I am sensing
Who I truly am,
And I stand to meet that test.
I am your Word within this life,
This lifetime
Know I this.

seasonal focus
Flowers announce the promise of fruit.

Saturday, June 15, 2024

morning focus
Our Earthly Mother

deepening
Hold a piece of local fruit which is ripe
in this season. Make it part of your next meal.

meditation
I feel the presence
Of our Earthly Mother within me,
And that presence is illuminated
By the warm rays of the Father of us all.
All about me are the gifts
Of the Mother's ripening fruits,
And I know that in my own way
I am ripening too.

today I will bring the spirit of Authenticity to my _____

feelings _____

the blessing
Even as my fruits ripen,
As my gifts become manifest,
As I mature in openness and love,
I remember that I have walked this path before,
And will again.
For the fruits of now
Contain the seeds of tomorrow,
And my seeds of bygone seasons
Have brought this day's joy to me.
My seeds, my fruits will come and go,
And I will carry on.

evening focus
The angel of Eternal Life

Sunday, June 16, 2024

seasonal focus
Flowers announce the promise of fruit.

morning focus
The angel of Earth

deepening
Hold a handful of moist, decaying,
living earth as you meditate.

meditation
What is the source
From whence gushes the frenzied growth
All about me?
What overlighting presence
Guides the living things of earth
Toward the zenith of their life?
I, as one of these living things,
Marvel at the perfection of our unfolding.
Blessed am I to be a part of the Plan.

today I will bring the spirit of Wholeness to my _____

feelings_____

evening focus
The angel of Creative Work

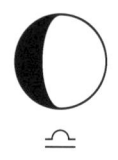

Father's Day

the blessing
My heart tells me
That the time of compromise
Has passed.
Now, the work I do
Must nourish me
And heal the earth
And free our common spirit.

seasonal focus
Flowers announce the promise of fruit.

Monday, June 17, 2024

morning focus
The angel of Life

opening
Meditate while touching a living plant,
bush, tree or pet. Exchange love with this being.

meditation
From the point from which all Life flows,
It flows to me.
My part is to accept this life consciously
As a manifestation of God on earth.
It is I
Who bring Light and Love into this existence.
No angelic being can do it for me.
Yes, heartily do I accept
This responsibility!
Yes, gladly do I accept
The God in me!

today I will bring the spirit of Responsibility to my _____

feelings _____

the blessing
Throughout me there is movement;
There is growth
Streaming to the outer bounds of my potential,
And I feel full and overflowing.
Yet at my center, at the very core of me,
There is a quiet place
From which my guidance comes.
Let me learn to seek this center
Often.

evening focus
The angel of Peace

♎ → ♏

Tuesday, June 18, 2024

seasonal focus
Flowers announce the promise of fruit.

morning focus
The angel of Joy

opening
Imagine someone whom you dislike.
Enfold that person's image in your *love*,
without forcing yourself to like them.

meditation
From each moment
I draw life.
From each living being
I draw love.
From the earth and the sun
I draw nourishment.
From each I receive
And to each I joyfully give,
For the web that connects each to me
Weaves its tapestry throughout my being,
Uniting me with all.
Separateness
Is an illusion.

today I will bring the spirit of Joy to my _____

feelings _____

evening focus
The angel of Power

the blessing
As our sun
Daily shares more and more of its power with me,
I stand in awe of the power
That also lies within me.
I take upon myself the yoke of responsibility for my power,
And direct that power
In the service of positive, liberating evolution
For myself and all beings.
So be it.

Wednesday, June 19, 2024

seasonal focus
Flowers announce the promise of fruit.

morning focus
The angel of the Sun

opening
Read the meditation and the blessing outside.
Be still and notice. . .

meditation
I enter into the season of the sun,
And the Sun within me responds in kind.
My heart tells me
To build my castles high with love and clarity.
My soul tells me
To bring the Plan to earth.
My mind tells me
To bring perfection to my work.
There is much to do and I am equal to the task.

today I will bring the spirit of Clarity to my _____
_____

feelings _____
_____
_____
_____
_____
_____
_____

the blessing
Many are the ways to share
The mystery that is me,
And the greatest of these is Love.
To love one another, truly,
Without expectation of gain,
Is to transform the world.
I am learning to move
Beyond possession and manipulation
And into the awareness of lovingness,
Where I need ask for naught
And simply share my love.

evening focus
The angel of Love

summer solstice

The sun now exerts its maximum power upon our part of the earth as its rays strike us head-on. The time of full outward physical manifestation is here. The powers of inner contemplation are at their lowest point, and everywhere are the energies of exerting the will, of "doing."

The sun moves from Gemini into Cancer, signaling the point of Solstice, of highest solar energy for this year. This was the ancient time of celebration, of outward joy in the fullness of life, the richness of our worldly blessings.

It is just as true for us today. As we experience the warm, full power of the solstice sun, we are called to make true on earth the words of the master Jesus, "I and the Father are One." To understand this is to recognize the divinity in everyone we meet. Use this day to see God in each face that you greet.

Thursday, June 20, 2024

seasonal focus
The tree bends with ripened fruit.

morning focus
The angel of Water

deepening
Hold water in your bowl as you read.
Sometime this day, wash the face of a dear one with it.

meditation
I live now
At the apex of the solar year,
Drenched in warmth and outer power.
I bathe
In the cleansing water of my Mother,
Naked and unashamed.
I need no garment to separate me
From the waters of the Spirit,
For my flesh and spirit are united,
And wholeness flows through me.

today I will bring the spirit of World Peace to my _____

feelings _____

At Solstice, the seed of winter tranforms into the ripe fruit of summer.

the blessing
In this time of outward activity,
Of creation on the physical plane,
I ask to remember that the wheel is ever-turning,
And I am propelled toward my inner nature
Even as I celebrate my outer nature.
For in the fullness of light
Rest the seeds of night,
And in darkness
The seeds of day.

evening focus
The angel of Wisdom

Friday, June 21, 2024

seasonal focus
The tree bends with ripened fruit.

morning focus
The angel of Air

opening
Practice deep breathing outside before meditation.
Expand your belly and chest, stretch your limits.

meditation
Sweet is the breath of nature
In my life,
Fragrant is the warm wind off the meadow
Where I lie.
All this is given to me.
But in my striving
For the illusory acquisitions of the world,
Are these treasures lost to me?
Simple joy is mine
If I but slow my pace.

today I will bring the spirit of Simplicity to my _____
_____

feelings_____
_____
_____
_____
_____
_____
_____

evening focus
Our Heavenly Father

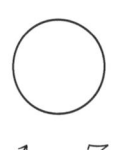

the blessing
There on the lush rolling land
Stands a stone, placed by human will
And pointed to the sky.
Its base is set to earth,
Its edges smoothed by the years.
Much like that Standing stone am I,
A channel
From the Father to the Mother,
A connector
Of the oceans of cosmic and earthly love.
This task I joyfully embrace.

Saturday, June 22, 2024

seasonal focus
The tree bends with ripened fruit.

morning focus
Our Earthly Mother

deepening
Hold a piece of local fruit which is ripe
in this season. Make it part of your next meal.

meditation
Lady, Mother of us all,
You are the source of all Love,
As the Father is the source of all Light.
You sustain me on my journey,
In my work,
In my service to my fellow beings.
May I be truly worthy
Of your Love.

today I will bring the spirit of Love For All Beings
to my _____

feelings _____

_____
_____
_____
_____
_____
_____

the blessing
There is a vibration
That emanates from me in whatever I do,
Mingling with,
Enhancing or detracting from
The universal vibration,
Depending upon the quality of my intent.
I commit myself
To a positive enhancement
Of the universal vibration
In each act and thought
That I create.

evening focus
The angel of Eternal Life

201

Sunday, June 23, 2024

seasonal focus
The tree bends with ripened fruit.

morning focus
The angel of Earth

deepening
Hold a handful of moist, decaying,
living earth as you meditate.

meditation
With the electric limits of my aura,
My personal energy field,
I tap the power
Of the earth in summer.
The earth current flows in me
And strengthens my body
For the work that only I can do
As a channel for the Light.
I feel it shine in me.

today I will bring the spirit of my Shining Light to my

feelings _____

_____

_____

_____

_____

_____

_____

_____

evening focus
The angel of Creative Work

the blessing
I am a builder,
A vehicle for creative perfection
To work itself upon the earth.
My task is clear and simple,
For I am the Plan unfolding,
And I am my work in progress.
The work goes well
And I give thanks.

seasonal focus
The tree bends with ripened fruit.

Monday, June 24, 2024

morning focus
The angel of Life

opening
Meditate while touching a living plant,
bush, tree or pet. Exchange love with this being.

meditation
There is a wholeness of my being
That I have come to know.
My life is the sum
Of my body, mind, and spirit
And more.
For I am immersed
In a cosmic ocean of Life
Which connects my life with All,
And I am All.

today I will bring the spirit of Connectedness to my
_____

feelings _____
_____
_____
_____
_____
_____
_____

the blessing
Awareness of the richness of my life
Draws forth in me a yearning
To share my gifts with all,
And the greatest of these is Peace.
To work actively for peace
Within my life
And to bring that peace
To those I know
Is to make real
My spirituality.

evening focus
The angel of Peace

Tuesday, June 25, 2024

seasonal focus
The tree bends with ripened fruit.

morning focus
The angel of Joy

opening
Imagine someone you fear or mistrust.
Enfold them in joy.
Feel your own ability to embrace joy.

meditation
It is my natural state
To be filled with joy,
A joy that knows from whence I came
And who I truly Am.
My moods may swing from up to down
But behind this flows
My joy in life.
Depressed emotions draw to me
Only more of the same.
I leave low vibrations behind
As I dance in the warm sun
Of this day.

today I will bring the spirit of Joyful Sharing to my _____

feelings _____

_____
_____
_____
_____
_____
_____

evening focus
The angel of Power

the blessing
As the tree shares its gifts of fruit,
So I, too, share the gifts of me.
For in me is the facilitator
Of a more loving world;
In me is the catalyst
For a greater social awareness.
In me is the power of the Word,
And I share that gift with all.

Wednesday, June 26, 2024

seasonal focus
The tree bends with ripened fruit.

morning focus
The angel of the Sun

opening
Read the meditation and the blessing outside.
Be still and notice. . .

meditation
Solar light,
Ancient source of power and life,
It is you who guides my path this day.
'Tis the season of your ruling,
And I, like you,
Must use this moment fully
To urge the world to grow.
And grow it will,
And grow I will
To the fullness of my potential,
For that is who I AM.

today I will bring the spirit of Fullness to my _____

feelings _____

the blessing
Does not the apple tree
Share its fruit with all,
Not choosing who is blest?
As my vessel overflows with love,
Do I not share this love with all?
For in our oneness
There exist no chosen ones.
Only fellow travellers do I see
On the path back home to God.

evening focus
The angel of Love

Thursday, June 27, 2024

seasonal focus
The tree bends with ripened fruit.

morning focus
The angel of Water

deepening
Hold water in your bowl as you read.
Sometime this day, wash the face of a dear one with it.

meditation
I live now
At the apex of the solar year,
Drenched in warmth and outer power.
I bathe
In the cleansing water of my Mother,
Naked and unashamed.
I need no garment to separate me
From the waters of the Spirit,
For my flesh and spirit are united,
And wholeness flows through me.

today I will bring the spirit of World Peace to my ____

feelings ____

---

evening focus
The angel of Wisdom

the blessing
In this time of outward activity,
Of creation on the physical plane,
I ask to remember that the wheel is ever-turning,
And I am propelled toward my inner nature
Even as I celebrate my outer nature.
For in the fullness of light
Rest the seeds of night,
And in darkness
The seeds of day.

seasonal focus
The tree bends with ripened fruit.

morning focus
The angel of Air

opening
Practice deep breathing outside before meditation. Expand your belly and chest, stretch your limits.

meditation
Sweet is the breath of nature
In my life,
Fragrant is the warm wind off the meadow
Where I lie.
All this is given to me.
But in my striving
For the illusory acquisitions of the world,
Are these treasures lost to me?
Simple joy is mine
If I but slow my pace.

today I will bring the spirit of Simplicity to my _____
_____

feelings _____
_____
_____
_____
_____
_____
_____

Friday, June 28, 2024

the blessing
There on the lush rolling land
Stands a stone, placed by human will
And pointed to the sky.
Its base is set to earth,
Its edges smoothed by the years.
Much like that Standing stone am I,
A channel
From the Father to the Mother,
A connector
Of the oceans of cosmic and earthly love.
This task I joyfully embrace.

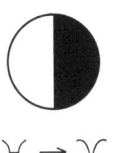

evening focus
Our Heavenly Father

Saturday, June 29, 2024

seasonal focus
The tree bends with ripened fruit.

morning focus
Our Earthly Mother

deepening
Hold a piece of local fruit which is ripe in this season. Make it part of your next meal.

meditation
Lady, Mother of us all,
You are the source of all Love,
As the Father is the source of all Light.
You sustain me on my journey,
In my work,
In my service to my fellow beings.
May I be truly worthy
Of your Love.

today I will bring the spirit of Love For All Beings to my _____

_____

feelings _____

_____

_____

_____

_____

_____

evening focus
The angel of Eternal Life

the blessing
There is a vibration
That emanates from me in whatever I do,
Mingling with,
Enhancing or detracting from
The universal vibration,
Depending upon the quality of my intent.
I commit myself
To a positive enhancement
Of the universal vibration
In each act and thought
That I create.

Sunday, June 30, 2024

seasonal focus
The tree bends with ripened fruit.

morning focus
The angel of Earth

deepening
Hold a handful of moist, decaying,
living earth as you meditate.

meditation
With the electric limits of my aura,
My personal energy field,
I tap the power
Of the earth in summer.
The earth current flows in me
And strengthens my body
For the work that only I can do
As a channel for the Light.
I feel it shine in me.

today I will bring the spirit of my Shining Light to my _____

feelings _____
_____
_____
_____
_____
_____
_____
_____

the blessing
I am a builder,
A vehicle for creative perfection
To work itself upon the earth.
My task is clear and simple,
For I am the Plan unfolding,
And I am my work in progress.
The work goes well
And I give thanks.

evening focus
The angel of Creative Work

♈ → ♉

209

Monday, July 1, 2024

seasonal focus
The tree bends with ripened fruit.

morning focus
The angel of Life

opening
Meditate while touching a living plant,
bush, tree or pet. Exchange love with this being.

meditation
There is a wholeness of my being
That I have come to know.
My life is the sum
Of my body, mind, and spirit
And more.
For I am immersed
In a cosmic ocean of Life
Which connects my life with All,
And I am All.

today I will bring the spirit of Connectedness to my
_____

feelings _____
_____
_____
_____
_____
_____

evening focus
The angel of Peace

the blessing
Awareness of the richness of my life
Draws forth in me a yearning
To share my gifts with all,
And the greatest of these is Peace.
To work actively for peace
Within my life
And to bring that peace
To those I know
Is to make real
My spirituality.

seasonal focus
The tree bends with ripened fruit.

morning focus
The angel of Joy

opening
Imagine someone you fear or mistrust.
Enfold them in joy.
Feel your own ability to embrace joy.

meditation
It is my natural state
To be filled with joy,
A joy that knows from whence I came
And who I truly Am.
My moods may swing from up to down
But behind this flows
My joy in life.
Depressed emotions draw to me
Only more of the same.
I leave low vibrations behind
As I dance in the warm sun
Of this day.

today I will bring the spirit of Joyful Sharing to my

feelings _____

Tuesday, July 2, 2024

the blessing
As the tree shares its gifts of fruit,
So I, too, share the gifts of me.
For in me is the facilitator
Of a more loving world;
In me is the catalyst
For a greater social awareness.
In me is the power of the Word,
And I share that gift with all.

evening focus
The angel of Power

Wednesday, July 3, 2024

seasonal focus
The tree bends with ripened fruit.

morning focus
The angel of the Sun

opening
Read the meditation and the blessing outside.
Be still and notice. . .

meditation
Solar light,
Ancient source of power and life,
It is you who guides my path this day.
'Tis the season of your ruling,
And I, like you,
Must use this moment fully
To urge the world to grow.
And grow it will,
And grow I will
To the fullness of my potential,
For that is who I AM.

today I will bring the spirit of Fullness to my _____
_____

feelings _____
_____
_____
_____
_____
_____

evening focus
The angel of Love

the blessing
Does not the apple tree
Share its fruit with all,
Not choosing who is blest?
As my vessel overflows with love,
Do I not share this love with all?
For in our oneness
There exist no chosen ones.
Only fellow travellers do I see
On the path back home to God.

212

seasonal focus
The tree bends with ripened fruit.

Thursday, July 4, 2024

morning focus
The angel of Water

deepening
Hold water in your bowl as you read.
Sometime this day, wash the face of a dear one with it.

meditation
I live now
At the apex of the solar year,
Drenched in warmth and outer power.
I bathe
In the cleansing water of my Mother,
Naked and unashamed.
I need no garment to separate me
From the waters of the Spirit,
For my flesh and spirit are united,
And wholeness flows through me.

today I will bring the spirit of World Peace to my _____

feelings _____

the blessing
In this time of outward activity,
Of creation on the physical plane,
I ask to remember that the wheel is ever-turning,
And I am propelled toward my inner nature
Even as I celebrate my outer nature.
For in the fullness of light
Rest the seeds of night,
And in darkness
The seeds of day.

evening focus
The angel of Wisdom

Friday, July 5, 2024

seasonal focus
The tree bends with ripened fruit.

morning focus
The angel of Air

opening
Practice deep breathing outside before meditation.
Expand your belly and chest, stretch your limits.

meditation
Sweet is the breath of nature
In my life,
Fragrant is the warm wind off the meadow
Where I lie.
All this is given to me.
But in my striving
For the illusory acquisitions of the world,
Are these treasures lost to me?
Simple joy is mine
If I but slow my pace.

today I will bring the spirit of Simplicity to my _____
_____

feelings_____
_____
_____
_____
_____
_____
_____

evening focus
Our Heavenly Father

the blessing
There on the lush rolling land
Stands a stone, placed by human will
And pointed to the sky.
Its base is set to earth,
Its edges smoothed by the years.
Much like that Standing stone am I,
A channel
From the Father to the Mother,
A connector
Of the oceans of cosmic and earthly love.
This task I joyfully embrace.

seasonal focus
The tree bends with ripened fruit.

morning focus
Our Earthly Mother

deepening
Hold a piece of local fruit which is ripe in this season. Make it part of your next meal.

meditation
Lady, Mother of us all,
You are the source of all Love,
As the Father is the source of all Light.
You sustain me on my journey,
In my work,
In my service to my fellow beings.
May I be truly worthy
Of your Love.

today I will bring the spirit of Love For All Beings to my _____

_____

feelings _____

_____

_____

_____

_____

_____

_____

the blessing
There is a vibration
That emanates from me in whatever I do,
Mingling with,
Enhancing or detracting from
The universal vibration,
Depending upon the quality of my intent.
I commit myself
To a positive enhancement
Of the universal vibration
In each act and thought
That I create.

Saturday, July 6, 2024

evening focus
The angel of Eternal Life

215

Sunday, July 7, 2024

seasonal focus
The tree bends with ripened fruit.

morning focus
The angel of Earth

deepening
Hold a handful of moist, decaying,
living earth as you meditate.

meditation
With the electric limits of my aura,
My personal energy field,
I tap the power
Of the earth in summer.
The earth current flows in me
And strengthens my body
For the work that only I can do
As a channel for the Light.
I feel it shine in me.

today I will bring the spirit of my Shining Light to my
_____

feelings _____
_____
_____
_____
_____
_____
_____
_____

evening focus
The angel of Creative Work

the blessing
I am a builder,
A vehicle for creative perfection
To work itself upon the earth.
My task is clear and simple,
For I am the Plan unfolding,
And I am my work in progress.
The work goes well
And I give thanks.

seasonal focus
The tree bends with ripened fruit.

morning focus
The angel of Life

opening
Meditate while touching a living plant,
bush, tree or pet. Exchange love with this being.

meditation
There is a wholeness of my being
That I have come to know.
My life is the sum
Of my body, mind, and spirit
And more.
For I am immersed
In a cosmic ocean of Life
Which connects my life with All,
And I am All.

today I will bring the spirit of Connectedness to my
_____

feelings _____
_____
_____
_____
_____
_____
_____

Monday, July 8, 2024

the blessing
Awareness of the richness of my life
Draws forth in me a yearning
To share my gifts with all,
And the greatest of these is Peace.
To work actively for peace
Within my life
And to bring that peace
To those I know
Is to make real
My spirituality.

evening focus
The angel of Peace

217

Tuesday, July 9, 2024

seasonal focus
The tree bends with ripened fruit.

morning focus
The angel of Joy

opening
Imagine someone you fear or mistrust.
Enfold them in joy.
Feel your own ability to embrace joy.

meditation
It is my natural state
To be filled with joy,
A joy that knows from whence I came
And who I truly Am.
My moods may swing from up to down
But behind this flows
My joy in life.
Depressed emotions draw to me
Only more of the same.
I leave low vibrations behind
As I dance in the warm sun
Of this day.

today I will bring the spirit of Joyful Sharing to my _____

feelings _____

_____

_____

_____

_____

_____

evening focus
The angel of Power

♌ → ♍

the blessing
As the tree shares its gifts of fruit,
So I, too, share the gifts of me.
For in me is the facilitator
Of a more loving world;
In me is the catalyst
For a greater social awareness.
In me is the power of the Word,
And I share that gift with all.

Wednesday, July 10, 2024

seasonal focus
The tree bends with ripened fruit.

morning focus
The angel of the Sun

opening
Read the meditation and the blessing outside.
Be still and notice. . .

meditation
Solar light,
Ancient source of power and life,
It is you who guides my path this day.
'Tis the season of your ruling,
And I, like you,
Must use this moment fully
To urge the world to grow.
And grow it will,
And grow I will
To the fullness of my potential,
For that is who I AM.

today I will bring the spirit of Fullness to my _____

feelings _____

the blessing
Does not the apple tree
Share its fruit with all,
Not choosing who is blest?
As my vessel overflows with love,
Do I not share this love with all?
For in our oneness
There exist no chosen ones.
Only fellow travellers do I see
On the path back home to God.

evening focus
The angel of Love

Thursday, July 11, 2024

seasonal focus
The tree bends with ripened fruit.

morning focus
The angel of Water

deepening
Hold water in your bowl as you read.
Sometime this day, wash the face of a dear one with it.

meditation
I live now
At the apex of the solar year,
Drenched in warmth and outer power.
I bathe
In the cleansing water of my Mother,
Naked and unashamed.
I need no garment to separate me
From the waters of the Spirit,
For my flesh and spirit are united,
And wholeness flows through me.

today I will bring the spirit of World Peace to my ____

feelings ____

evening focus
The angel of Wisdom

♍ → ♎

the blessing
In this time of outward activity,
Of creation on the physical plane,
I ask to remember that the wheel is ever-turning,
And I am propelled toward my inner nature
Even as I celebrate my outer nature.
For in the fullness of light
Rest the seeds of night,
And in darkness
The seeds of day.

seasonal focus
The tree bends with ripened fruit.

Friday, July 12, 2024

morning focus
The angel of Air

opening
Practice deep breathing outside before meditation.
Expand your belly and chest, stretch your limits.

meditation
Sweet is the breath of nature
In my life,
Fragrant is the warm wind off the meadow
Where I lie.
All this is given to me.
But in my striving
For the illusory acquisitions of the world,
Are these treasures lost to me?
Simple joy is mine
If I but slow my pace.

today I will bring the spirit of Simplicity to my _____

feelings _____

the blessing
There on the lush rolling land
Stands a stone, placed by human will
And pointed to the sky.
Its base is set to earth,
Its edges smoothed by the years.
Much like that Standing stone am I,
A channel
From the Father to the Mother,
A connector
Of the oceans of cosmic and earthly love.
This task I joyfully embrace.

evening focus
Our Heavenly Father

Saturday, July 13, 2024

seasonal focus
The tree bends with ripened fruit.

morning focus
Our Earthly Mother

deepening
Hold a piece of local fruit which is ripe in this season. Make it part of your next meal.

meditation
Lady, Mother of us all,
You are the source of all Love,
As the Father is the source of all Light.
You sustain me on my journey,
In my work,
In my service to my fellow beings.
May I be truly worthy
Of your Love.

today I will bring the spirit of Love For All Beings to my _____

_____

feelings _____

_____

_____

_____

_____

_____

_____

evening focus
The angel of Eternal Life

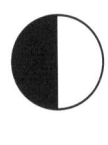

the blessing
There is a vibration
That emanates from me in whatever I do,
Mingling with,
Enhancing or detracting from
The universal vibration,
Depending upon the quality of my intent.
I commit myself
To a positive enhancement
Of the universal vibration
In each act and thought
That I create.

seasonal focus
The tree bends with ripened fruit.

morning focus
The angel of Earth

deepening
Hold a handful of moist, decaying, living earth as you meditate.

meditation
With the electric limits of my aura,
My personal energy field,
I tap the power
Of the earth in summer.
The earth current flows in me
And strengthens my body
For the work that only I can do
As a channel for the Light.
I feel it shine in me.

today I will bring the spirit of my Shining Light to my _____

feelings _____

_____
_____
_____
_____
_____
_____
_____

the blessing
I am a builder,
A vehicle for creative perfection
To work itself upon the earth.
My task is clear and simple,
For I am the Plan unfolding,
And I am my work in progress.
The work goes well
And I give thanks.

evening focus
The angel of Creative Work

♎ → ♏

Monday, July 15, 2024

seasonal focus
The tree bends with ripened fruit.

morning focus
The angel of Life

opening
Meditate while touching a living plant,
bush, tree or pet. Exchange love with this being.

meditation
There is a wholeness of my being
That I have come to know.
My life is the sum
Of my body, mind, and spirit
And more.
For I am immersed
In a cosmic ocean of Life
Which connects my life with All,
And I am All.

today I will bring the spirit of Connectedness to my
_____

feelings _____
_____
_____
_____
_____
_____
_____

evening focus
The angel of Peace

the blessing
Awareness of the richness of my life
Draws forth in me a yearning
To share my gifts with all,
And the greatest of these is Peace.
To work actively for peace
Within my life
And to bring that peace
To those I know
Is to make real
My spirituality.

224

seasonal focus
The tree bends with ripened fruit.

morning focus
The angel of Joy

opening
Imagine someone you fear or mistrust.
Enfold them in joy.
Feel your own ability to embrace joy.

meditation
It is my natural state
To be filled with joy,
A joy that knows from whence I came
And who I truly Am.
My moods may swing from up to down
But behind this flows
My joy in life.
Depressed emotions draw to me
Only more of the same.
I leave low vibrations behind
As I dance in the warm sun
Of this day.

today I will bring the spirit of Joyful Sharing to my _____

feelings _____

_____

_____

_____

_____

_____

the blessing
As the tree shares its gifts of fruit,
So I, too, share the gifts of me.
For in me is the facilitator
Of a more loving world;
In me is the catalyst
For a greater social awareness.
In me is the power of the Word,
And I share that gift with all.

evening focus
The angel of Power

Tuesday, July 16, 2024

Wednesday, July 17, 2024

seasonal focus
The tree bends with ripened fruit.

morning focus
The angel of the Sun

opening
Read the meditation and the blessing outside.
Be still and notice...

meditation
Solar light,
Ancient source of power and life,
It is you who guides my path this day.
'Tis the season of your ruling,
And I, like you,
Must use this moment fully
To urge the world to grow.
And grow it will,
And grow I will
To the fullness of my potential,
For that is who I AM.

today I will bring the spirit of Fullness to my _____
_____

feelings _____
_____
_____
_____
_____
_____

evening focus
The angel of Love

the blessing
Does not the apple tree
Share its fruit with all,
Not choosing who is blest?
As my vessel overflows with love,
Do I not share this love with all?
For in our oneness
There exist no chosen ones.
Only fellow travellers do I see
On the path back home to God.

seasonal focus
The tree bends with ripened fruit.

Thursday, July 18, 2024

morning focus
The angel of Water

deepening
Hold water in your bowl as you read.
Sometime this day, wash the face of a dear one with it.

meditation
I live now
At the apex of the solar year,
Drenched in warmth and outer power.
I bathe
In the cleansing water of my Mother,
Naked and unashamed.
I need no garment to separate me
From the waters of the Spirit,
For my flesh and spirit are united,
And wholeness flows through me.

today I will bring the spirit of World Peace to my _____

feelings _____

the blessing
In this time of outward activity,
Of creation on the physical plane,
I ask to remember that the wheel is ever-turning,
And I am propelled toward my inner nature
Even as I celebrate my outer nature.
For in the fullness of light
Rest the seeds of night,
And in darkness
The seeds of day.

evening focus
The angel of Wisdom

Friday, July 19, 2024

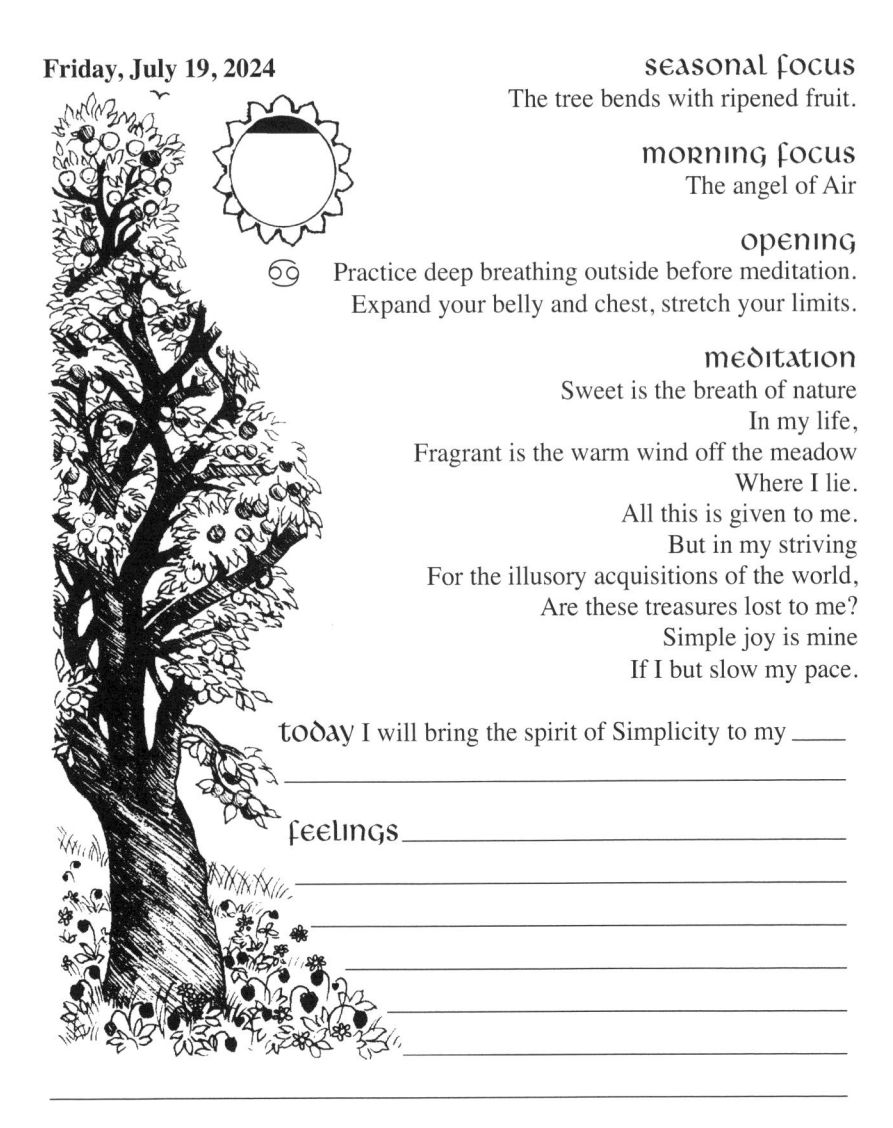

seasonal focus
The tree bends with ripened fruit.

morning focus
The angel of Air

opening
Practice deep breathing outside before meditation.
Expand your belly and chest, stretch your limits.

meditation
Sweet is the breath of nature
In my life,
Fragrant is the warm wind off the meadow
Where I lie.
All this is given to me.
But in my striving
For the illusory acquisitions of the world,
Are these treasures lost to me?
Simple joy is mine
If I but slow my pace.

today I will bring the spirit of Simplicity to my ____
_____

feelings _____
_____
_____
_____
_____
_____
_____

evening focus
Our Heavenly Father

the blessing
There on the lush rolling land
Stands a stone, placed by human will
And pointed to the sky.
Its base is set to earth,
Its edges smoothed by the years.
Much like that Standing stone am I,
A channel
From the Father to the Mother,
A connector
Of the oceans of cosmic and earthly love.
This task I joyfully embrace.

Saturday, July 20, 2024

seasonal focus
The tree bends with ripened fruit.

morning focus
Our Earthly Mother

deepening
Hold a piece of local fruit which is ripe
in this season. Make it part of your next meal.

meditation
Lady, Mother of us all,
You are the source of all Love,
As the Father is the source of all Light.
You sustain me on my journey,
In my work,
In my service to my fellow beings.
May I be truly worthy
Of your Love.

today I will bring the spirit of Love For All Beings
to my _____

feelings _____

_____

_____

_____

_____

_____

_____

the blessing
There is a vibration
That emanates from me in whatever I do,
Mingling with,
Enhancing or detracting from
The universal vibration,
Depending upon the quality of my intent.
I commit myself
To a positive enhancement
Of the universal vibration
In each act and thought
That I create.

evening focus
The angel of Eternal Life

Sunday, July 21, 2024

seasonal focus
The tree bends with ripened fruit.

morning focus
The angel of Earth

deepening
Hold a handful of moist, decaying,
living earth as you meditate.

meditation
With the electric limits of my aura,
My personal energy field,
I tap the power
Of the earth in summer.
The earth current flows in me
And strengthens my body
For the work that only I can do
As a channel for the Light.
I feel it shine in me.

today I will bring the spirit of my Shining Light to my
_____

feelings _____
_____
_____
_____
_____
_____
_____
_____

evening focus
The angel of Creative Work

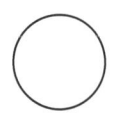

the blessing
I am a builder,
A vehicle for creative perfection
To work itself upon the earth.
My task is clear and simple,
For I am the Plan unfolding,
And I am my work in progress.
The work goes well
And I give thanks.

seasonal focus
The tree bends with ripened fruit.

morning focus
The angel of Life

opening
Meditate while touching a living plant,
bush, tree or pet. Exchange love with this being.

meditation
There is a wholeness of my being
That I have come to know.
My life is the sum
Of my body, mind, and spirit
And more.
For I am immersed
In a cosmic ocean of Life
Which connects my life with All,
And I am All.

today I will bring the spirit of Connectedness to my
_____

feelings _____
_____
_____
_____
_____
_____
_____

Monday, July 22, 2024

the blessing
Awareness of the richness of my life
Draws forth in me a yearning
To share my gifts with all,
And the greatest of these is Peace.
To work actively for peace
Within my life
And to bring that peace
To those I know
Is to make real
My spirituality.

evening focus
The angel of Peace

231

Tuesday, July 23, 2024

seasonal focus
The tree bends with ripened fruit.

morning focus
The angel of Joy

opening
Imagine someone you fear or mistrust.
Enfold them in joy.
Feel your own ability to embrace joy.

meditation
It is my natural state
To be filled with joy,
A joy that knows from whence I came
And who I truly Am.
My moods may swing from up to down
But behind this flows
My joy in life.
Depressed emotions draw to me
Only more of the same.
I leave low vibrations behind
As I dance in the warm sun
Of this day.

today I will bring the spirit of Joyful Sharing to my

feelings _____

_____

_____

_____

_____

_____

evening focus
The angel of Power

the blessing
As the tree shares its gifts of fruit,
So I, too, share the gifts of me.
For in me is the facilitator
Of a more loving world;
In me is the catalyst
For a greater social awareness.
In me is the power of the Word,
And I share that gift with all.

seasonal focus
The tree bends with ripened fruit.

morning focus
The angel of the Sun

opening
Read the meditation and the blessing outside.
Be still and notice. . .

meditation
Solar light,
Ancient source of power and life,
It is you who guides my path this day.
'Tis the season of your ruling,
And I, like you,
Must use this moment fully
To urge the world to grow.
And grow it will,
And grow I will
To the fullness of my potential,
For that is who I AM.

today I will bring the spirit of Fullness to my _____

feelings _____

Wednesday, July 24, 2024

the blessing
Does not the apple tree
Share its fruit with all,
Not choosing who is blest?
As my vessel overflows with love,
Do I not share this love with all?
For in our oneness
There exist no chosen ones.
Only fellow travellers do I see
On the path back home to God.

evening focus
The angel of Love

Thursday, July 25, 2024

seasonal focus
The tree bends with ripened fruit.

morning focus
The angel of Water

deepening
Hold water in your bowl as you read.
Sometime this day, wash the face of a dear one with it.

meditation
I live now
At the apex of the solar year,
Drenched in warmth and outer power.
I bathe
In the cleansing water of my Mother,
Naked and unashamed.
I need no garment to separate me
From the waters of the Spirit,
For my flesh and spirit are united,
And wholeness flows through me.

today I will bring the spirit of World Peace to my ____

feelings ____

evening focus
The angel of Wisdom

the blessing
In this time of outward activity,
Of creation on the physical plane,
I ask to remember that the wheel is ever-turning,
And I am propelled toward my inner nature
Even as I celebrate my outer nature.
For in the fullness of light
Rest the seeds of night,
And in darkness
The seeds of day.

seasonal focus
The tree bends with ripened fruit.

Friday, July 26, 2024

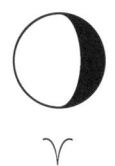

morning focus
The angel of Air

opening
Practice deep breathing outside before meditation.
Expand your belly and chest, stretch your limits.

meditation
Sweet is the breath of nature
In my life,
Fragrant is the warm wind off the meadow
Where I lie.
All this is given to me.
But in my striving
For the illusory acquisitions of the world,
Are these treasures lost to me?
Simple joy is mine
If I but slow my pace.

today I will bring the spirit of Simplicity to my _____

feelings _____

the blessing
There on the lush rolling land
Stands a stone, placed by human will
And pointed to the sky.
Its base is set to earth,
Its edges smoothed by the years.
Much like that Standing stone am I,
A channel
From the Father to the Mother,
A connector
Of the oceans of cosmic and earthly love.
This task I joyfully embrace.

evening focus
Our Heavenly Father

Saturday, July 27, 2024

seasonal focus
The tree bends with ripened fruit.

morning focus
Our Earthly Mother

deepening
Hold a piece of local fruit which is ripe in this season. Make it part of your next meal.

meditation
Lady, Mother of us all,
You are the source of all Love,
As the Father is the source of all Light.
You sustain me on my journey,
In my work,
In my service to my fellow beings.
May I be truly worthy
Of your Love.

today I will bring the spirit of Love For All Beings to my _____

_____

feelings _____

_____

_____

_____

_____

_____

evening focus
The angel of Eternal Life

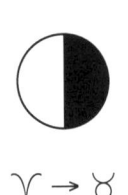

the blessing
There is a vibration
That emanates from me in whatever I do,
Mingling with,
Enhancing or detracting from
The universal vibration,
Depending upon the quality of my intent.
I commit myself
To a positive enhancement
Of the universal vibration
In each act and thought
That I create.

seasonal focus
The tree bends with ripened fruit.

morning focus
The angel of Earth

deepening
Hold a handful of moist, decaying, living earth as you meditate.

meditation
With the electric limits of my aura,
My personal energy field,
I tap the power
Of the earth in summer.
The earth current flows in me
And strengthens my body
For the work that only I can do
As a channel for the Light.
I feel it shine in me.

Sunday, July 28, 2024

today I will bring the spirit of my Shining Light to my
_____

feelings _____
_____
_____
_____
_____
_____
_____
_____

the blessing
I am a builder,
A vehicle for creative perfection
To work itself upon the earth.
My task is clear and simple,
For I am the Plan unfolding,
And I am my work in progress.
The work goes well
And I give thanks.

evening focus
The angel of Creative Work

Monday, July 29, 2024

seasonal focus
The tree bends with ripened fruit.

morning focus
The angel of Life

opening
Meditate while touching a living plant,
bush, tree or pet. Exchange love with this being.

meditation
There is a wholeness of my being
That I have come to know.
My life is the sum
Of my body, mind, and spirit
And more.
For I am immersed
In a cosmic ocean of Life
Which connects my life with All,
And I am All.

today I will bring the spirit of Connectedness to my
_____

feelings _____
_____
_____
_____
_____
_____
_____

evening focus
The angel of Peace

♉ → ♊

the blessing
Awareness of the richness of my life
Draws forth in me a yearning
To share my gifts with all,
And the greatest of these is Peace.
To work actively for peace
Within my life
And to bring that peace
To those I know
Is to make real
My spirituality.

seasonal focus
The tree bends with ripened fruit.

morning focus
The angel of Joy

opening
Imagine someone you fear or mistrust.
Enfold them in joy.
Feel your own ability to embrace joy.

meditation
It is my natural state
To be filled with joy,
A joy that knows from whence I came
And who I truly Am.
My moods may swing from up to down
But behind this flows
My joy in life.
Depressed emotions draw to me
Only more of the same.
I leave low vibrations behind
As I dance in the warm sun
Of this day.

today I will bring the spirit of Joyful Sharing to my _____

feelings _____

the blessing
As the tree shares its gifts of fruit,
So I, too, share the gifts of me.
For in me is the facilitator
Of a more loving world;
In me is the catalyst
For a greater social awareness.
In me is the power of the Word,
And I share that gift with all.

evening focus
The angel of Power

Tuesday, July 30, 2024

Wednesday, July 31, 2024

seasonal focus
The tree bends with ripened fruit.

morning focus
The angel of the Sun

opening
Read the meditation and the blessing outside.
Be still and notice...

meditation
Solar light,
Ancient source of power and life,
It is you who guides my path this day.
'Tis the season of your ruling,
And I, like you,
Must use this moment fully
To urge the world to grow.
And grow it will,
And grow I will
To the fullness of my potential,
For that is who I AM.

today I will bring the spirit of Fullness to my _____
_____
feelings _____
_____
_____
_____
_____
_____

evening focus
The angel of Love

the blessing
Does not the apple tree
Share its fruit with all,
Not choosing who is blest?
As my vessel overflows with love,
Do I not share this love with all?
For in our oneness
There exist no chosen ones.
Only fellow travellers do I see
On the path back home to God.

teltane

Even as the fullness of the sun hung heavy in the summer sky, our ancestors noticed that each succeeding day saw the sun rising later and setting earlier. As an assurance that the sun would retain its power until the harvest was complete, the Celts celebrated a ritual marriage on this day between Lugh, the sun, and Eire, the earth. This cosmic mating of the male and female energies was vital to the maintenance of harmony and abundance.

We have seen in our time the effects of imbalance of yin and yang. The restoration of this harmony and abundance in our lives and on our planet is a sacred task that each of us must shoulder. The male and female in each of us must learn to love itself and, from that, to love the other.

On Teltane (or Lammas, or Lughnassad), Lugh, the Celtic god of Light, buried his foster mother Tailltiu beneath a great mound in Ireland. This signifies the withdrawal of the Mother Goddess into the earth in preparation for the falling seeds that will need her care if they are to germinate in winter.

Thursday, August 1, 2024

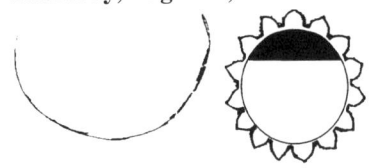

seasonal focus
The bountiful harvest is gathered.

morning focus
The angel of Water

deepening
Hold water in your bowl as you read.
Sometime today sprinkle it
on one whom you are *not* close to
(or perhaps cleanse their hands or face).

meditation
As the wave of summer's glory
Reaches crest and then flows on,
I gain perspective on my doing-nature.
A half-turn of the wheel ago
Saw me emerging from winter,
With visions, plans, and dreams.
Where have the visions led me,
What plans have been realized?
What of my life? I ask.
What of today?

today I will bring the spirit of Assertiveness to my
_____

feelings _____

_____
_____
_____
_____

This is Teltane, when ripened fruits are lovingly picked from heavily laden trees.

evening focus
The angel of Wisdom

the blessing
In this season of outer work,
My twofold task is clear.
My work is learning and also teaching,
For I have much to share.
No false humility will block the rhythm of this cycle,
This flow of wisdom to me, through me.
The inbreath-outbreath finds me
Now learning, now teaching;
The cycle is complete.

seasonal focus
The bountiful harvest is gathered.

morning focus
The angel of Air

Friday, August 2, 2024

opening
Practice deep breathing outside
before meditation. Expand your belly
and chest, stretch your limits.

meditation
This morning brings a different breeze,
A breath of change and newness.
What do I sense,
What blurry vision flickers, tempting me?
The winds of change blow in my life,
And I must now decide.
Do I unfurl my sails to catch them
Or keep the sails furled?
My choice this season will set the course
Of many seasons' journeys.
Let meditation be my guide;
Let calmness lead the way.

today I will bring the spirit of Change to my ___

feelings ___

the blessing
"Thy Will Be Done"
Is the name of the River
That carries me along.
This day, I surrender my ego
To that eternal river
As I will surrender my spirit to it
At the last breath of this body.
The river will carry me then
Until my next work is clear.

evening focus
Our Heavenly Father

243

Saturday, August 3, 2024

seasonal focus
The bountiful harvest is gathered.

morning focus
Our Earthly Mother

deepening
Hold grapes or other late-ripening fruit.
Make this a part of your next meal.

meditation
The richness of my Mother's garden
Surrounds me on this morning.
The nature forces toil unendingly
For me,
And I am blessed.
The elemental kingdom,
Which guides and nurtures the plants and trees,
Is yet another manifestation
Of my Mother's love for me.
And I,
Within my kingdom,
What do I guide and nourish,
As I return the gifts of Love?

today I will bring the spirit of Abundance to my

feelings _____

_____

_____

_____

_____

evening focus
The angel of Eternal Life

the blessing
The food upon my table
Shares its life with me.
I ask that this life nourish me,
As I shall one day nourish the earth
With my body
And as I now nourish the earth
With my love.

244

seasonal focus
The bountiful harvest is gathered.

morning focus
The angel of Earth

deepening
Hold a stone during the reading.
Explore it intimately, sensuously.

meditation
I feel my body become the earth,
The richness and the rock.
From my scant depth of dark topsoil
Spring the fruits for all.
But rock am I
As well as soil,
And at my center flows
The fire of molten mystery
That was kindled long ago.
What consciousness
Began that fire,
Bringing me to now?

today I will bring the spirit of Perfection to my _____

feelings _____

Sunday, August 4, 2024

the blessing
The table in my house is full
And I have much to share.
As I gather in the fruits of my labors,
As I work with the talents that I have,
I see that it is in the gathering
That fulfillment lies.
It is in the labor of right livelihood
That I find greater joy
Than in the security of an overflowing cupboard.

evening focus
The angel of Creative Work

Monday, August 5, 2024

seasonal focus
The bountiful harvest is gathered.

morning focus
The angel of Life

opening
Having gathered leaves, notice their veins.
Study the veins in your own arms and hands.

meditation
The late summer days fill me with warmth,
And I am content.
My life flows as a river,
Rushing to the sea
Wherein all become One.
As I go, I share the waters of my life
As the laden trees share their fruits with all.
And as the river does not wish
To be a mountain,
So, too, am I content with me.
For in the river is mirrored
The essence of All.

today I will bring the spirit of Fullness to my __
_____

feelings_____
_____
_____
_____
_____
_____

evening focus
The angel of Peace

the blessing
As the richness of my life brings peace to my soul,
So do I actively share this peace with all.
Peace with those I love,
Peace with those who trouble me,
Peace with those I fear,
Peace with beings far and near.
For it is I who chain the dove of peace
Or I who let it fly.

seasonal focus
The bountiful harvest is gathered.

Tuesday, August 6, 2024

morning focus
The angel of Joy

opening
Before the reading, meditate on the image of a newborn child, looking out at the world in awe. Experience *your* newness.

meditation
This day lies before me, a newborn child.
What shall this child experience
As it grows from day to night,
From new to old?
Will it be a clone of yesterday's child
And of the day before?
Or is there newness in this day
To match the newness of a child?
Is there joy awaiting to match the joy of expectation
Twinkling in this newborn eye?
I am the child;
The choice is mine.

today I will bring the spirit of Newness to my ___

feelings ___

the blessing
Within me lives the be-er and the do-er,
The meditating monastic
And the builder of temples.
In this season of outward manifestation,
As the rich ripe fruits are gathered,
It is my monk that keeps me centered
As my builder builds castles of love.
How right it is to work my wonders in the world,
Empowered by the chant within.

evening focus
The angel of Power

Wednesday, August 7, 2024

seasonal focus
The bountiful harvest is gathered.

morning focus
The angel of the Sun

opening
Read the meditation and the blessing outside.
Be still and notice. . .

meditation
This day brings to me
The gift of glorious sun,
Of warmth and light
And growth.
How mindlessly I go about the day,
Protected from this nourishment,
Unconscious of this joyful gift!
Surely I will find time this day
To take the sun to me,
And surely will I find a way
To shine *my* light with love.

today I will bring the spirit of Sharing to my ___

feelings___

evening focus
The angel of Love

the blessing
The warmth of this day has filled me,
And how natural it is
To allow this warmth to radiate
Back into the world.
I smile at you,
And you are no stranger to my heart.
I gaze at my own reflection in the eyes of the other,
And there is no other,
Only our shared divinity.
The boundaries disappear.

seasonal focus
The bountiful harvest is gathered.

Thursday, August 8, 2024

morning focus
The angel of Water

deepening
Hold water in your bowl as you read.
Sometime today sprinkle it
on one whom you are *not* close to
(or perhaps cleanse their hands or face).

meditation
As the wave of summer's glory
Reaches crest and then flows on,
I gain perspective on my doing-nature.
A half-turn of the wheel ago
Saw me emerging from winter,
With visions, plans, and dreams.
Where have the visions led me,
What plans have been realized?
What of my life? I ask.
What of today?

today I will bring the spirit of Assertiveness to my

feelings _____

_____

_____

_____

_____

_____

the blessing
In this season of outer work,
My twofold task is clear.
My work is learning and also teaching,
For I have much to share.
No false humility will block the rhythm of this cycle,
This flow of wisdom to me, through me.
The inbreath-outbreath finds me
Now learning, now teaching;
The cycle is complete.

evening focus
The angel of Wisdom

Friday, August 9, 2024

seasonal focus
The bountiful harvest is gathered.

morning focus
The angel of Air

opening
Practice deep breathing outside
before meditation. Expand your belly
and chest, stretch your limits.

meditation
This morning brings a different breeze,
A breath of change and newness.
What do I sense,
What blurry vision flickers, tempting me?
The winds of change blow in my life,
And I must now decide.
Do I unfurl my sails to catch them
Or keep the sails furled?
My choice this season will set the course
Of many seasons' journeys.
Let meditation be my guide;
Let calmness lead the way.

today I will bring the spirit of Change to my ___
_____

feelings _____
_____
_____
_____
_____
_____
_____

evening focus
Our Heavenly Father

the blessing
"Thy Will Be Done"
Is the name of the River
That carries me along.
This day, I surrender my ego
To that eternal river
As I will surrender my spirit to it
At the last breath of this body.
The river will carry me then
Until my next work is clear.

seasonal focus
The bountiful harvest is gathered.

morning focus
Our Earthly Mother

deepening
Hold grapes or other late-ripening fruit.
Make this a part of your next meal.

meditation
The richness of my Mother's garden
Surrounds me on this morning.
The nature forces toil unendingly
For me,
And I am blessed.
The elemental kingdom,
Which guides and nurtures the plants and trees,
Is yet another manifestation
Of my Mother's love for me.
And I,
Within my kingdom,
What do I guide and nourish,
As I return the gifts of Love?

today I will bring the spirit of Abundance to my

feelings _____

Saturday, August 10, 2024

the blessing
The food upon my table
Shares its life with me.
I ask that this life nourish me,
As I shall one day nourish the earth
With my body
And as I now nourish the earth
With my love.

evening focus
The angel of Eternal Life

♎ → ♏

251

Sunday, August 11, 2024

seasonal focus
The bountiful harvest is gathered.

morning focus
The angel of Earth

deepening
Hold a stone during the reading.
Explore it intimately, sensuously.

meditation
I feel my body become the earth,
The richness and the rock.
From my scant depth of dark topsoil
Spring the fruits for all.
But rock am I
As well as soil,
And at my center flows
The fire of molten mystery
That was kindled long ago.
What consciousness
Began that fire,
Bringing me to now?

today I will bring the spirit of Perfection to my _____

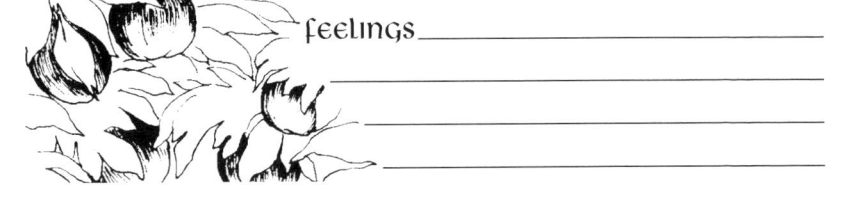

feelings _____

_____
_____
_____
_____
_____

evening focus
The angel of Creative Work

the blessing
The table in my house is full
And I have much to share.
As I gather in the fruits of my labors,
As I work with the talents that I have,
I see that it is in the gathering
That fulfillment lies.
It is in the labor of right livelihood
That I find greater joy
Than in the security of an overflowing cupboard.

seasonal focus

The bountiful harvest is gathered.

Monday, August 12, 2024

morning focus

The angel of Life

opening

Having gathered leaves, notice their veins.
Study the veins in your own arms and hands.

meditation

The late summer days fill me with warmth,
And I am content.
My life flows as a river,
Rushing to the sea
Wherein all become One.
As I go, I share the waters of my life
As the laden trees share their fruits with all.
And as the river does not wish
To be a mountain,
So, too, am I content with me.
For in the river is mirrored
The essence of All.

today I will bring the spirit of Fullness to my ___

feelings ___

the blessing

As the richness of my life brings peace to my soul,
So do I actively share this peace with all.
Peace with those I love,
Peace with those who trouble me,
Peace with those I fear,
Peace with beings far and near.
For it is I who chain the dove of peace
Or I who let it fly.

evening focus

The angel of Peace

Tuesday, August 13, 2024

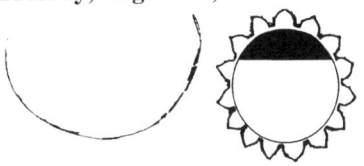

seasonal focus
The bountiful harvest is gathered.

morning focus
The angel of Joy

opening
Before the reading, meditate on the image
of a newborn child, looking out at the
world in awe. Experience *your* newness.

meditation
This day lies before me, a newborn child.
What shall this child experience
As it grows from day to night,
From new to old?
Will it be a clone of yesterday's child
And of the day before?
Or is there newness in this day
To match the newness of a child?
Is there joy awaiting to match the joy of expectation
Twinkling in this newborn eye?
I am the child;
The choice is mine.

today I will bring the spirit of Newness to my
_____

feelings_____
_____
_____
_____
_____
_____
_____

evening focus
The angel of Power

the blessing
Within me lives the be-er and the do-er,
The meditating monastic
And the builder of temples.
In this season of outward manifestation,
As the rich ripe fruits are gathered,
It is my monk that keeps me centered
As my builder builds castles of love.
How right it is to work my wonders in the world,
Empowered by the chant within.

seasonal focus
The bountiful harvest is gathered.

morning focus
The angel of the Sun

Wednesday, August 14, 2024

opening
Read the meditation and the blessing outside.
Be still and notice. . .

meditation
This day brings to me
The gift of glorious sun,
Of warmth and light
And growth.
How mindlessly I go about the day,
Protected from this nourishment,
Unconscious of this joyful gift!
Surely I will find time this day
To take the sun to me,
And surely will I find a way
To shine *my* light with love.

today I will bring the spirit of Sharing to my ___

feelings ___

the blessing
The warmth of this day has filled me,
And how natural it is
To allow this warmth to radiate
Back into the world.
I smile at you,
And you are no stranger to my heart.
I gaze at my own reflection in the eyes of the other,
And there is no other,
Only our shared divinity.
The boundaries disappear.

evening focus
The angel of Love

Thursday, August 15, 2024

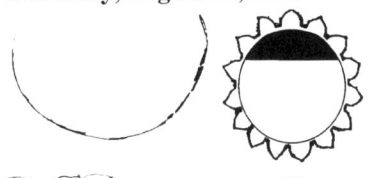

seasonal focus
The bountiful harvest is gathered.

morning focus
The angel of Water

deepening
Hold water in your bowl as you read.
Sometime today sprinkle it
on one whom you are *not* close to
(or perhaps cleanse their hands or face).

meditation
As the wave of summer's glory
Reaches crest and then flows on,
I gain perspective on my doing-nature.
A half-turn of the wheel ago
Saw me emerging from winter,
With visions, plans, and dreams.
Where have the visions led me,
What plans have been realized?
What of my life? I ask.
What of today?

today I will bring the spirit of Assertiveness to my
_____

feelings_____
_____
_____
_____
_____
_____
_____

evening focus
The angel of Wisdom

the blessing
In this season of outer work,
My twofold task is clear.
My work is learning and also teaching,
For I have much to share.
No false humility will block the rhythm of this cycle,
This flow of wisdom to me, through me.
The inbreath-outbreath finds me
Now learning, now teaching;
The cycle is complete.

seasonal focus
The bountiful harvest is gathered.

Friday, August 16, 2024

morning focus
The angel of Air

opening
Practice deep breathing outside
before meditation. Expand your belly
and chest, stretch your limits.

meditation
This morning brings a different breeze,
A breath of change and newness.
What do I sense,
What blurry vision flickers, tempting me?
The winds of change blow in my life,
And I must now decide.
Do I unfurl my sails to catch them
Or keep the sails furled?
My choice this season will set the course
Of many seasons' journeys.
Let meditation be my guide;
Let calmness lead the way.

today I will bring the spirit of Change to my ___

feelings ___

the blessing
"Thy Will Be Done"
Is the name of the River
That carries me along.
This day, I surrender my ego
To that eternal river
As I will surrender my spirit to it
At the last breath of this body.
The river will carry me then
Until my next work is clear.

evening focus
Our Heavenly Father

Saturday, August 17, 2024

seasonal focus
The bountiful harvest is gathered.

morning focus
Our Earthly Mother

deepening
Hold grapes or other late-ripening fruit.
Make this a part of your next meal.

meditation
The richness of my Mother's garden
Surrounds me on this morning.
The nature forces toil unendingly
For me,
And I am blessed.
The elemental kingdom,
Which guides and nurtures the plants and trees,
Is yet another manifestation
Of my Mother's love for me.
And I,
Within my kingdom,
What do I guide and nourish,
As I return the gifts of Love?

today I will bring the spirit of Abundance to my
_____

feelings_____
_____
_____
_____
_____
_____
_____

evening focus
The angel of Eternal Life

♑ → ≈

the blessing
The food upon my table
Shares its life with me.
I ask that this life nourish me,
As I shall one day nourish the earth
With my body
And as I now nourish the earth
With my love.

seasonal focus
The bountiful harvest is gathered.

morning focus
The angel of Earth

deepening
Hold a stone during the reading.
Explore it intimately, sensuously.

meditation
I feel my body become the earth,
The richness and the rock.
From my scant depth of dark topsoil
Spring the fruits for all.
But rock am I
As well as soil,
And at my center flows
The fire of molten mystery
That was kindled long ago.
What consciousness
Began that fire,
Bringing me to now?

today I will bring the spirit of Perfection to my _____

feelings _____

Sunday, August 18, 2024

the blessing
The table in my house is full
And I have much to share.
As I gather in the fruits of my labors,
As I work with the talents that I have,
I see that it is in the gathering
That fulfillment lies.
It is in the labor of right livelihood
That I find greater joy
Than in the security of an overflowing cupboard.

evening focus
The angel of Creative Work

259

Monday, August 19, 2024

seasonal focus
The bountiful harvest is gathered.

morning focus
The angel of Life

opening
Having gathered leaves, notice their veins.
Study the veins in your own arms and hands.

meditation
The late summer days fill me with warmth,
And I am content.
My life flows as a river,
Rushing to the sea
Wherein all become One.
As I go, I share the waters of my life
As the laden trees share their fruits with all.
And as the river does not wish
To be a mountain,
So, too, am I content with me.
For in the river is mirrored
The essence of All.

today I will bring the spirit of Fullness to my ___

feelings ___

___

___

___

___

___

___

evening focus
The angel of Peace

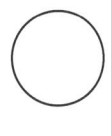

the blessing
As the richness of my life brings peace to my soul,
So do I actively share this peace with all.
Peace with those I love,
Peace with those who trouble me,
Peace with those I fear,
Peace with beings far and near.
For it is I who chain the dove of peace
Or I who let it fly.

seasonal focus
The bountiful harvest is gathered.

Tuesday, August 20, 2024

morning focus
The angel of Joy

opening
Before the reading, meditate on the image of a newborn child, looking out at the world in awe. Experience *your* newness.

meditation
This day lies before me, a newborn child.
What shall this child experience
As it grows from day to night,
From new to old?
Will it be a clone of yesterday's child
And of the day before?
Or is there newness in this day
To match the newness of a child?
Is there joy awaiting to match the joy of expectation
Twinkling in this newborn eye?
I am the child;
The choice is mine.

today I will bring the spirit of Newness to my ___

feelings

the blessing
Within me lives the be-er and the do-er,
The meditating monastic
And the builder of temples.
In this season of outward manifestation,
As the rich ripe fruits are gathered,
It is my monk that keeps me centered
As my builder builds castles of love.
How right it is to work my wonders in the world,
Empowered by the chant within.

evening focus
The angel of Power

Wednesday, August 21, 2024

seasonal focus
The bountiful harvest is gathered.

morning focus
The angel of the Sun

opening
Read the meditation and the blessing outside.
Be still and notice...

meditation
This day brings to me
The gift of glorious sun,
Of warmth and light
And growth.
How mindlessly I go about the day,
Protected from this nourishment,
Unconscious of this joyful gift!
Surely I will find time this day
To take the sun to me,
And surely will I find a way
To shine *my* light with love.

today I will bring the spirit of Sharing to my ___
_____

feelings_____
_____
_____
_____
_____
_____
_____

evening focus
The angel of Love

the blessing
The warmth of this day has filled me,
And how natural it is
To allow this warmth to radiate
Back into the world.
I smile at you,
And you are no stranger to my heart.
I gaze at my own reflection in the eyes of the other,
And there is no other,
Only our shared divinity.
The boundaries disappear.

seasonal focus
The bountiful harvest is gathered.

Thursday, August 22, 2024

morning focus
The angel of Water

deepening
Hold water in your bowl as you read.
Sometime today sprinkle it
on one whom you are *not* close to
(or perhaps cleanse their hands or face).

meditation
As the wave of summer's glory
Reaches crest and then flows on,
I gain perspective on my doing-nature.
A half-turn of the wheel ago
Saw me emerging from winter,
With visions, plans, and dreams.
Where have the visions led me,
What plans have been realized?
What of my life? I ask.
What of today?

today I will bring the spirit of Assertiveness to my _____

feelings _____
_____
_____
_____
_____
_____
_____

the blessing
In this season of outer work,
My twofold task is clear.
My work is learning and also teaching,
For I have much to share.
No false humility will block the rhythm of this cycle,
This flow of wisdom to me, through me.
The inbreath-outbreath finds me
Now learning, now teaching;
The cycle is complete.

evening focus
The angel of Wisdom

Friday, August 23, 2024

seasonal focus
The bountiful harvest is gathered.

morning focus
The angel of Air

opening
Practice deep breathing outside
before meditation. Expand your belly
and chest, stretch your limits.

meditation
This morning brings a different breeze,
A breath of change and newness.
What do I sense,
What blurry vision flickers, tempting me?
The winds of change blow in my life,
And I must now decide.
Do I unfurl my sails to catch them
Or keep the sails furled?
My choice this season will set the course
Of many seasons' journeys.
Let meditation be my guide;
Let calmness lead the way.

today I will bring the spirit of Change to my ___

feelings ___

evening focus
Our Heavenly Father

♈ → ♉

the blessing
"Thy Will Be Done"
Is the name of the River
That carries me along.
This day, I surrender my ego
To that eternal river
As I will surrender my spirit to it
At the last breath of this body.
The river will carry me then
Until my next work is clear.

seasonal focus
The bountiful harvest is gathered.

morning focus
Our Earthly Mother

deepening
Hold grapes or other late-ripening fruit.
Make this a part of your next meal.

Saturday, August 24, 2024

meditation
The richness of my Mother's garden
Surrounds me on this morning.
The nature forces toil unendingly
For me,
And I am blessed.
The elemental kingdom,
Which guides and nurtures the plants and trees,
Is yet another manifestation
Of my Mother's love for me.
And I,
Within my kingdom,
What do I guide and nourish,
As I return the gifts of Love?

today I will bring the spirit of Abundance to my

feelings _____

the blessing
The food upon my table
Shares its life with me.
I ask that this life nourish me,
As I shall one day nourish the earth
With my body
And as I now nourish the earth
With my love.

evening focus
The angel of Eternal Life

Sunday, August 25, 2024

seasonal focus
The bountiful harvest is gathered.

morning focus
The angel of Earth

deepening
Hold a stone during the reading.
Explore it intimately, sensuously.

meditation
I feel my body become the earth,
The richness and the rock.
From my scant depth of dark topsoil
Spring the fruits for all.
But rock am I
As well as soil,
And at my center flows
The fire of molten mystery
That was kindled long ago.
What consciousness
Began that fire,
Bringing me to now?

today I will bring the spirit of Perfection to my _____

feelings_____

_____

_____

_____

_____

_____

evening focus
The angel of Creative Work

♉ → ♊

the blessing
The table in my house is full
And I have much to share.
As I gather in the fruits of my labors,
As I work with the talents that I have,
I see that it is in the gathering
That fulfillment lies.
It is in the labor of right livelihood
That I find greater joy
Than in the security of an overflowing cupboard.

seasonal focus
The bountiful harvest is gathered.

Monday, August 26, 2024

morning focus
The angel of Life

opening
Having gathered leaves, notice their veins.
Study the veins in your own arms and hands.

meditation
The late summer days fill me with warmth,
And I am content.
My life flows as a river,
Rushing to the sea
Wherein all become One.
As I go, I share the waters of my life
As the laden trees share their fruits with all.
And as the river does not wish
To be a mountain,
So, too, am I content with me.
For in the river is mirrored
The essence of All.

today I will bring the spirit of Fullness to my ____

feelings ____

the blessing
As the richness of my life brings peace to my soul,
So do I actively share this peace with all.
Peace with those I love,
Peace with those who trouble me,
Peace with those I fear,
Peace with beings far and near.
For it is I who chain the dove of peace
Or I who let it fly.

evening focus
The angel of Peace

267

Tuesday, August 27, 2024

seasonal focus
The bountiful harvest is gathered.

morning focus
The angel of Joy

opening
Before the reading, meditate on the image
of a newborn child, looking out at the
world in awe. Experience *your* newness.

meditation
This day lies before me, a newborn child.
What shall this child experience
As it grows from day to night,
From new to old?
Will it be a clone of yesterday's child
And of the day before?
Or is there newness in this day
To match the newness of a child?
Is there joy awaiting to match the joy of expectation
Twinkling in this newborn eye?
I am the child;
The choice is mine.

today I will bring the spirit of Newness to my
_____

feelings _____
_____
_____
_____
_____
_____
_____

evening focus
The angel of Power

the blessing
Within me lives the be-er and the do-er,
The meditating monastic
And the builder of temples.
In this season of outward manifestation,
As the rich ripe fruits are gathered,
It is my monk that keeps me centered
As my builder builds castles of love.
How right it is to work my wonders in the world,
Empowered by the chant within.

seasonal focus
The bountiful harvest is gathered.

morning focus
The angel of the Sun

Wednesday, August 28, 2024

opening
Read the meditation and the blessing outside.
Be still and notice. . .

meditation
This day brings to me
The gift of glorious sun,
Of warmth and light
And growth.
How mindlessly I go about the day,
Protected from this nourishment,
Unconscious of this joyful gift!
Surely I will find time this day
To take the sun to me,
And surely will I find a way
To shine *my* light with love.

today I will bring the spirit of Sharing to my ___

feelings ___

the blessing
The warmth of this day has filled me,
And how natural it is
To allow this warmth to radiate
Back into the world.
I smile at you,
And you are no stranger to my heart.
I gaze at my own reflection in the eyes of the other,
And there is no other,
Only our shared divinity.
The boundaries disappear.

evening focus
The angel of Love

269

Thursday, August 29, 2024

seasonal focus
The bountiful harvest is gathered.

morning focus
The angel of Water

deepening
Hold water in your bowl as you read.
Sometime today sprinkle it
on one whom you are *not* close to
(or perhaps cleanse their hands or face).

meditation
As the wave of summer's glory
Reaches crest and then flows on,
I gain perspective on my doing-nature.
A half-turn of the wheel ago
Saw me emerging from winter,
With visions, plans, and dreams.
Where have the visions led me,
What plans have been realized?
What of my life? I ask.
What of today?

today I will bring the spirit of Assertiveness to my
_____

feelings_____
_____
_____
_____
_____
_____
_____

evening focus
The angel of Wisdom

the blessing
In this season of outer work,
My twofold task is clear.
My work is learning and also teaching,
For I have much to share.
No false humility will block the rhythm of this cycle,
This flow of wisdom to me, through me.
The inbreath-outbreath finds me
Now learning, now teaching;
The cycle is complete.

seasonal focus
The bountiful harvest is gathered.

morning focus
The angel of Air

opening
Practice deep breathing outside
before meditation. Expand your belly
and chest, stretch your limits.

meditation
This morning brings a different breeze,
A breath of change and newness.
What do I sense,
What blurry vision flickers, tempting me?
The winds of change blow in my life,
And I must now decide.
Do I unfurl my sails to catch them
Or keep the sails furled?
My choice this season will set the course
Of many seasons' journeys.
Let meditation be my guide;
Let calmness lead the way.

today I will bring the spirit of Change to my ___

feelings ___

Friday, August 30, 2024

the blessing
"Thy Will Be Done"
Is the name of the River
That carries me along.
This day, I surrender my ego
To that eternal river
As I will surrender my spirit to it
At the last breath of this body.
The river will carry me then
Until my next work is clear.

evening focus
Our Heavenly Father

Saturday, August 31, 2024

seasonal focus
The bountiful harvest is gathered.

morning focus
Our Earthly Mother

deepening
Hold grapes or other late-ripening fruit.
Make this a part of your next meal.

meditation
The richness of my Mother's garden
Surrounds me on this morning.
The nature forces toil unendingly
For me,
And I am blessed.
The elemental kingdom,
Which guides and nurtures the plants and trees,
Is yet another manifestation
Of my Mother's love for me.
And I,
Within my kingdom,
What do I guide and nourish,
As I return the gifts of Love?

today I will bring the spirit of Abundance to my
_____
feelings_____
_____
_____
_____
_____
_____
_____

evening focus
The angel of Eternal Life

the blessing
The food upon my table
Shares its life with me.
I ask that this life nourish me,
As I shall one day nourish the earth
With my body
And as I now nourish the earth
With my love.

one world family

There seem to be certain moments in our history, certain rare magical moments, where all of the forces impinging on our species combine to create a "potential," a possible pregnant ripeness for something completely new. The idea that this period in our human evolution is such a period is not a new one. Marilyn Ferguson's paradigm shift, Ken Keyes Jr.'s 100th Monkey Effect, and the quantum leap and avalanche effect of the new physics all give us models of the transformation that can, if we choose, come out of the chaos of the present.

How to do it? If we are to actually create this shift, we must have a dream, a common vision. We must dream a dream that is concrete enough to be imagined in our minds while still being universal enough to activate our collective hearts and spirits. I want to offer to you such a dream. It is the dream of a One World Family. The dream of a planet where everyone is seen as family isn't a new one, and that speaks of its power. I believe it is a dream that every human being holds somewhere deep inside. For some, it is buried far from consciousness, layered over by generations of fear and mistrust. For some it has bubbled to the surface, but it is frustrated by the conflicts that arise just from trying to communicate to those close to us, no less to the entire family of humankind.

Perhaps what we need is a simple (not easy, but simple) shift in our perception. I think that one of the biggest stumbling blocks to the recognition of our interconnections as "one big family" is the idea that if that's true, we then will all have to like each other. That's not necessarily so. Think about your own nuclear family. I'm thinking about *mine* right now. There are some cousins in New Jersey that I can't stand! But I would never kill them. And if they were starving, I probably wouldn't let politics or geography get in my way of assisting them. They are blood. They're blood relatives and, regardless of what I think about them at a personality level, I just don't let blood relatives suffer if I can possibly help it.

We are *all* blood relatives! Every human on this planet is your blood relative. Can you feel that perceptual shift? Can you experience those unknown, strange, different-from-you folks out there as your own blood? In *Seven Mysteries of Life,* Guy Murchie weaves a fairly solid case of the idea that every human alive on this planet today is indeed closely related. His statement is that we are all *at least* 16th cousins. That's right, even those funny looking whatchamacallems over in whatever, they're at the very least your 16th cousins.

Sure, cousins, and brothers and sisters and even parents and off spring have killed and abused each other throughout history, but not much, and not without drawing the outrage of the entire society. When the blood we spill is "family blood," we think about it a lot more than when "outsider" blood flows. Genetics and quantum physics and anthropology and spiritual wisdom now seem to agree that there are *no* outsiders. We are all blood relatives. And if enough of us can make this truth an intimate part of our daily consciousness, then perhaps the "critical mass" effect will cause a perceptual shift in every human consciousness. That is a dream worth manifesting.

I want to ask you to take a few minutes right now to read *There is But One Human Heart* on the next page. I ask that you read it as if the dream has already come true.

there is but one human heart

Can you feel it?
The rich red blood
your heart sends coursing
through your human body?

Can you feel it?
This same rich blood of life
being pumped by every human heart
in every mountain, valley, plain
on our common home — the earth?

From the sea, from the caves,
from the death-point in the battle sphere,
we have struggled and survived.
We have borne one another and killed one another
and we have, in some incredible way,
passed onward the tenuous thread
of our common human life.

We have a history, you and I
We are the human ones.
We have come to learn from and move beyond
our arrogance and our separateness
We have come here to go home.
Together.

The political boundaries, the walls we have made,
they will crumble.
Our common blood will remain.
We will come together as One World Family,
even as you and I now come together
to challenge the wall we have built between us.
We will share our love for all our family
just as you and I now reach out
to touch the place of oneness within our common heart.

seasonal focus
The bountiful harvest is gathered.

Sunday, September 1, 2024

morning focus
The angel of Earth

deepening
Hold a stone during the reading.
Explore it intimately, sensuously.

meditation
I feel my body become the earth,
The richness and the rock.
From my scant depth of dark topsoil
Spring the fruits for all.
But rock am I
As well as soil,
And at my center flows
The fire of molten mystery
That was kindled long ago.
What consciousness
Began that fire,
Bringing me to now?

today I will bring the spirit of Perfection to my _____

feelings _____

the blessing
The table in my house is full
And I have much to share.
As I gather in the fruits of my labors,
As I work with the talents that I have,
I see that it is in the gathering
That fulfillment lies.
It is in the labor of right livelihood
That I find greater joy
Than in the security of an overflowing cupboard.

evening focus
The angel of Creative Work

275

Monday, September 2, 2024

seasonal focus
The bountiful harvest is gathered.

morning focus
The angel of Life

opening
Having gathered leaves, notice their veins.
Study the veins in your own arms and hands.

meditation
The late summer days fill me with warmth,
And I am content.
My life flows as a river,
Rushing to the sea
Wherein all become One.
As I go, I share the waters of my life
As the laden trees share their fruits with all.
And as the river does not wish
To be a mountain,
So, too, am I content with me.
For in the river is mirrored
The essence of All.

today I will bring the spirit of Fullness to my __
_____

feelings _____
_____
_____
_____
_____
_____
_____

evening focus
The angel of Peace

the blessing
As the richness of my life brings peace to my soul,
So do I actively share this peace with all.
Peace with those I love,
Peace with those who trouble me,
Peace with those I fear,
Peace with beings far and near.
For it is I who chain the dove of peace
Or I who let it fly.

seasonal focus
The bountiful harvest is gathered.

Tuesday, September 3, 2024

morning focus
The angel of Joy

opening
Before the reading, meditate on the image of a newborn child, looking out at the world in awe. Experience *your* newness.

meditation
This day lies before me, a newborn child.
What shall this child experience
As it grows from day to night,
From new to old?
Will it be a clone of yesterday's child
And of the day before?
Or is there newness in this day
To match the newness of a child?
Is there joy awaiting to match the joy of expectation
Twinkling in this newborn eye?
I am the child;
The choice is mine.

today I will bring the spirit of Newness to my ___

feelings ___

the blessing
Within me lives the be-er and the do-er,
The meditating monastic
And the builder of temples.
In this season of outward manifestation,
As the rich ripe fruits are gathered,
It is my monk that keeps me centered
As my builder builds castles of love.
How right it is to work my wonders in the world,
Empowered by the chant within.

evening focus
The angel of Power

277

Wednesday, September 4, 2024

seasonal focus
The bountiful harvest is gathered.

morning focus
The angel of the Sun

opening
Read the meditation and the blessing outside.
Be still and notice. . .

meditation
This day brings to me
The gift of glorious sun,
Of warmth and light
And growth.
How mindlessly I go about the day,
Protected from this nourishment,
Unconscious of this joyful gift!
Surely I will find time this day
To take the sun to me,
And surely will I find a way
To shine *my* light with love.

today I will bring the spirit of Sharing to my ___
_____

feelings_____
_____
_____
_____
_____
_____

evening focus
The angel of Love

the blessing
The warmth of this day has filled me,
And how natural it is
To allow this warmth to radiate
Back into the world.
I smile at you,
And you are no stranger to my heart.
I gaze at my own reflection in the eyes of the other,
And there is no other,
Only our shared divinity.
The boundaries disappear.

Thursday, September 5, 2024

seasonal focus
The bountiful harvest is gathered.

morning focus
The angel of Water

deepening
Hold water in your bowl as you read.
Sometime today sprinkle it
on one whom you are *not* close to
(or perhaps cleanse their hands or face).

meditation
As the wave of summer's glory
Reaches crest and then flows on,
I gain perspective on my doing-nature.
A half-turn of the wheel ago
Saw me emerging from winter,
With visions, plans, and dreams.
Where have the visions led me,
What plans have been realized?
What of my life? I ask.
What of today?

today I will bring the spirit of Assertiveness to my

feelings _____

_____

_____

_____

_____

_____

the blessing
In this season of outer work,
My twofold task is clear.
My work is learning and also teaching,
For I have much to share.
No false humility will block the rhythm of this cycle,
This flow of wisdom to me, through me.
The inbreath-outbreath finds me
Now learning, now teaching;
The cycle is complete.

evening focus
The angel of Wisdom

Friday, September 6, 2024

seasonal focus
The bountiful harvest is gathered.

morning focus
The angel of Air

opening
Practice deep breathing outside
before meditation. Expand your belly
and chest, stretch your limits.

meditation
This morning brings a different breeze,
A breath of change and newness.
What do I sense,
What blurry vision flickers, tempting me?
The winds of change blow in my life,
And I must now decide.
Do I unfurl my sails to catch them
Or keep the sails furled?
My choice this season will set the course
Of many seasons' journeys.
Let meditation be my guide;
Let calmness lead the way.

today I will bring the spirit of Change to my ___
_____

feelings _____
_____
_____
_____
_____
_____
_____

evening focus
Our Heavenly Father

the blessing
"Thy Will Be Done"
Is the name of the River
That carries me along.
This day, I surrender my ego
To that eternal river
As I will surrender my spirit to it
At the last breath of this body.
The river will carry me then
Until my next work is clear.

Saturday, September 7, 2024

seasonal focus
The bountiful harvest is gathered.

morning focus
Our Earthly Mother

deepening
Hold grapes or other late-ripening fruit.
Make this a part of your next meal.

meditation
The richness of my Mother's garden
Surrounds me on this morning.
The nature forces toil unendingly
For me,
And I am blessed.
The elemental kingdom,
Which guides and nurtures the plants and trees,
Is yet another manifestation
Of my Mother's love for me.
And I,
Within my kingdom,
What do I guide and nourish,
As I return the gifts of Love?

today I will bring the spirit of Abundance to my _____

feelings _____

_____
_____
_____
_____
_____
_____

the blessing
The food upon my table
Shares its life with me.
I ask that this life nourish me,
As I shall one day nourish the earth
With my body
And as I now nourish the earth
With my love.

evening focus
The angel of Eternal Life

Sunday, September 8, 2024

seasonal focus
The bountiful harvest is gathered.

morning focus
The angel of Earth

deepening
Hold a stone during the reading.
Explore it intimately, sensuously.

meditation
I feel my body become the earth,
The richness and the rock.
From my scant depth of dark topsoil
Spring the fruits for all.
But rock am I
As well as soil,
And at my center flows
The fire of molten mystery
That was kindled long ago.
What consciousness
Began that fire,
Bringing me to now?

today I will bring the spirit of Perfection to my _____

feelings _____

_____

_____

_____

_____

_____

evening focus
The angel of Creative Work

the blessing
The table in my house is full
And I have much to share.
As I gather in the fruits of my labors,
As I work with the talents that I have,
I see that it is in the gathering
That fulfillment lies.
It is in the labor of right livelihood
That I find greater joy
Than in the security of an overflowing cupboard.

seasonal focus
The bountiful harvest is gathered.

morning focus
The angel of Life

Monday, September 9, 2024

opening
Having gathered leaves, notice their veins.
Study the veins in your own arms and hands.

meditation
The late summer days fill me with warmth,
And I am content.
My life flows as a river,
Rushing to the sea
Wherein all become One.
As I go, I share the waters of my life
As the laden trees share their fruits with all.
And as the river does not wish
To be a mountain,
So, too, am I content with me.
For in the river is mirrored
The essence of All.

today I will bring the spirit of Fullness to my ___

feelings _____

the blessing
As the richness of my life brings peace to my soul,
So do I actively share this peace with all.
Peace with those I love,
Peace with those who trouble me,
Peace with those I fear,
Peace with beings far and near.
For it is I who chain the dove of peace
Or I who let it fly.

evening focus
The angel of Peace

Tuesday, September 10, 2024

seasonal focus
The bountiful harvest is gathered.

morning focus
The angel of Joy

opening
Before the reading, meditate on the image of a newborn child, looking out at the world in awe. Experience *your* newness.

meditation
This day lies before me, a newborn child.
What shall this child experience
As it grows from day to night,
From new to old?
Will it be a clone of yesterday's child
And of the day before?
Or is there newness in this day
To match the newness of a child?
Is there joy awaiting to match the joy of expectation
Twinkling in this newborn eye?
I am the child;
The choice is mine.

today I will bring the spirit of Newness to my

_____

feelings _____

_____
_____
_____
_____
_____
_____

evening focus
The angel of Power

the blessing
Within me lives the be-er and the do-er,
The meditating monastic
And the builder of temples.
In this season of outward manifestation,
As the rich ripe fruits are gathered,
It is my monk that keeps me centered
As my builder builds castles of love.
How right it is to work my wonders in the world,
Empowered by the chant within.

Wednesday, September 11, 2024

seasonal focus
The bountiful harvest is gathered.

morning focus
The angel of the Sun

opening
Read the meditation and the blessing outside.
Be still and notice...

meditation
This day brings to me
The gift of glorious sun,
Of warmth and light
And growth.
How mindlessly I go about the day,
Protected from this nourishment,
Unconscious of this joyful gift!
Surely I will find time this day
To take the sun to me,
And surely will I find a way
To shine *my* light with love.

today I will bring the spirit of Sharing to my ___

feelings ___

the blessing
The warmth of this day has filled me,
And how natural it is
To allow this warmth to radiate
Back into the world.
I smile at you,
And you are no stranger to my heart.
I gaze at my own reflection in the eyes of the other,
And there is no other,
Only our shared divinity.
The boundaries disappear.

evening focus
The angel of Love

Thursday, September 12, 2024

seasonal focus
The bountiful harvest is gathered.

morning focus
The angel of Water

deepening
Hold water in your bowl as you read.
Sometime today sprinkle it
on one whom you are *not* close to
(or perhaps cleanse their hands or face).

meditation
As the wave of summer's glory
Reaches crest and then flows on,
I gain perspective on my doing-nature.
A half-turn of the wheel ago
Saw me emerging from winter,
With visions, plans, and dreams.
Where have the visions led me,
What plans have been realized?
What of my life? I ask.
What of today?

today I will bring the spirit of Assertiveness to my
_____

feelings_____
_____
_____
_____
_____
_____
_____

evening focus
The angel of Wisdom

the blessing
In this season of outer work,
My twofold task is clear.
My work is learning and also teaching,
For I have much to share.
No false humility will block the rhythm of this cycle,
This flow of wisdom to me, through me.
The inbreath-outbreath finds me
Now learning, now teaching;
The cycle is complete.

seasonal focus
The bountiful harvest is gathered.

morning focus
The angel of Air

Friday, September 13, 2024

opening
Practice deep breathing outside
before meditation. Expand your belly
and chest, stretch your limits.

meditation
This morning brings a different breeze,
A breath of change and newness.
What do I sense,
What blurry vision flickers, tempting me?
The winds of change blow in my life,
And I must now decide.
Do I unfurl my sails to catch them
Or keep the sails furled?
My choice this season will set the course
Of many seasons' journeys.
Let meditation be my guide;
Let calmness lead the way.

today I will bring the spirit of Change to my ___

feelings ___

the blessing
"Thy Will Be Done"
Is the name of the River
That carries me along.
This day, I surrender my ego
To that eternal river
As I will surrender my spirit to it
At the last breath of this body.
The river will carry me then
Until my next work is clear.

evening focus
Our Heavenly Father

Saturday, September 14, 2024

seasonal focus
The bountiful harvest is gathered.

morning focus
Our Earthly Mother

deepening
Hold grapes or other late-ripening fruit.
Make this a part of your next meal.

meditation
The richness of my Mother's garden
Surrounds me on this morning.
The nature forces toil unendingly
For me,
And I am blessed.
The elemental kingdom,
Which guides and nurtures the plants and trees,
Is yet another manifestation
Of my Mother's love for me.
And I,
Within my kingdom,
What do I guide and nourish,
As I return the gifts of Love?

today I will bring the spirit of Abundance to my
_____

feelings_____
_____
_____
_____
_____
_____
_____

evening focus
The angel of Eternal Life

the blessing
The food upon my table
Shares its life with me.
I ask that this life nourish me,
As I shall one day nourish the earth
With my body
And as I now nourish the earth
With my love.

seasonal focus
The bountiful harvest is gathered.

Sunday, September 15, 2024

morning focus
The angel of Earth

deepening
Hold a stone during the reading.
Explore it intimately, sensuously.

meditation
I feel my body become the earth,
The richness and the rock.
From my scant depth of dark topsoil
Spring the fruits for all.
But rock am I
As well as soil,
And at my center flows
The fire of molten mystery
That was kindled long ago.
What consciousness
Began that fire,
Bringing me to now?

today I will bring the spirit of Perfection to my _____

feelings _____

_____

_____

_____

_____

the blessing
The table in my house is full
And I have much to share.
As I gather in the fruits of my labors,
As I work with the talents that I have,
I see that it is in the gathering
That fulfillment lies.
It is in the labor of right livelihood
That I find greater joy
Than in the security of an overflowing cupboard.

evening focus
The angel of Creative Work

Monday, September 16, 2024

seasonal focus
The bountiful harvest is gathered.

morning focus
The angel of Life

opening
Having gathered leaves, notice their veins.
Study the veins in your own arms and hands.

meditation
The late summer days fill me with warmth,
And I am content.
My life flows as a river,
Rushing to the sea
Wherein all become One.
As I go, I share the waters of my life
As the laden trees share their fruits with all.
And as the river does not wish
To be a mountain,
So, too, am I content with me.
For in the river is mirrored
The essence of All.

today I will bring the spirit of Fullness to my __

feelings __

evening focus
The angel of Peace

the blessing
As the richness of my life brings peace to my soul,
So do I actively share this peace with all.
Peace with those I love,
Peace with those who trouble me,
Peace with those I fear,
Peace with beings far and near.
For it is I who chain the dove of peace
Or I who let it fly.

seasonal focus
The bountiful harvest is gathered.

Tuesday, September 17, 2024

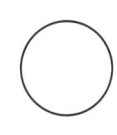

morning focus
The angel of Joy

opening
Before the reading, meditate on the image of a newborn child, looking out at the world in awe. Experience *your* newness.

meditation
This day lies before me, a newborn child.
What shall this child experience
As it grows from day to night,
From new to old?
Will it be a clone of yesterday's child
And of the day before?
Or is there newness in this day
To match the newness of a child?
Is there joy awaiting to match the joy of expectation
Twinkling in this newborn eye?
I am the child;
The choice is mine.

today I will bring the spirit of Newness to my ___

feelings ___

the blessing
Within me lives the be-er and the do-er,
The meditating monastic
And the builder of temples.
In this season of outward manifestation,
As the rich ripe fruits are gathered,
It is my monk that keeps me centered
As my builder builds castles of love.
How right it is to work my wonders in the world,
Empowered by the chant within.

evening focus
The angel of Power

Wednesday, September 18, 2024

seasonal focus
The bountiful harvest is gathered.

morning focus
The angel of the Sun

opening
Read the meditation and the blessing outside.
Be still and notice. . .

meditation
This day brings to me
The gift of glorious sun,
Of warmth and light
And growth.
How mindlessly I go about the day,
Protected from this nourishment,
Unconscious of this joyful gift!
Surely I will find time this day
To take the sun to me,
And surely will I find a way
To shine *my* light with love.

today I will bring the spirit of Sharing to my ___

feelings ___

evening focus
The angel of Love

the blessing
The warmth of this day has filled me,
And how natural it is
To allow this warmth to radiate
Back into the world.
I smile at you,
And you are no stranger to my heart.
I gaze at my own reflection in the eyes of the other,
And there is no other,
Only our shared divinity.
The boundaries disappear.

Thursday, September 19, 2024

seasonal focus
The bountiful harvest is gathered.

morning focus
The angel of Water

deepening
Hold water in your bowl as you read.
Sometime today sprinkle it
on one whom you are *not* close to
(or perhaps cleanse their hands or face).

meditation
As the wave of summer's glory
Reaches crest and then flows on,
I gain perspective on my doing-nature.
A half-turn of the wheel ago
Saw me emerging from winter,
With visions, plans, and dreams.
Where have the visions led me,
What plans have been realized?
What of my life? I ask.
What of today?

today I will bring the spirit of Assertiveness to my
_____

feelings _____
_____
_____
_____
_____
_____
_____

the blessing
In this season of outer work,
My twofold task is clear.
My work is learning and also teaching,
For I have much to share.
No false humility will block the rhythm of this cycle,
This flow of wisdom to me, through me.
The inbreath-outbreath finds me
Now learning, now teaching;
The cycle is complete.

evening focus
The angel of Wisdom

Friday, September 20, 2024

seasonal focus
The bountiful harvest is gathered.

morning focus
The angel of Air

opening
Practice deep breathing outside
before meditation. Expand your belly
and chest, stretch your limits.

meditation
This morning brings a different breeze,
A breath of change and newness.
What do I sense,
What blurry vision flickers, tempting me?
The winds of change blow in my life,
And I must now decide.
Do I unfurl my sails to catch them
Or keep the sails furled?
My choice this season will set the course
Of many seasons' journeys.
Let meditation be my guide;
Let calmness lead the way.

today I will bring the spirit of Change to my ___

_____

feelings _____

_____

_____

_____

_____

_____

_____

evening focus
Our Heavenly Father

the blessing
"Thy Will Be Done"
Is the name of the River
That carries me along.
This day, I surrender my ego
To that eternal river
As I will surrender my spirit to it
At the last breath of this body.
The river will carry me then
Until my next work is clear.

seasonal focus
The bountiful harvest is gathered.

morning focus
Our Earthly Mother

deepening
Hold grapes or other late-ripening fruit.
Make this a part of your next meal.

meditation
The richness of my Mother's garden
Surrounds me on this morning.
The nature forces toil unendingly
For me,
And I am blessed.
The elemental kingdom,
Which guides and nurtures the plants and trees,
Is yet another manifestation
Of my Mother's love for me.
And I,
Within my kingdom,
What do I guide and nourish,
As I return the gifts of Love?

today I will bring the spirit of Abundance to my

feelings _____

the blessing
The food upon my table
Shares its life with me.
I ask that this life nourish me,
As I shall one day nourish the earth
With my body
And as I now nourish the earth
With my love.

evening focus
The angel of Eternal Life

autumn equinox

This is the point on the wheel of the year when there is a balance between the energies of outward, physical, yang manifestation and inward, psychic, yin creativity. There will be equal hours of daylight and darkness this day.

This balance point of the rational and the intuitive will exist for a moment, and then the forces of intuitive, dark, inner contemplation will slowly ascend and rule the seasonal wheel through the winter. At Winter Solstice, the inner world of yin will be at its zenith.

We now enter the all-important time of inner growth. During summer, there was little time for the juices of contemplative creativity to bubble up from deep within us. Now is the time to prepare for this to occur most fruitfully. Only when we surrender to our inner nature can we begin to hear the still small voice within, and we must set our outer affairs in order now to be ready when it calls.

seasonal focus
The harvest is stored.

Sunday, September 22, 2024

morning focus
The angel of Earth

deepening
Gather fallen leaves and take them into your meditation. Let their surrender teach you.

meditation
Let me use the wisdom of my senses
To understand the earth
In this season of preparation.
For as the earth prepares its life forms,
So, too, shall I prepare.
The nature kingdom is my teacher,
And I have much to learn.
I learn of letting go
My grip on yesterday
And free myself for the wonder
Of tomorrow's subtle joy.

today I will bring the spirit of Learning From Everything to my _____

feelings _____

Autumn Equinox occurs today when summer fruits are taken inside and stored.

the blessing
Fulfillment and completeness
Are gifts I give to me.
They come from focused labor
And perfection as my guide.
How well I see the power
That my own acts have on me,
And I create my world of joy
or a world of misery.
Perfection is my natural state;
How easily I forget!

evening focus
The angel of Creative Work

Monday, September 23, 2024

seasonal focus
The harvest is stored.

morning focus
The angel of Life

opening
Before reading, study your face in a mirror.
What do you really see?

meditation
I have grown in wisdom
As this yearly wheel has turned.
I see
That freedom in my life
Is tied to that of all.
The springtime sense of Me Alone
Has mellowed and matured
Into the deeper knowing
That We are One.
Only when I respect the sacredness
Of all life shall I be truly free.

today I will bring the spirit of Freedom to my _____

feelings _____

evening focus
The angel of Peace

the blessing
The core of peace
Lives not in thoughts,
Nor in the deeds I do.
It lives inside my heart,
In how I feel about me.
When I have learned to be at peace
Within myself,
Then shall I radiate that peace to all.
Let me now go within
To calm the inner sea.

seasonal focus
The harvest is stored.

Tuesday, September 24, 2024

morning focus
The angel of Joy

opening
At this moment, what do you need more of?
This day, give that needed something to
someone else. Find a way to give it away.

meditation
Softness fills my days
In this season of autumn light.
Gentle joy of life returning
To know its roots again.
Joyful completion
Of the outward surge of growth,
Preparing me for that to come
In the darkness before birth.
Who will I laugh with on this day,
Expecting nothing,
Sharing all?

today I will bring the spirit of Intimacy to my _____

feelings _____

the blessing
The shifting balance
From outward straightline movement
To inner spiral flow
Spins the wheel of my life inward,
And I must now transform
My restless yearnings
Into quiet contemplation
To aid me in the winter's inner journey
To the abundant core of me.

evening focus
The angel of Power

Wednesday, September 25, 2024

seasonal focus
The harvest is stored.

morning focus
The angel of the Sun

opening
Intently notice the light and shadow of
your world. Light a candle after the reading
and allow the flame to warm your hands.

meditation
This day will offer me another chance
To take within me
The lifeblood of the sun.
These lengthened rays of solar fire
Will be stored within my heart
If I but use this time to full advantage.
Let me study all the colors,
The shadings and the hues,
So that, when deep in winter's womb,
I may paint the portrait of the sun with a memory
And share that scene with all.

today I will bring the spirit of Contentment to my ____

feelings ____

evening focus
The angel of Love

the blessing
Out of the dance of summer
Comes the gathering of autumn
More gently now, more softly,
I gather with my friends
And touch the hands that form the circle
And look into wiser eyes.
My love in comfort flows from my life
To color all that is,
And blessed by other forms of God,
It flows quietly back to me.

seasonal focus
The harvest is stored.

morning focus
The angel of Water

deepening
Pour water from your old favored bowl
into a new bowl. Back and forth, from old to new.
Same water. Drink it with respect.

meditation
There is a trickling of time in my life,
A cascading mountain stream of moments
That connect each spring and fall,
Each blossoming and harvesting.
What will be the colors of my flower
Come next Beltane time?
The answer lies in the ways
That I now prepare the soil
Of my inner garden,
And in how lovingly I water the seeds
From summer's fruit.

today I will bring the spirit of Expectancy to my _____

feelings _____

Thursday, September 26, 2024

the blessing
It has been said
That each of us has deep within
The knowledge of all things,
And when we are ready to remember
Then the knowledge is there to be known.
This is the season of readying,
Of challenging old beliefs
That bind us to the past.
The millennium calls to me
To live the wisdom deep within me.

evening focus
The angel of Wisdom

Friday, September 27, 2024

seasonal focus
The harvest is stored.

morning focus
The angel of Air

opening
Before reading, do alternate nasal breathing.
Five inhalations through left nostril only,
then five through right. Do five times and notice.

meditation
There is a yearning in me now,
Which follows a season of outbreath.
It is the longing for the sweet inbreath
Of my spiritual nature.
And as my physical nature still urges me
To *do*,
Yet in my heart I know my path leads me to *be*.
And I humbly honor the do-er in me
That makes my world revolve.
But now I prepare to take my inbreath
At the center
Of my Self.

today I will bring the spirit of Surrender to my _____

feelings _____

evening focus
Our Heavenly Father

the blessing
You have brought me to the sun
And have filled me with its light.
You have strengthened my Will
And clarified my sight.
And now the eagle must fly
Back to the earth
And make ready to surrender
To the season of new birth.

seasonal focus
The harvest is stored.

morning focus
Our Earthly Mother

deepening
Hold a squash or other late local vegetable as you read. Use this in your evening meal.

meditation
The colors change, so slowly at first.
The mood is changing,
With subtle shifts of softness.
My Mother's garden shows to me
The procession of all life.
The life in me responds,
For I, too, am of this garden,
And subject to its call.
No fool am I that fights this journey,
Missing the inner wealth to come.

today I will bring the spirit of Softness to my _____

feelings _____

Saturday, September 28, 2024

the blessing
As the wheel of the seasons
Turns me ever forward
Toward my last season,
My heart tells me that there is more.
My eyes observe the seed as it grows
Into the tree.
And from this tree more seeds will come
To once again be trees.
The essence of my spirit lives within each seed,
And my tree will grow anew.
Blessed is my spirit, for it will never die.

evening focus
The angel of Eternal Life

Sunday, September 29, 2024

seasonal focus
The harvest is stored.

morning focus
The angel of Earth

deepening
Gather fallen leaves and take them into your meditation. Let their surrender teach you.

meditation
Let me use the wisdom of my senses
To understand the earth
In this season of preparation.
For as the earth prepares its life forms,
So, too, shall I prepare.
The nature kingdom is my teacher,
And I have much to learn.
I learn of letting go
My grip on yesterday
And free myself for the wonder
Of tomorrow's subtle joy.

today I will bring the spirit of Learning From Everything to my _____

feelings _____

evening focus
The angel of Creative Work

♌ → ♍

the blessing
Fulfillment and completeness
Are gifts I give to me.
They come from focused labor
And perfection as my guide.
How well I see the power
That my own acts have on me,
And I create my world of joy
or a world of misery.
Perfection is my natural state;
How easily I forget!

ORDERING A BOOK FOR NEXT YEAR?

You may order directly from our website: **www.earthstewards.org**.
Or you may call **1-800-561-2909** to order by phone, and with questions related to Danaan's books. Our email address is **publishing@earthstewards.org**.

The mailing address is
Earthstewards
1425 Cowgill Ave
Bellingham, WA 98225-8016

To order online from other sources in the U.S. and internationally, search for **"Essene Book of Days 2025."** Your local bookstore may also be able to order the book for you.

All orders shipped to Washington State will need to include the appropriate sales tax for the address to which it is sent.

Name & Address	email address - used to notify you when we the have the next calendar book
	Phone

ITEM	PRICE EACH	QTY.	TOTAL
Essene Book of Days 2025	$19.95		
*Essene Book of Days 2025, 2 or more *	*$18.00*		
Essene Book of Meditations & Blessings	$ 8.95		
*Essene Book of Med/Bless, 5 or more *	*$ 7.00*		
Warriors of the Heart-6th edition	$14.95		

* Discounts for multiple books apply only when shipped to the same address.

For more information about books, shipping, sales tax and donations, see the back of this form.

Book Total
Shipping
Subtotal
WA orders only — add your sales tax on Subtotal
Donation
TOTAL ENCLOSED

Payment Information: ___ **Visa/Mastercard or Check #** _____

Card Number   Exp. Date

Security Code

305

Earthstewards Network Publications

· Books ·

The Essene Book of Days is a journal, calendar and guide for those on a path of personal and spiritual growth. 416 pp. *Danaan Parry* ($19.95). Two or more books sent to one address, $18.00 each.

The **Essene Book of Meditations & Blessings** is a handy pocket-size book featuring all the daily meditations and blessings in *The Essene Book of Days*. A great travel companion! Fourth edition. 144 pp. *Danaan Parry* ($8.95). **5-pack:** Five or more books sent to one address are $7 each.

Warriors of the Heart is a handbook for bringing healing, passion and meaning to your life and relationships. Based on Danaan's conflict resolution work around the world. 224 pp. *Danaan Parry* ($14.95).

· Shipping ·

- No charge for USPS Media Mail or books sent standard shipping from our printer, within the US. At this time of year, delivery should be within 10 days after shipment of your order, except for Alaska and Hawaii.
- We charge for shipping by USPS Priority Mail, and to addresses outside the US. Priority Mail takes about 3 days. The charge is the difference between Media Mail postage and the actual cost for the shipping.

The USPS has raised rates the last several years, so we cannot predict the additional cost if we ship other than Media Mail. In 2023, the additional charge for Priority Mail within the US was $5.60. Email publishing@earthstewards.org or call us at 800-561-2909 to get the actual shipping charge for Priority Mail or mail outside the US.

· If You Live Outside the US ·

Many Amazon sites carry Danaan's books. You should be able to save substantially on shipping costs if you buy on their sites.

· Sales Tax ·

We collect sales tax only in Washington. The rate is determined by the address to which we ship your order. If you don't know the rate, contact us for the information.

· Donations ·

The Earthstewards Network was co-founded by Danaan Parry, and still lives on in the connection of people drawn to his concepts and philosophy. Workshops continued for a few years after his death, but now the only sources of income are sales of his books and donations. See www.earthstewards.org or page 410 for more information.

seasonal focus
The harvest is stored

Monday, September 30, 2024

morning focus
The angel of Life

opening
Before reading, study your face in a mirror.
What do you really see?

meditation
I have grown in wisdom
As this yearly wheel has turned.
I see
That freedom in my life
Is tied to that of all.
The springtime sense of Me Alone
Has mellowed and matured
Into the deeper knowing
That We are One.
Only when I respect the sacredness
Of all life shall I be truly free.

today I will bring the spirit of Freedom to my _____

feelings _____

the blessing
The core of peace
Lives not in thoughts,
Nor in the deeds I do.
It lives inside my heart,
In how I feel about me.
When I have learned to be at peace
Within myself,
Then shall I radiate that peace to all.
Let me now go within
To calm the inner sea.

evening focus
The angel of Peace

307

Tuesday, October 1, 2024

seasonal focus
The harvest is stored.

morning focus
The angel of Joy

opening
At this moment, what do you need more of?
This day, give that needed something to
someone else. Find a way to give it away.

meditation
Softness fills my days
In this season of autumn light.
Gentle joy of life returning
To know its roots again.
Joyful completion
Of the outward surge of growth,
Preparing me for that to come
In the darkness before birth.
Who will I laugh with on this day,
Expecting nothing,
Sharing all?

today I will bring the spirit of Intimacy to my_____

feelings_____

evening focus
The angel of Power

the blessing
The shifting balance
From outward straightline movement
To inner spiral flow
Spins the wheel of my life inward,
And I must now transform
My restless yearnings
Into quiet contemplation
To aid me in the winter's inner journey
To the abundant core of me.

seasonal focus
The harvest is stored.

morning focus
The angel of the Sun

Wednesday, October 2, 2024

opening
Intently notice the light and shadow of your world. Light a candle after the reading and allow the flame to warm your hands.

meditation
This day will offer me another chance
To take within me
The lifeblood of the sun.
These lengthened rays of solar fire
Will be stored within my heart
If I but use this time to full advantage.
Let me study all the colors,
The shadings and the hues,
So that, when deep in winter's womb,
I may paint the portrait of the sun with a memory
And share that scene with all.

today I will bring the spirit of Contentment to my _____

feelings _____

the blessing
Out of the dance of summer
Comes the gathering of autumn
More gently now, more softly,
I gather with my friends
And touch the hands that form the circle
And look into wiser eyes.
My love in comfort flows from my life
To color all that is,
And blessed by other forms of God,
It flows quietly back to me.

evening focus
The angel of Love

Rosh Hasana

Thursday, October 3, 2024

seasonal focus
The harvest is stored.

morning focus
The angel of Water

deepening
Pour water from your old favored bowl
into a new bowl. Back and forth, from old to new.
Same water. Drink it with respect.

meditation
There is a trickling of time in my life,
A cascading mountain stream of moments
That connect each spring and fall,
Each blossoming and harvesting.
What will be the colors of my flower
Come next Beltane time?
The answer lies in the ways
That I now prepare the soil
Of my inner garden,
And in how lovingly I water the seeds
From summer's fruit.

today I will bring the spirit of Expectancy to my _____
_____

feelings _____
_____
_____
_____
_____
_____
_____

evening focus
The angel of Wisdom

the blessing
It has been said
That each of us has deep within
The knowledge of all things,
And when we are ready to remember
Then the knowledge is there to be known.
This is the season of readying,
Of challenging old beliefs
That bind us to the past.
The millennium calls to me
To live the wisdom deep within me.

seasonal focus
The harvest is stored.

Friday, October 4, 2024

morning focus
The angel of Air

opening
Before reading, do alternate nasal breathing.
Five inhalations through left nostril only,
then five through right. Do five times and notice.

meditation
There is a yearning in me now,
Which follows a season of outbreath.
It is the longing for the sweet inbreath
Of my spiritual nature.
And as my physical nature still urges me
To *do*,
Yet in my heart I know my path leads me to *be*.
And I humbly honor the do-er in me
That makes my world revolve.
But now I prepare to take my inbreath
At the center
Of my Self.

today I will bring the spirit of Surrender to my _____

feelings _____

the blessing
You have brought me to the sun
And have filled me with its light.
You have strengthened my Will
And clarified my sight.
And now the eagle must fly
Back to the earth
And make ready to surrender
To the season of new birth.

evening focus
Our Heavenly Father

♎ → ♏

Saturday, October 5, 2024

seasonal focus
The harvest is stored.

morning focus
Our Earthly Mother

deepening
Hold a squash or other late local vegetable
as you read. Use this in your evening meal.

meditation
The colors change, so slowly at first.
The mood is changing,
With subtle shifts of softness.
My Mother's garden shows to me
The procession of all life.
The life in me responds,
For I, too, am of this garden,
And subject to its call.
No fool am I that fights this journey,
Missing the inner wealth to come.

today I will bring the spirit of Softness to my _____

feelings _____

_____

_____

_____

_____

_____

evening focus
The angel of Eternal Life

the blessing
As the wheel of the seasons
Turns me ever forward
Toward my last season,
My heart tells me that there is more.
My eyes observe the seed as it grows
Into the tree.
And from this tree more seeds will come
To once again be trees.
The essence of my spirit lives within each seed,
And my tree will grow anew.
Blessed is my spirit, for it will never die.

312

seasonal focus
The harvest is stored.

Sunday, October 6, 2024

morning focus
The angel of Earth

deepening
Gather fallen leaves and take them into your meditation. Let their surrender teach you.

meditation
Let me use the wisdom of my senses
To understand the earth
In this season of preparation.
For as the earth prepares its life forms,
So, too, shall I prepare.
The nature kingdom is my teacher,
And I have much to learn.
I learn of letting go
My grip on yesterday
And free myself for the wonder
Of tomorrow's subtle joy.

today I will bring the spirit of Learning From Everything to my _____

feelings _____

the blessing
Fulfillment and completeness
Are gifts I give to me.
They come from focused labor
And perfection as my guide.
How well I see the power
That my own acts have on me,
And I create my world of joy
or a world of misery.
Perfection is my natural state;
How easily I forget!

evening focus
The angel of Creative Work

Monday, October 7, 2024

seasonal focus
The harvest is stored.

morning focus
The angel of Life

opening
Before reading, study your face in a mirror.
What do you really see?

meditation
I have grown in wisdom
As this yearly wheel has turned.
I see
That freedom in my life
Is tied to that of all.
The springtime sense of Me Alone
Has mellowed and matured
Into the deeper knowing
That We are One.
Only when I respect the sacredness
Of all life shall I be truly free.

today I will bring the spirit of Freedom to my _____

feelings _____
_____
_____
_____
_____
_____
_____

evening focus
The angel of Peace

the blessing
The core of peace
Lives not in thoughts,
Nor in the deeds I do.
It lives inside my heart,
In how I feel about me.
When I have learned to be at peace
Within myself,
Then shall I radiate that peace to all.
Let me now go within
To calm the inner sea.

seasonal focus
The harvest is stored.

Tuesday, October 8, 2024

morning focus
The angel of Joy

opening
At this moment, what do you need more of? This day, give that needed something to someone else. Find a way to give it away.

meditation
Softness fills my days
In this season of autumn light.
Gentle joy of life returning
To know its roots again.
Joyful completion
Of the outward surge of growth,
Preparing me for that to come
In the darkness before birth.
Who will I laugh with on this day,
Expecting nothing,
Sharing all?

today I will bring the spirit of Intimacy to my _____

feelings _____

the blessing
The shifting balance
From outward straightline movement
To inner spiral flow
Spins the wheel of my life inward,
And I must now transform
My restless yearnings
Into quiet contemplation
To aid me in the winter's inner journey
To the abundant core of me.

evening focus
The angel of Power

Wednesday, October 9, 2024

seasonal focus
The harvest is stored.

morning focus
The angel of the Sun

opening
Intently notice the light and shadow of
your world. Light a candle after the reading
and allow the flame to warm your hands.

meditation
This day will offer me another chance
To take within me
The lifeblood of the sun.
These lengthened rays of solar fire
Will be stored within my heart
If I but use this time to full advantage.
Let me study all the colors,
The shadings and the hues,
So that, when deep in winter's womb,
I may paint the portrait of the sun with a memory
And share that scene with all.

today I will bring the spirit of Contentment to my ____
_____

feelings _____
_____
_____
_____
_____
_____
_____

evening focus
The angel of Love

the blessing
Out of the dance of summer
Comes the gathering of autumn
More gently now, more softly,
I gather with my friends
And touch the hands that form the circle
And look into wiser eyes.
My love in comfort flows from my life
To color all that is,
And blessed by other forms of God,
It flows quietly back to me.

seasonal focus
The harvest is stored.

Thursday, October 10, 2024

morning focus
The angel of Water

deepening
Pour water from your old favored bowl
into a new bowl. Back and forth, from old to new.
Same water. Drink it with respect.

meditation
There is a trickling of time in my life,
A cascading mountain stream of moments
That connect each spring and fall,
Each blossoming and harvesting.
What will be the colors of my flower
Come next Beltane time?
The answer lies in the ways
That I now prepare the soil
Of my inner garden,
And in how lovingly I water the seeds
From summer's fruit.

today I will bring the spirit of Expectancy to my _____

feelings _____

_____

_____

_____

_____

_____

the blessing
It has been said
That each of us has deep within
The knowledge of all things,
And when we are ready to remember
Then the knowledge is there to be known.
This is the season of readying,
Of challenging old beliefs
That bind us to the past.
The millennium calls to me
To live the wisdom deep within me.

evening focus
The angel of Wisdom

Friday, October 11, 2024

seasonal focus
The harvest is stored.

morning focus
The angel of Air

opening
Before reading, do alternate nasal breathing.
Five inhalations through left nostril only,
then five through right. Do five times and notice.

meditation
There is a yearning in me now,
Which follows a season of outbreath.
It is the longing for the sweet inbreath
Of my spiritual nature.
And as my physical nature still urges me
To *do*,
Yet in my heart I know my path leads me to *be*.
And I humbly honor the do-er in me
That makes my world revolve.
But now I prepare to take my inbreath
At the center
Of my Self.

today I will bring the spirit of Surrender to my _____

feelings _____

evening focus
Our Heavenly Father

Yom Kippur

the Blessing
You have brought me to the sun
And have filled me with its light.
You have strengthened my Will
And clarified my sight.
And now the eagle must fly
Back to the earth
And make ready to surrender
To the season of new birth.

seasonal focus
The harvest is stored.

morning focus
Our Earthly Mother

deepening
Hold a squash or other late local vegetable as you read. Use this in your evening meal.

meditation
The colors change, so slowly at first.
The mood is changing,
With subtle shifts of softness.
My Mother's garden shows to me
The procession of all life.
The life in me responds,
For I, too, am of this garden,
And subject to its call.
No fool am I that fights this journey,
Missing the inner wealth to come.

today I will bring the spirit of Softness to my _____

feelings _____

Saturday, October 12, 2024

the blessing
As the wheel of the seasons
Turns me ever forward
Toward my last season,
My heart tells me that there is more.
My eyes observe the seed as it grows
Into the tree.
And from this tree more seeds will come
To once again be trees.
The essence of my spirit lives within each seed,
And my tree will grow anew.
Blessed is my spirit, for it will never die.

evening focus
The angel of Eternal Life

Sunday, October 13, 2024

seasonal focus
The harvest is stored.

morning focus
The angel of Earth

deepening
Gather fallen leaves and take them into your meditation. Let their surrender teach you.

meditation
Let me use the wisdom of my senses
To understand the earth
In this season of preparation.
For as the earth prepares its life forms,
So, too, shall I prepare.
The nature kingdom is my teacher,
And I have much to learn.
I learn of letting go
My grip on yesterday
And free myself for the wonder
Of tomorrow's subtle joy.

today I will bring the spirit of Learning From Everything to my _____

feelings _____

_____

_____

_____

_____

evening focus
The angel of Creative Work

the blessing
Fulfillment and completeness
Are gifts I give to me.
They come from focused labor
And perfection as my guide.
How well I see the power
That my own acts have on me,
And I create my world of joy
or a world of misery.
Perfection is my natural state;
How easily I forget!

seasonal focus
The harvest is stored

morning focus
The angel of Life

opening
Before reading, study your face in a mirror.
What do you really see?

meditation
I have grown in wisdom
As this yearly wheel has turned.
I see
That freedom in my life
Is tied to that of all.
The springtime sense of Me Alone
Has mellowed and matured
Into the deeper knowing
That We are One.
Only when I respect the sacredness
Of all life shall I be truly free.

today I will bring the spirit of Freedom to my _____

feelings _____

the blessing
The core of peace
Lives not in thoughts,
Nor in the deeds I do.
It lives inside my heart,
In how I feel about me.
When I have learned to be at peace
Within myself,
Then shall I radiate that peace to all.
Let me now go within
To calm the inner sea.

evening focus
The angel of Peace

Monday, October 14, 2024

Tuesday, October 15, 2024

seasonal focus
The harvest is stored.

morning focus
The angel of Joy

opening
At this moment, what do you need more of?
This day, give that needed something to
someone else. Find a way to give it away.

meditation
Softness fills my days
In this season of autumn light.
Gentle joy of life returning
To know its roots again.
Joyful completion
Of the outward surge of growth,
Preparing me for that to come
In the darkness before birth.
Who will I laugh with on this day,
Expecting nothing,
Sharing all?

today I will bring the spirit of Intimacy to my_____
_____

feelings_____
_____
_____
_____

_____
_____

evening focus
The angel of Power

♓ → ♈

the blessing
The shifting balance
From outward straightline movement
To inner spiral flow
Spins the wheel of my life inward,
And I must now transform
My restless yearnings
Into quiet contemplation
To aid me in the winter's inner journey
To the abundant core of me.

seasonal focus
The harvest is stored.

Wednesday, October 16, 2024

morning focus
The angel of the Sun

opening
Intently notice the light and shadow of your world. Light a candle after the reading and allow the flame to warm your hands.

meditation
This day will offer me another chance
To take within me
The lifeblood of the sun.
These lengthened rays of solar fire
Will be stored within my heart
If I but use this time to full advantage.
Let me study all the colors,
The shadings and the hues,
So that, when deep in winter's womb,
I may paint the portrait of the sun with a memory
And share that scene with all.

today I will bring the spirit of Contentment to my _____

feelings _____

the blessing
Out of the dance of summer
Comes the gathering of autumn
More gently now, more softly,
I gather with my friends
And touch the hands that form the circle
And look into wiser eyes.
My love in comfort flows from my life
To color all that is,
And blessed by other forms of God,
It flows quietly back to me.

evening focus
The angel of Love

Thursday, October 17, 2024

seasonal focus
The harvest is stored.

morning focus
The angel of Water

deepening
Pour water from your old favored bowl
into a new bowl. Back and forth, from old to new.
Same water. Drink it with respect.

meditation
There is a trickling of time in my life,
A cascading mountain stream of moments
That connect each spring and fall,
Each blossoming and harvesting.
What will be the colors of my flower
Come next Beltane time?
The answer lies in the ways
That I now prepare the soil
Of my inner garden,
And in how lovingly I water the seeds
From summer's fruit.

today I will bring the spirit of Expectancy to my _____

feelings _____

evening focus
The angel of Wisdom

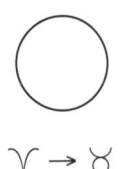

the blessing
It has been said
That each of us has deep within
The knowledge of all things,
And when we are ready to remember
Then the knowledge is there to be known.
This is the season of readying,
Of challenging old beliefs
That bind us to the past.
The millennium calls to me
To live the wisdom deep within me.

seasonal focus
The harvest is stored.

Friday, October 18, 2024

morning focus
The angel of Air

opening
Before reading, do alternate nasal breathing.
Five inhalations through left nostril only,
then five through right. Do five times and notice.

meditation
There is a yearning in me now,
Which follows a season of outbreath.
It is the longing for the sweet inbreath
Of my spiritual nature.
And as my physical nature still urges me
To *do*,
Yet in my heart I know my path leads me to *be*.
And I humbly honor the do-er in me
That makes my world revolve.
But now I prepare to take my inbreath
At the center
Of my Self.

today I will bring the spirit of Surrender to my _____

feelings _____

the blessing
You have brought me to the sun
And have filled me with its light.
You have strengthened my Will
And clarified my sight.
And now the eagle must fly
Back to the earth
And make ready to surrender
To the season of new birth.

evening focus
Our Heavenly Father

Saturday, October 19, 2024

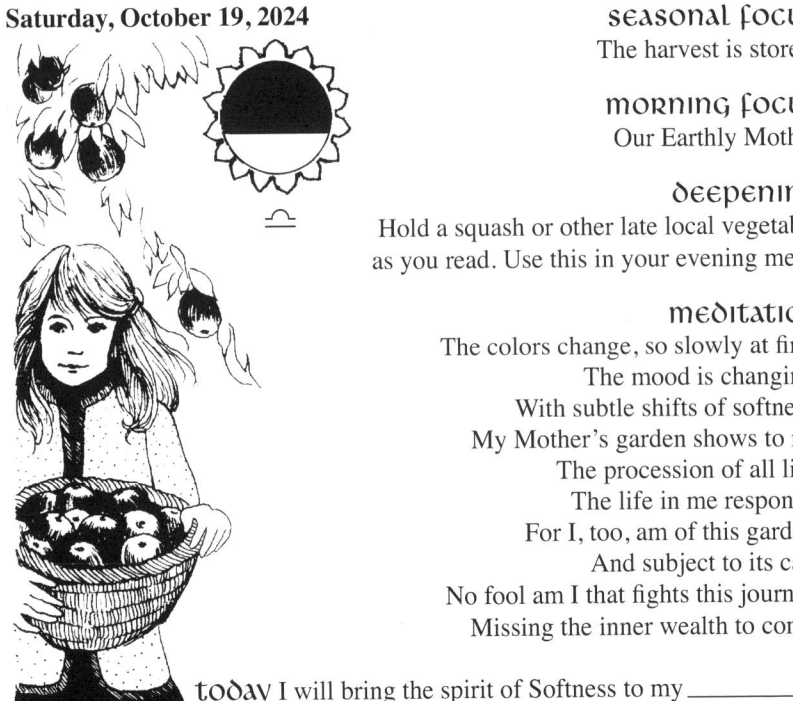

seasonal focus
The harvest is stored.

morning focus
Our Earthly Mother

deepening
Hold a squash or other late local vegetable as you read. Use this in your evening meal.

meditation
The colors change, so slowly at first.
The mood is changing,
With subtle shifts of softness.
My Mother's garden shows to me
The procession of all life.
The life in me responds,
For I, too, am of this garden,
And subject to its call.
No fool am I that fights this journey,
Missing the inner wealth to come.

today I will bring the spirit of Softness to my _____

feelings _____
_____
_____
_____
_____
_____

evening focus
The angel of Eternal Life

♉ → ♊

the blessing
As the wheel of the seasons
Turns me ever forward
Toward my last season,
My heart tells me that there is more.
My eyes observe the seed as it grows
Into the tree.
And from this tree more seeds will come
To once again be trees.
The essence of my spirit lives within each seed,
And my tree will grow anew.
Blessed is my spirit, for it will never die.

seasonal focus
The harvest is stored.

morning focus
The angel of Earth

deepening
Gather fallen leaves and take them into
your meditation. Let their surrender teach you.

meditation
Let me use the wisdom of my senses
To understand the earth
In this season of preparation.
For as the earth prepares its life forms,
So, too, shall I prepare.
The nature kingdom is my teacher,
And I have much to learn.
I learn of letting go
My grip on yesterday
And free myself for the wonder
Of tomorrow's subtle joy.

today I will bring the spirit of Learning From Everything to my _____

feelings _____

the blessing
Fulfillment and completeness
Are gifts I give to me.
They come from focused labor
And perfection as my guide.
How well I see the power
That my own acts have on me,
And I create my world of joy
or a world of misery.
Perfection is my natural state;
How easily I forget!

Sunday, October 20, 2024

evening focus
The angel of Creative Work

Monday, October 21, 2024

seasonal focus
The harvest is stored.

morning focus
The angel of Life

opening
Before reading, study your face in a mirror.
What do you really see?

meditation
I have grown in wisdom
As this yearly wheel has turned.
I see
That freedom in my life
Is tied to that of all.
The springtime sense of Me Alone
Has mellowed and matured
Into the deeper knowing
That We are One.
Only when I respect the sacredness
Of all life shall I be truly free.

today I will bring the spirit of Freedom to my _____

feelings _____

evening focus
The angel of Peace

the blessing
The core of peace
Lives not in thoughts,
Nor in the deeds I do.
It lives inside my heart,
In how I feel about me.
When I have learned to be at peace
Within myself,
Then shall I radiate that peace to all.
Let me now go within
To calm the inner sea.

328

seasonal focus
The harvest is stored.

Tuesday, October 22, 2024

morning focus
The angel of Joy

opening
At this moment, what do you need more of? This day, give that needed something to someone else. Find a way to give it away.

meditation
Softness fills my days
In this season of autumn light.
Gentle joy of life returning
To know its roots again.
Joyful completion
Of the outward surge of growth,
Preparing me for that to come
In the darkness before birth.
Who will I laugh with on this day,
Expecting nothing,
Sharing all?

today I will bring the spirit of Intimacy to my _____

feelings _____

_____

_____

_____

_____

_____

the blessing
The shifting balance
From outward straightline movement
To inner spiral flow
Spins the wheel of my life inward,
And I must now transform
My restless yearnings
Into quiet contemplation
To aid me in the winter's inner journey
To the abundant core of me.

evening focus
The angel of Power

329

Wednesday, October 23, 2024

seasonal focus
The harvest is stored.

morning focus
The angel of the Sun

opening
Intently notice the light and shadow of your world. Light a candle after the reading and allow the flame to warm your hands.

meditation
This day will offer me another chance
To take within me
The lifeblood of the sun.
These lengthened rays of solar fire
Will be stored within my heart
If I but use this time to full advantage.
Let me study all the colors,
The shadings and the hues,
So that, when deep in winter's womb,
I may paint the portrait of the sun with a memory
And share that scene with all.

today I will bring the spirit of Contentment to my ___

feelings ___

evening focus
The angel of Love

the blessing
Out of the dance of summer
Comes the gathering of autumn
More gently now, more softly,
I gather with my friends
And touch the hands that form the circle
And look into wiser eyes.
My love in comfort flows from my life
To color all that is,
And blessed by other forms of God,
It flows quietly back to me.

seasonal focus
The harvest is stored.

Thursday, October 24, 2024

morning focus
The angel of Water

deepening
Pour water from your old favored bowl
into a new bowl. Back and forth, from old to new.
Same water. Drink it with respect.

meditation
There is a trickling of time in my life,
A cascading mountain stream of moments
That connect each spring and fall,
Each blossoming and harvesting.
What will be the colors of my flower
Come next Beltane time?
The answer lies in the ways
That I now prepare the soil
Of my inner garden,
And in how lovingly I water the seeds
From summer's fruit.

today I will bring the spirit of Expectancy to my _____

feelings _____

the blessing
It has been said
That each of us has deep within
The knowledge of all things,
And when we are ready to remember
Then the knowledge is there to be known.
This is the season of readying,
Of challenging old beliefs
That bind us to the past.
The millennium calls to me
To live the wisdom deep within me.

evening focus
The angel of Wisdom

331

Friday, October 25, 2024

seasonal focus
The harvest is stored.

morning focus
The angel of Air

opening
Before reading, do alternate nasal breathing.
Five inhalations through left nostril only,
then five through right. Do five times and notice.

meditation
There is a yearning in me now,
Which follows a season of outbreath.
It is the longing for the sweet inbreath
Of my spiritual nature.
And as my physical nature still urges me
To *do*,
Yet in my heart I know my path leads me to *be*.
And I humbly honor the do-er in me
That makes my world revolve.
But now I prepare to take my inbreath
At the center
Of my Self.

today I will bring the spirit of Surrender to my _____

feelings _____

evening focus
Our Heavenly Father

the blessing
You have brought me to the sun
And have filled me with its light.
You have strengthened my Will
And clarified my sight.
And now the eagle must fly
Back to the earth
And make ready to surrender
To the season of new birth.

seasonal focus
The harvest is stored.

morning focus
Our Earthly Mother

deepening
Hold a squash or other late local vegetable as you read. Use this in your evening meal.

meditation
The colors change, so slowly at first.
The mood is changing,
With subtle shifts of softness.
My Mother's garden shows to me
The procession of all life.
The life in me responds,
For I, too, am of this garden,
And subject to its call.
No fool am I that fights this journey,
Missing the inner wealth to come.

today I will bring the spirit of Softness to my _____

feelings _____

Saturday, October 26, 2024

the blessing
As the wheel of the seasons
Turns me ever forward
Toward my last season,
My heart tells me that there is more.
My eyes observe the seed as it grows
Into the tree.
And from this tree more seeds will come
To once again be trees.
The essence of my spirit lives within each seed,
And my tree will grow anew.
Blessed is my spirit, for it will never die.

evening focus
The angel of Eternal Life

Sunday, October 27, 2024

seasonal focus
The harvest is stored.

morning focus
The angel of Earth

deepening
Gather fallen leaves and take them into your meditation. Let their surrender teach you.

meditation
Let me use the wisdom of my senses
To understand the earth
In this season of preparation.
For as the earth prepares its life forms,
So, too, shall I prepare.
The nature kingdom is my teacher,
And I have much to learn.
I learn of letting go
My grip on yesterday
And free myself for the wonder
Of tomorrow's subtle joy.

today I will bring the spirit of Learning From Everything to my _____

feelings _____

_____

_____

_____

_____

evening focus
The angel of Creative Work

the blessing
Fulfillment and completeness
Are gifts I give to me.
They come from focused labor
And perfection as my guide.
How well I see the power
That my own acts have on me,
And I create my world of joy
or a world of misery.
Perfection is my natural state;
How easily I forget!

seasonal focus
The harvest is stored

morning focus
The angel of Life

opening
Before reading, study your face in a mirror.
What do you really see?

meditation
I have grown in wisdom
As this yearly wheel has turned.
I see
That freedom in my life
Is tied to that of all.
The springtime sense of Me Alone
Has mellowed and matured
Into the deeper knowing
That We are One.
Only when I respect the sacredness
Of all life shall I be truly free.

today I will bring the spirit of Freedom to my _____

feelings _____

Monday, October 28, 2024

the blessing
The core of peace
Lives not in thoughts,
Nor in the deeds I do.
It lives inside my heart,
In how I feel about me.
When I have learned to be at peace
Within myself,
Then shall I radiate that peace to all.
Let me now go within
To calm the inner sea.

evening focus
The angel of Peace

Tuesday, October 29, 2024

seasonal focus
The harvest is stored.

morning focus
The angel of Joy

opening
At this moment, what do you need more of?
This day, give that needed something to
someone else. Find a way to give it away.

meditation
Softness fills my days
In this season of autumn light.
Gentle joy of life returning
To know its roots again.
Joyful completion
Of the outward surge of growth,
Preparing me for that to come
In the darkness before birth.
Who will I laugh with on this day,
Expecting nothing,
Sharing all?

today I will bring the spirit of Intimacy to my _____

feelings _____

evening focus
The angel of Power

the blessing
The shifting balance
From outward straightline movement
To inner spiral flow
Spins the wheel of my life inward,
And I must now transform
My restless yearnings
Into quiet contemplation
To aid me in the winter's inner journey
To the abundant core of me.

seasonal focus
The harvest is stored.

Wednesday, October 30, 2024

morning focus
The angel of the Sun

opening
Intently notice the light and shadow of your world. Light a candle after the reading and allow the flame to warm your hands.

meditation
This day will offer me another chance
To take within me
The lifeblood of the sun.
These lengthened rays of solar fire
Will be stored within my heart
If I but use this time to full advantage.
Let me study all the colors,
The shadings and the hues,
So that, when deep in winter's womb,
I may paint the portrait of the sun with a memory
And share that scene with all.

today I will bring the spirit of Contentment to my ___

feelings ___

the blessing
Out of the dance of summer
Comes the gathering of autumn
More gently now, more softly,
I gather with my friends
And touch the hands that form the circle
And look into wiser eyes.
My love in comfort flows from my life
To color all that is,
And blessed by other forms of God,
It flows quietly back to me.

evening focus
The angel of Love

Thursday, October 31, 2024

seasonal focus
The harvest is stored.

morning focus
The angel of Water

deepening
Pour water from your old favored bowl
into a new bowl. Back and forth, from old to new.
Same water. Drink it with respect.

meditation
There is a trickling of time in my life,
A cascading mountain stream of moments
That connect each spring and fall,
Each blossoming and harvesting.
What will be the colors of my flower
Come next Beltane time?
The answer lies in the ways
That I now prepare the soil
Of my inner garden,
And in how lovingly I water the seeds
From summer's fruit.

today I will bring the spirit of Expectancy to my _____

feelings _____

evening focus
The angel of Wisdom

Halloween

the blessing
It has been said
That each of us has deep within
The knowledge of all things,
And when we are ready to remember
Then the knowledge is there to be known.
This is the season of readying,
Of challenging old beliefs
That bind us to the past.
The millennium calls to me
To live the wisdom deep within me.

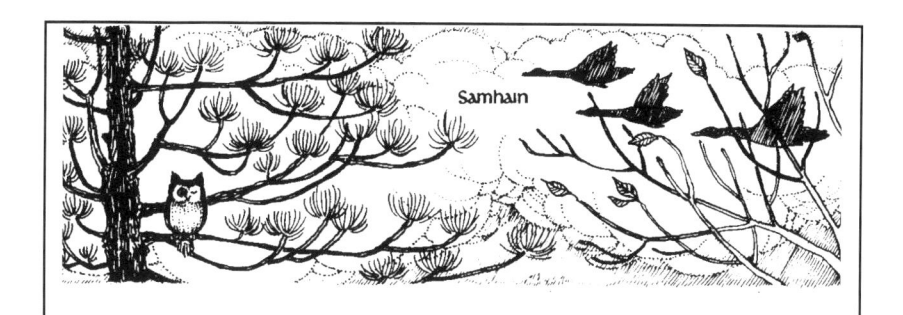

samhain

We have come to a very important point in the cycle of the seasons. Samhain (pronounced SOW-WAIN) is the doorway to the sanctum sanctorum. Beyond this doorway lies the deep cavern of the Earth Mother's womb, the creative abyss, from which grows all that is intuitive and contemplative and natural on this earth.

For the ancient Celtic peoples, it was the beginning of the new year, and a huge ritual bonfire was used to burn away the images of the old year, freeing the people from the fears and worries of the past.

On this day, the world of our physical reality and the world of spirit reality come together and communicate. This has given rise to Halloween and the masquerading as ghosts and goblins. In ancient days, the costumes were actually the horns and skins of game animals, which were worn to show respect for the life that had given itself so that the tribe might survive.

Samhain marks the end of a cycle. The seed now begins its time of gestation in the rich, dark earth.

Friday, November 1, 2024

seasonal focus
Outer darkness calls for nourishment within.

morning focus
The angel of Air

opening
Do alternate nasal breathing slowly.
Allow yourself to die after each outbreath and
to be born anew at each inbreath.

meditation
Each life upon this earthly plane
Knows beginning and knows ending.
Each turn of the yearly wheel as well
Brings birth and death.
Each breath I take reminds me, too,
That I must die each moment
So as to bring a blessed newness
To the next breath that I take.
For if each outbreath ends in death,
Each inbreath sees me born anew,
And present to that moment.

✦ today I will bring the spirit of Clarity to my _____
_____

feelings _____
_____
_____
_____
_____

At Samhain, the tree draws energy deep within and begins a new seed.

evening focus
Our Heavenly Father

the blessing
Throughout the flow of passing seasons,
You have shared your Light with me.
No middle-person have I required
To walk the path with you.
For in my heart
You dwell forever,
Not in some mansion high,
And the blessings that you give to me
Come from deep inside.

seasonal focus
Outer darkness calls for nourishment within.

morning focus
Our Earthly Mother

deepening
Hold a bare twig as you meditate. Empty yourself.

meditation
The morning calls to me
To slow my pace and be,
To ease my crowded schedule
And perhaps just sit and stare.
To focus on a burning log,
On a raindrop on a leaf,
Or to find my own image
In a flickering candle flame.
The Mother's weather urges me
To let it go, let go.
A deep primal inner voice
Is whispering…within.

Saturday, November 2, 2024

today I will bring the spirit of Focused Awareness to my _____

_____

feelings _____

_____

_____

_____

_____

_____

the blessing
I have seen the maple tree;
The leaves have left its limbs.
It stands bare and brittle now, its spirit gone within.
And in my mind I know that deep within the earth
Its lifeblood pulses in its roots, rejuvenating strength.
How like that maple tree am I, as I go within my core,
Experiencing outer death
And inner depth once more.

evening focus
The angel of Eternal Life

Sunday, November 3, 2024

seasonal focus
Outer darkness calls for nourishment within.

morning focus
The angel of Earth

deepening
Hold moist earth in your hand as you read,
for your own new seed to grow in — alone.

meditation
The seed within the earth
Lies alone, awaiting.
It knows not loneliness,
But strength of purpose.
Throughout the year
I have known loneliness in crowds,
But aloneness is quite different.
I must pass through the gate
To the inner temple
Alone.

today I will bring the spirit of Aloneness to my _____
_____

feelings _____

evening focus
The angel of Creative Work

the blessing
My inner wellspring bubbles over,
And the more I share the more I have.
Help me to be of valued service,
Yet not attached to being a server.
For the tools of service are compassion and humility,
And these are born in a loving heart,
Which is open enough to take as well as give.
From you I receive, to you I give,
Together we share, from this we live.

seasonal focus
Outer darkness calls for nourishment within.

morning focus
The angel of Life

deepening
Do nothing. Simply *be*.

meditation
As leaves fall to the earth
And surrender to the soil,
So I, too, move my attention
From my outward stance
To my inner Buddha nature.
The life in me flows back and forth
From exerting my will
To flowing with the Will of All.
And in this season of stillness,
My direction is clear
As I return unto my source.
The stillness calls to me.

today I will bring the spirit of New Beginnings to my _____

feelings _____

_____

_____

_____

_____

_____

_____

Monday, November 4, 2024

the blessing
The whispering of the candle flame
Invokes the peace within,
Reminding me of the quiet journey that I seem to be on.
I have been given a peaceful heart and a path to take me there.
May I joyfully take up this task
To reach the core of me,
And there to find all beings
Residing in my heart.

evening focus
The angel of Peace

343

Tuesday, November 5, 2024

seasonal focus
Outer darkness calls for nourishment within.

morning focus
The angel of Joy

opening
Surrender to the joy hidden within you
through a song or chant that sings you.
Just open your mouth and let it out.

meditation
This morning gives a song to me,
A lovely melody for me to play
Within my heart,
To give my spirit wings.
And I must close my eyes
To let the music come.
Unhurried, without force,
It yields its gift to me.
And just as gently I share this gift,
I hum this melody.
The air accepts, the world is nourished,
And I become my song.
*(Allow some song or chant to come
to you in meditation and give it wings.)*

today I will bring the spirit of Joyful Music to my _____

feelings _____

evening focus
The angel of Power

the blessing
Within my being lives a silent power,
A firm, sound frame of wise and compassionate strength.
How often do I deny this gift,
This blessing from my Source?
Perhaps as the outward power of the sun recedes in winter,
I will learn to own the strength within.

seasonal focus
Outer darkness calls for nourishment within.

Wednesday, November 6, 2024

morning focus
The angel of the Sun

deepening
Focus intently on a candle flame
until you sense a merging of you and flame.

meditation
You run from me,
You who have showered me with light and warmth.
In summer's fullness was I nourished by your glow,
But now I must provide this warmth myself.
The glow must be found within my heart,
The light within my spirit.
When next we meet in summer's glory,
I will wiser be.
Till then I take your light inwardly with me.

today I will bring the spirit of Inner Glow to my _____

feelings _____

the blessing
(On this evening, we use the form of a love song, in the higher sense of Love.)

Love is the o-cean, Love is the o-cean, I am one with thee

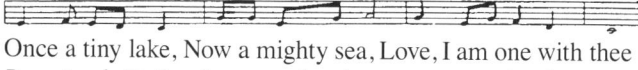

Once a tiny lake, Now a mighty sea, Love, I am one with thee

Repeat, substituting the name of each person present for the word Love. If you sing the Blessing alone, use your name, and repeat the verse until you can allow it to be true for you.

evening focus
The angel of Love

Thursday, November 7, 2024

seasonal focus
Outer darkness calls for nourishment within.

morning focus
The angel of Water

deepening
Hold water in your cupped hand as you read.
Drink it in a sacred manner.

meditation
As I enter the sacred temple of inner knowing,
I purify my being to prepare myself for the initiation
That I have longed to find.
I cleanse my mind and heart
As I strip away
Whatever stands between my spirit and the source of All.
I make myself ready.
And I wait.
And it will come to me.

today I will bring the spirit of Purification to my _____
_____

feelings _____
_____
_____
_____
_____
_____

evening focus
The angel of Wisdom

the blessing
Ancient is the one in me
That the spirit of this season,
With its quiet murmur,
Calls.
Beyond, beneath the outer me,
My wise old seer
Looks out upon the dance with compassion,
With a smile.
And the ancient one waits
For the young one to knock upon the door.
And both of them
Are me.

seasonal focus
Outer darkness calls for nourishment within.

Friday, November 8, 2024

morning focus
The angel of Air

opening
Do alternate nasal breathing slowly.
Allow yourself to die after each outbreath
and to be born anew at each inbreath.

meditation
Each life upon this earthly plane
Knows beginning and knows ending.
Each turn of the yearly wheel as well
Brings birth and death.
Each breath I take reminds me, too,
That I must die each moment
So as to bring a blessed newness
To the next breath that I take.
For if each outbreath ends in death,
Each inbreath sees me born anew,
And present to that moment.

today I will bring the spirit of Clarity to my _____

_____

feelings _____

_____

_____

_____

_____

the blessing
Throughout the flow of passing seasons,
You have shared your Light with me.
No middle-person have I required
To walk the path with you.
For in my heart
You dwell forever,
Not in some mansion high,
And the blessings that you give to me
Come from deep inside.

evening focus
Our Heavenly Father

Saturday, November 9, 2024

seasonal focus
Outer darkness calls for nourishment within.

morning focus
Our Earthly Mother

deepening
Hold a bare twig as you meditate.
Empty yourself.

meditation
The morning calls to me
To slow my pace and be,
To ease my crowded schedule
And perhaps just sit and stare.
To focus on a burning log,
On a raindrop on a leaf,
Or to find my own image
In a flickering candle flame.
The Mother's weather urges me
To let it go, let go.
A deep primal inner voice
Is whispering…within.

today I bring the spirit of Focused Awareness to my
_____

feelings _____
_____
_____
_____
_____
_____
_____

evening focus
The angel of Eternal Life

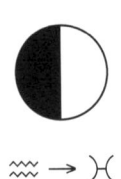

the blessing
I have seen the maple tree;
The leaves have left its limbs.
It stands bare and brittle now, its spirit gone within.
And in my mind I know that deep within the earth
Its lifeblood pulses in its roots, rejuvenating strength.
How like that maple tree am I, as I go within my core,
Experiencing outer death
And inner depth once more.

seasonal focus
Outer darkness calls for nourishment within.

Sunday, November 10, 2024

morning focus
The angel of Earth

deepening
Hold moist earth in your hand as you read,
for your own new seed to grow in — alone.

meditation
The seed within the earth
Lies alone, awaiting.
It knows not loneliness,
But strength of purpose.
Throughout the year
I have known loneliness in crowds,
But aloneness is quite different.
I must pass through the gate
To the inner temple
Alone.

today I will bring the spirit of Aloneness to my _____

feelings _____

the blessing
My inner wellspring bubbles over,
And the more I share the more I have.
Help me to be of valued service,
Yet not attached to being a server.
For the tools of service are compassion and humility,
And these are born in a loving heart,
Which is open enough to take as well as give.
From you I receive, to you I give,
Together we share, from this we live.

evening focus
The angel of Creative Work

Monday, November 11, 2024

seasonal focus
Outer darkness calls for nourishment within.

morning focus
The angel of Life

deepening
Do nothing. Simply *be*.

meditation
As leaves fall to the earth
And surrender to the soil,
So I, too, move my attention
From my outward stance
To my inner Buddha nature.
The life in me flows back and forth
From exerting my will
To flowing with the Will of All.
And in this season of stillness,
My direction is clear
As I return unto my source.
The stillness calls to me.

today I will bring the spirit of New Beginnings to my

feelings _____
_____
_____
_____
_____
_____
_____
_____

evening focus
The angel of Peace

the blessing
The whispering of the candle flame
Invokes the peace within,
Reminding me of the quiet journey that I seem to be on.
I have been given a peaceful heart and a path to take me there.
May I joyfully take up this task
To reach the core of me,
And there to find all beings
Residing in my heart.

seasonal focus
Outer darkness calls for nourishment within.

Tuesday, November 12, 2024

morning focus
The angel of Joy

opening
Surrender to the joy hidden within you
through a song or chant that sings you.
Just open your mouth and let it out.

meditation
This morning gives a song to me,
A lovely melody for me to play
Within my heart,
To give my spirit wings.
And I must close my eyes
To let the music come.
Unhurried, without force,
It yields its gift to me.
And just as gently I share this gift,
I hum this melody.
The air accepts, the world is nourished,
And I become my song.
*(Allow some song or chant to come
to you in meditation and give it wings.)*

today I will bring the spirit of Joyful Music to my _____

feelings _____

_____
_____
_____
_____
_____

the blessing
Within my being lives a silent power,
A firm, sound frame of wise and compassionate strength.
How often do I deny this gift,
This blessing from my Source?
Perhaps as the outward power of the sun recedes in winter,
I will learn to own the strength within.

evening focus
The angel of Power

Wednesday, November 13, 2024

seasonal focus
Outer darkness calls for nourishment within.

morning focus
The angel of the Sun

deepening
Focus intently on a candle flame
until you sense a merging of you and flame.

meditation
You run from me,
You who have showered me with light and warmth.
In summer's fullness was I nourished by your glow,
But now I must provide this warmth myself.
The glow must be found within my heart,
The light within my spirit.
When next we meet in summer's glory,
I will wiser be.
Till then I take your light inwardly with me.

today I will bring the spirit of Inner Glow to my _____
_____

★ feelings _____
_____
_____
_____
_____
_____

the blessing
(On this evening, we use the form of a love song, in the higher sense of Love.)

Love is the o-cean, Love is the o-cean, I am one with thee

Once a tiny lake, Now a mighty sea, Love, I am one with thee

Repeat, substituting the name of each person present for the word Love. If you sing the Blessing alone, use your name, and repeat the verse until you can allow it to be true for you.

evening focus
The angel of Love

seasonal focus
Outer darkness calls for nourishment within.

Thursday, November 14, 2024

morning focus
The angel of Water

deepening
Hold water in your cupped hand as you read.
Drink it in a sacred manner.

meditation
As I enter the sacred temple of inner knowing,
I purify my being to prepare myself for the initiation
That I have longed to find.
I cleanse my mind and heart
As I strip away
Whatever stands between my spirit and the source of All.
I make myself ready.
And I wait.
And it will come to me.

today I will bring the spirit of Purification to my _____
_____

feelings _____
_____
_____
_____
_____
_____
_____

the blessing
Ancient is the one in me
That the spirit of this season,
With its quiet murmur,
Calls.
Beyond, beneath the outer me,
My wise old seer
Looks out upon the dance with compassion,
With a smile.
And the ancient one waits
For the young one to knock upon the door.
And both of them
Are me.

evening focus
The angel of Wisdom

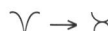

Friday, November 15, 2024

seasonal focus
Outer darkness calls for nourishment within.

morning focus
The angel of Air

opening
Do alternate nasal breathing slowly.
Allow yourself to die after each outbreath and
to be born anew at each inbreath.

meditation
Each life upon this earthly plane
Knows beginning and knows ending.
Each turn of the yearly wheel as well
Brings birth and death.
Each breath I take reminds me, too,
That I must die each moment
So as to bring a blessed newness
To the next breath that I take.
For if each outbreath ends in death,
Each inbreath sees me born anew,
And present to that moment.

today I will bring the spirit of Clarity to my ____
_____

feelings _____
_____
_____
_____
_____
_____

evening focus
Our Heavenly Father

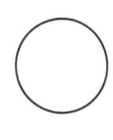

the blessing
Throughout the flow of passing seasons,
You have shared your Light with me.
No middle-person have I required
To walk the path with you.
For in my heart
You dwell forever,
Not in some mansion high,
And the blessings that you give to me
Come from deep inside.

seasonal focus
Outer darkness calls for nourishment within.

Saturday, November 16, 2024

morning focus
Our Earthly Mother

deepening
Hold a bare twig as you meditate. Empty yourself.

meditation
The morning calls to me
To slow my pace and be,
To ease my crowded schedule
And perhaps just sit and stare.
To focus on a burning log,
On a raindrop on a leaf,
Or to find my own image
In a flickering candle flame.
The Mother's weather urges me
To let it go, let go.
A deep primal inner voice
Is whispering…within.

today I will bring the spirit of Focused Awareness to my _____

feelings _____

_____

_____

_____

_____

_____

_____

the blessing
I have seen the maple tree;
The leaves have left its limbs.
It stands bare and brittle now, its spirit gone within.
And in my mind I know that deep within the earth
Its lifeblood pulses in its roots, rejuvenating strength.
How like that maple tree am I, as I go within my core,
Experiencing outer death
And inner depth once more.

evening focus
The angel of Eternal Life

♉ → ♊

Sunday, November 17, 2024

seasonal focus
Outer darkness calls for nourishment within.

morning focus
The angel of Earth

deepening
Hold moist earth in your hand as you read,
for your own new seed to grow in — alone.

meditation
The seed within the earth
Lies alone, awaiting.
It knows not loneliness,
But strength of purpose.
Throughout the year
I have known loneliness in crowds,
But aloneness is quite different.
I must pass through the gate
To the inner temple
Alone.

today I will bring the spirit of Aloneness to my _____
_____

feelings _____
_____
_____
_____
_____
_____
_____

evening focus
The angel of Creative Work

the blessing
My inner wellspring bubbles over,
And the more I share the more I have.
Help me to be of valued service,
Yet not attached to being a server.
For the tools of service are compassion and humility,
And these are born in a loving heart,
Which is open enough to take as well as give.
From you I receive, to you I give,
Together we share, from this we live.

seasonal focus
Outer darkness calls for nourishment within.

Monday, November 18, 2024

morning focus
The angel of Life

deepening
Do nothing. Simply *be*.

meditation
As leaves fall to the earth
And surrender to the soil,
So I, too, move my attention
From my outward stance
To my inner Buddha nature.
The life in me flows back and forth
From exerting my will
To flowing with the Will of All.
And in this season of stillness,
My direction is clear
As I return unto my source.
The stillness calls to me.

today I will bring the spirit of New Beginnings to my

feelings

the blessing
The whispering of the candle flame
Invokes the peace within,
Reminding me of the quiet journey that I seem to be on.
I have been given a peaceful heart and a path to take me there.
May I joyfully take up this task
To reach the core of me,
And there to find all beings
Residing in my heart.

evening focus
The angel of Peace

357

Tuesday, November 19, 2024

seasonal focus
Outer darkness calls for nourishment within.

morning focus
The angel of Joy

opening
Surrender to the joy hidden within you
through a song or chant that sings you.
Just open your mouth and let it out.

meditation
This morning gives a song to me,
A lovely melody for me to play
Within my heart,
To give my spirit wings.
And I must close my eyes
To let the music come.
Unhurried, without force,
It yields its gift to me.
And just as gently I share this gift,
I hum this melody.
The air accepts, the world is nourished,
And I become my song.
*(Allow some song or chant to come
to you in meditation and give it wings.)*

today I will bring the spirit of Joyful Music to my
_____

feelings _____

_____
_____
_____
_____
_____

evening focus
The angel of Power

the blessing
Within my being lives a silent power,
A firm, sound frame of wise and compassionate strength.
How often do I deny this gift,
This blessing from my Source?
Perhaps as the outward power of the sun recedes in winter,
I will learn to own the strength within.

seasonal focus
Outer darkness calls for nourishment within.

Wednesday, November 20, 2024

morning focus
The angel of the Sun

deepening
Focus intently on a candle flame
until you sense a merging of you and flame.

meditation
You run from me,
You who have showered me with light and warmth.
In summer's fullness was I nourished by your glow,
But now I must provide this warmth myself.
The glow must be found within my heart,
The light within my spirit.
When next we meet in summer's glory,
I will wiser be.
Till then I take your light inwardly with me.

today I will bring the spirit of Inner Glow to my _____

feelings _____

the blessing
(On this evening, we use the form of a love song, in the higher sense of Love.)

Love is the o-cean, Love is the o-cean, I am one with thee

Once a tiny lake, Now a mighty sea, Love, I am one with thee

Repeat, substituting the name of each person present for the word Love. If you sing the Blessing alone, use your name, and repeat the verse until you can allow it to be true for you.

evening focus
The angel of Love

Thursday, November 21, 2024

♏ → ♐

seasonal focus
Outer darkness calls for nourishment within.

morning focus
The angel of Water

deepening
Hold water in your cupped hand as you read.
Drink it in a sacred manner.

meditation
As I enter the sacred temple of inner knowing,
I purify my being to prepare myself for the initiation
That I have longed to find.
I cleanse my mind and heart
As I strip away
Whatever stands between my spirit and the source of All.
I make myself ready.
And I wait.
And it will come to me.

today I will bring the spirit of Purification to my _____
_____

✦ feelings _____
_____
_____
_____
_____
_____

evening focus
The angel of Wisdom

♌

the blessing
Ancient is the one in me
That the spirit of this season,
With its quiet murmur,
Calls.
Beyond, beneath the outer me,
My wise old seer
Looks out upon the dance with compassion,
With a smile.
And the ancient one waits
For the young one to knock upon the door.
And both of them
Are me.

seasonal focus
Outer darkness calls for nourishment within.

Friday, November 22, 2024

morning focus
The angel of Air

opening
Do alternate nasal breathing slowly.
Allow yourself to die after each outbreath
and to be born anew at each inbreath.

meditation
Each life upon this earthly plane
Knows beginning and knows ending.
Each turn of the yearly wheel as well
Brings birth and death.
Each breath I take reminds me, too,
That I must die each moment
So as to bring a blessed newness
To the next breath that I take.
For if each outbreath ends in death,
Each inbreath sees me born anew,
And present to that moment.

today I will bring the spirit of Clarity to my _____

feelings _____

the blessing
Throughout the flow of passing seasons,
You have shared your Light with me.
No middle-person have I required
To walk the path with you.
For in my heart
You dwell forever,
Not in some mansion high,
And the blessings that you give to me
Come from deep inside.

evening focus
Our Heavenly Father

♌ → ♍

361

Saturday, November 23, 2024

seasonal focus
Outer darkness calls for nourishment within.

morning focus
Our Earthly Mother

deepening
Hold a bare twig as you meditate.
Empty yourself.

meditation
The morning calls to me
To slow my pace and be,
To ease my crowded schedule
And perhaps just sit and stare.
To focus on a burning log,
On a raindrop on a leaf,
Or to find my own image
In a flickering candle flame.
The Mother's weather urges me
To let it go, let go.
A deep primal inner voice
Is whispering…within.

today I bring the spirit of Focused Awareness to my
_____

✦ feelings _____

_____

_____

_____

_____

_____

_____

evening focus
The angel of Eternal Life

the blessing
I have seen the maple tree;
The leaves have left its limbs.
It stands bare and brittle now, its spirit gone within.
And in my mind I know that deep within the earth
Its lifeblood pulses in its roots, rejuvenating strength.
How like that maple tree am I, as I go within my core,
Experiencing outer death
And inner depth once more.

seasonal focus
Outer darkness calls for nourishment within.

Sunday, November 24, 2024

morning focus
The angel of Earth

deepening
Hold moist earth in your hand as you read,
for your own new seed to grow in — alone.

meditation
The seed within the earth
Lies alone, awaiting.
It knows not loneliness,
But strength of purpose.
Throughout the year
I have known loneliness in crowds,
But aloneness is quite different.
I must pass through the gate
To the inner temple
Alone.

today I will bring the spirit of Aloneness to my _____

feelings _____

the blessing
My inner wellspring bubbles over,
And the more I share the more I have.
Help me to be of valued service,
Yet not attached to being a server.
For the tools of service are compassion and humility,
And these are born in a loving heart,
Which is open enough to take as well as give.
From you I receive, to you I give,
Together we share, from this we live.

evening focus
The angel of Creative Work

Monday, November 25, 2024

seasonal focus
Outer darkness calls for nourishment within.

morning focus
The angel of Life

deepening
Do nothing. Simply *be*.

meditation
As leaves fall to the earth
And surrender to the soil,
So I, too, move my attention
From my outward stance
To my inner Buddha nature.
The life in me flows back and forth
From exerting my will
To flowing with the Will of All.
And in this season of stillness,
My direction is clear
As I return unto my source.
The stillness calls to me.

today I will bring the spirit of New Beginnings to my
_____

feelings _____

_____

_____

_____

_____

_____

_____

evening focus
The angel of Peace

the blessing
The whispering of the candle flame
Invokes the peace within,
Reminding me of the quiet journey that I seem to be on.
I have been given a peaceful heart and a path to take me there.
May I joyfully take up this task
To reach the core of me,
And there to find all beings
Residing in my heart.

seasonal focus
Outer darkness calls for nourishment within.

Tuesday, November 26, 2024

morning focus
The angel of Joy

opening
Surrender to the joy hidden within you
through a song or chant that sings you.
Just open your mouth and let it out.

meditation
This morning gives a song to me,
A lovely melody for me to play
Within my heart,
To give my spirit wings.
And I must close my eyes
To let the music come.
Unhurried, without force,
It yields its gift to me.
And just as gently I share this gift,
I hum this melody.
The air accepts, the world is nourished,
And I become my song.
*(Allow some song or chant to come
to you in meditation and give it wings.)*

today I will bring the spirit of Joyful Music to my _____

feelings _____
_____
_____
_____
_____
_____

the blessing
Within my being lives a silent power,
A firm, sound frame of wise and compassionate strength.
How often do I deny this gift,
This blessing from my Source?
Perhaps as the outward power of the sun recedes in winter,
I will learn to own the strength within.

evening focus
The angel of Power

365

Wednesday, November 27, 2024

seasonal focus
Outer darkness calls for nourishment within.

morning focus
The angel of the Sun

deepening
Focus intently on a candle flame
until you sense a merging of you and flame.

meditation
You run from me,
You who have showered me with light and warmth.
In summer's fullness was I nourished by your glow,
But now I must provide this warmth myself.
The glow must be found within my heart,
The light within my spirit.
When next we meet in summer's glory,
I will wiser be.
Till then I take your light inwardly with me.

today I will bring the spirit of Inner Glow to my _____

✱ feelings _____

the blessing
(On this evening, we use the form of a love song, in the higher sense of Love.)

Love is the o-cean, Love is the o-cean, I am one with thee

Once a tiny lake, Now a mighty sea, Love, I am one with thee

Repeat, substituting the name of each person present for the word Love. If you sing the Blessing alone, use your name, and repeat the verse until you can allow it to be true for you.

evening focus
The angel of Love

♎ → ♏

seasonal focus
Outer darkness calls for nourishment within.

Thursday, November 28, 2024

morning focus
The angel of Water

deepening
Hold water in your cupped hand as you read.
Drink it in a sacred manner.

meditation
As I enter the sacred temple of inner knowing,
I purify my being to prepare myself for the initiation
That I have longed to find.
I cleanse my mind and heart
As I strip away
Whatever stands between my spirit and the source of All.
I make myself ready.
And I wait.
And it will come to me.

today I will bring the spirit of Purification to my _____
_____

feelings _____
_____
_____
_____
_____
_____
_____

the blessing
Ancient is the one in me
That the spirit of this season,
With its quiet murmur,
Calls.
Beyond, beneath the outer me,
My wise old seer
Looks out upon the dance with compassion,
With a smile.
And the ancient one waits
For the young one to knock upon the door.
And both of them
Are me.

evening focus
The angel of Wisdom

Thanksgiving

367

Friday, November 29, 2024

seasonal focus
Outer darkness calls for nourishment within.

morning focus
The angel of Air

opening
Do alternate nasal breathing slowly.
Allow yourself to die after each outbreath and
to be born anew at each inbreath.

meditation
Each life upon this earthly plane
Knows beginning and knows ending.
Each turn of the yearly wheel as well
Brings birth and death.
Each breath I take reminds me, too,
That I must die each moment
So as to bring a blessed newness
To the next breath that I take.
For if each outbreath ends in death,
Each inbreath sees me born anew,
And present to that moment.

today I will bring the spirit of Clarity to my _____
_____

feelings _____
_____
_____
_____
_____
_____

evening focus
Our Heavenly Father

the blessing
Throughout the flow of passing seasons,
You have shared your Light with me.
No middle-person have I required
To walk the path with you.
For in my heart
You dwell forever,
Not in some mansion high,
And the blessings that you give to me
Come from deep inside.

have you ordered?

You may order directly from our website: **www.earthstewards.org**.
Or you may call **1-800-561-2909** to order by phone, and with questions related to Danaan's books. Our email address is **publishing@earthstewards.org**.

The mailing address is
Earthstewards
1425 Cowgill Ave
Bellingham, WA 98225-8016

To order online from other sources in the U.S. and internationally, search for **"Essene Book of Days 2025."** Your local bookstore may also be able to order the book for you.

All orders shipped to Washington State will need to include the appropriate sales tax for the address to which it is sent.

Name & Address	email address - used to notify you when we the have the next calendar book
	Phone

ITEM	PRICE EACH	QTY.	TOTAL
Essene Book of Days 2025	$19.95		
Essene Book of Days 2025 2 or more *	**$18.00**		
Essene Book of Meditations & Blessings	$ 8.95		
Essene Book of Med/Bless, 5 or more *	**$ 7.00**		
Warriors of the Heart-6th edition	$14.95		

* Discounts for multiple books apply only when shipped to the same address.

For more information about books, shipping, sales tax and donations, see the back of this form.

Book Total	
Shipping	
Subtotal	
WA orders only — add your sales tax on Subtotal	
Donation	
TOTAL ENCLOSED	

Payment Information: ___ **Visa/Mastercard or Check #** _____

Card Number   Exp. Date

Security Code

369

earthstewards network publications

· books ·

The Essene Book of Days is a journal, calendar and guide for those on a path of personal and spiritual growth. 416 pp. *Danaan Parry* ($19.95). Two or more books sent to one address, $18.00 each.

The **Essene Book of Meditations & Blessings** is a handy pocket-size book featuring all the daily meditations and blessings in *The Essene Book of Days*. A great travel companion! Fourth edition. 144 pp. *Danaan Parry* ($8.95). **5-pack:** Five or more books sent to one address are $7 each.

Warriors of the Heart is a handbook for bringing healing, passion and meaning to your life and relationships. Based on Danaan's conflict resolution work around the world. 224 pp. *Danaan Parry* ($14.95).

· shipping ·

- No charge for USPS Media Mail or books sent standard shipping from our printer, within the US. At this time of year, delivery can take two weeks or more, and Alaska and Hawaii are much slower.
- We charge for shipping by USPS Priority Mail, and to addresses outside the US. Priority Mail takes about 3 days. The charge is the difference between Media Mail postage and the actual cost for the shipping.

The USPS has raised rates the last several years, so we cannot predict the additional cost if we ship other than Media Mail. In 2023, the additional charge for Priority Mail within the US was $5.60. Email publishing@earthstewards.org or call us at 800-561-2909 to get the actual shipping charge for Priority Mail or mail outside the US.

· if you live outside the us ·

Many Amazon sites carry Danaan's books. You should be able to save substantially on shipping costs if you buy on their sites.

· sales tax ·

We collect sales tax only in Washington. The rate is determined by the address to which we ship your order. If you don't know the rate, contact us for the information.

· donations ·

The Earthstewards Network was co-founded by Danaan Parry, and still lives on in the connection of people drawn to his concepts and philosophy. Workshops continued for a few years after his death, but now the only sources of income are sales of his books and donations. See www.earthstewards.org or page 410 for more information.

seasonal focus
Outer darkness calls for nourishment within.

Saturday, November 30, 2024

morning focus
Our Earthly Mother

deepening
Hold a bare twig as you meditate. Empty yourself.

meditation
The morning calls to me
To slow my pace and be,
To ease my crowded schedule
And perhaps just sit and stare.
To focus on a burning log,
On a raindrop on a leaf,
Or to find my own image
In a flickering candle flame.
The Mother's weather urges me
To let it go, let go.
A deep primal inner voice
Is whispering…within.

today I will bring the spirit of Focused Awareness to my _____

feelings _____

the blessing
I have seen the maple tree;
The leaves have left its limbs.
It stands bare and brittle now, its spirit gone within.
And in my mind I know that deep within the earth
Its lifeblood pulses in its roots, rejuvenating strength.
How like that maple tree am I, as I go within my core,
Experiencing outer death
And inner depth once more.

evening focus
The angel of Eternal Life

371

Sunday, December 1, 2024

seasonal focus
Outer darkness calls for nourishment within.

morning focus
The angel of Earth

deepening
Hold moist earth in your hand as you read,
for your own new seed to grow in — alone.

meditation
The seed within the earth
Lies alone, awaiting.
It knows not loneliness,
But strength of purpose.
Throughout the year
I have known loneliness in crowds,
But aloneness is quite different.
I must pass through the gate
To the inner temple
Alone.

today I will bring the spirit of Aloneness to my _____
_____

feelings _____
_____
_____
_____
_____
_____
_____
_____

evening focus
The angel of Creative Work

the blessing
My inner wellspring bubbles over,
And the more I share the more I have.
Help me to be of valued service,
Yet not attached to being a server.
For the tools of service are compassion and humility,
And these are born in a loving heart,
Which is open enough to take as well as give.
From you I receive, to you I give,
Together we share, from this we live.

seasonal focus
Outer darkness calls for nourishment within.

Monday, December 2, 2024

morning focus
The angel of Life

deepening
Do nothing. Simply *be*.

meditation
As leaves fall to the earth
And surrender to the soil,
So I, too, move my attention
From my outward stance
To my inner Buddha nature.
The life in me flows back and forth
From exerting my will
To flowing with the Will of All.
And in this season of stillness,
My direction is clear
As I return unto my source.
The stillness calls to me.

today I will bring the spirit of New Beginnings to my

feelings _____

the blessing
The whispering of the candle flame
Invokes the peace within,
Reminding me of the quiet journey that I seem to be on.
I have been given a peaceful heart and a path to take me there.
May I joyfully take up this task
To reach the core of me,
And there to find all beings
Residing in my heart.

evening focus
The angel of Peace

Tuesday, December 3, 2024

seasonal focus
Outer darkness calls for nourishment within.

morning focus
The angel of Joy

opening
Surrender to the joy hidden within you
through a song or chant that sings you.
Just open your mouth and let it out.

meditation
This morning gives a song to me,
A lovely melody for me to play
Within my heart,
To give my spirit wings.
And I must close my eyes
To let the music come.
Unhurried, without force,
It yields its gift to me.
And just as gently I share this gift,
I hum this melody.
The air accepts, the world is nourished,
And I become my song.
*(Allow some song or chant to come
to you in meditation and give it wings.)*

today I will bring the spirit of Joyful Music to my
_____

feelings _____
_____
_____
_____
_____
_____
_____

evening focus
The angel of Power

the blessing
Within my being lives a silent power,
A firm, sound frame of wise and compassionate strength.
How often do I deny this gift,
This blessing from my Source?
Perhaps as the outward power of the sun recedes in winter,
I will learn to own the strength within.

seasonal focus

Wednesday, December 4, 2024

Outer darkness calls for nourishment within.

morning focus
The angel of the Sun

deepening
Focus intently on a candle flame
until you sense a merging of you and flame.

meditation
You run from me,
You who have showered me with light and warmth.
In summer's fullness was I nourished by your glow,
But now I must provide this warmth myself.
The glow must be found within my heart,
The light within my spirit.
When next we meet in summer's glory,
I will wiser be.
Till then I take your light inwardly with me.

today I will bring the spirit of Inner Glow to my _____
_____

feelings _____
_____
_____
_____
_____
_____

the blessing
(On this evening, we use the form of a love song, in the higher sense of Love.)

Love is the o-cean, Love is the o-cean, I am one with thee

Once a tiny lake, Now a mighty sea, Love, I am one with thee

Repeat, substituting the name of each person present for the word Love. If you sing the Blessing alone, use your name, and repeat the verse until you can allow it to be true for you.

evening focus
The angel of Love

Thursday, December 5, 2024

seasonal focus
Outer darkness calls for nourishment within.

morning focus
The angel of Water

deepening
Hold water in your cupped hand as you read.
Drink it in a sacred manner.

meditation
As I enter the sacred temple of inner knowing,
I purify my being to prepare myself for the initiation
That I have longed to find.
I cleanse my mind and heart
As I strip away
Whatever stands between my spirit and the source of All.
I make myself ready.
And I wait.
And it will come to me.

today I will bring the spirit of Purification to my _____
_____

★ feelings _____
_____
_____
_____
_____

_____
_____

evening focus
The angel of Wisdom

the blessing
Ancient is the one in me
That the spirit of this season,
With its quiet murmur,
Calls.
Beyond, beneath the outer me,
My wise old seer
Looks out upon the dance with compassion,
With a smile.
And the ancient one waits
For the young one to knock upon the door.
And both of them
Are me.

seasonal focus
Outer darkness calls for nourishment within.

Friday, December 6, 2024

morning focus
The angel of Air

opening
Do alternate nasal breathing slowly.
Allow yourself to die after each outbreath
and to be born anew at each inbreath.

meditation
Each life upon this earthly plane
Knows beginning and knows ending.
Each turn of the yearly wheel as well
Brings birth and death.
Each breath I take reminds me, too,
That I must die each moment
So as to bring a blessed newness
To the next breath that I take.
For if each outbreath ends in death,
Each inbreath sees me born anew,
And present to that moment.

today I will bring the spirit of Clarity to my _____

feelings _____

the blessing
Throughout the flow of passing seasons,
You have shared your Light with me.
No middle-person have I required
To walk the path with you.
For in my heart
You dwell forever,
Not in some mansion high,
And the blessings that you give to me
Come from deep inside.

evening focus
Our Heavenly Father

Saturday, December 7, 2024

seasonal focus
Outer darkness calls for nourishment within.

morning focus
Our Earthly Mother

deepening
Hold a bare twig as you meditate.
Empty yourself.

meditation
The morning calls to me
To slow my pace and be,
To ease my crowded schedule
And perhaps just sit and stare.
To focus on a burning log,
On a raindrop on a leaf,
Or to find my own image
In a flickering candle flame.
The Mother's weather urges me
To let it go, let go.
A deep primal inner voice
Is whispering…within.

today I bring the spirit of Focused Awareness to my
_____

feelings _____
_____
_____
_____
_____
_____
_____

evening focus
The angel of Eternal Life

the blessing
I have seen the maple tree;
The leaves have left its limbs.
It stands bare and brittle now, its spirit gone within.
And in my mind I know that deep within the earth
Its lifeblood pulses in its roots, rejuvenating strength.
How like that maple tree am I, as I go within my core,
Experiencing outer death
And inner depth once more.

seasonal focus
Outer darkness calls for nourishment within.

Sunday, December 8, 2024

morning focus
The angel of Earth

deepening
Hold moist earth in your hand as you read,
for your own new seed to grow in — alone.

meditation
The seed within the earth
Lies alone, awaiting.
It knows not loneliness,
But strength of purpose.
Throughout the year
I have known loneliness in crowds,
But aloneness is quite different.
I must pass through the gate
To the inner temple
Alone.

today I will bring the spirit of Aloneness to my _____

_____

feelings _____

_____

_____

_____

_____

_____

_____

_____

the blessing
My inner wellspring bubbles over,
And the more I share the more I have.
Help me to be of valued service,
Yet not attached to being a server.
For the tools of service are compassion and humility,
And these are born in a loving heart,
Which is open enough to take as well as give.
From you I receive, to you I give,
Together we share, from this we live.

evening focus
The angel of Creative Work

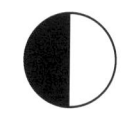

Monday, December 9, 2024

seasonal focus
Outer darkness calls for nourishment within.

morning focus
The angel of Life

deepening
Do nothing. Simply *be*.

meditation
As leaves fall to the earth
And surrender to the soil,
So I, too, move my attention
From my outward stance
To my inner Buddha nature.
The life in me flows back and forth
From exerting my will
To flowing with the Will of All.
And in this season of stillness,
My direction is clear
As I return unto my source.
The stillness calls to me.

today I will bring the spirit of New Beginnings to my
_____

feelings _____
_____
_____
_____
_____
_____
_____

evening focus
The angel of Peace

the blessing
The whispering of the candle flame
Invokes the peace within,
Reminding me of the quiet journey that I seem to be on.
I have been given a peaceful heart and a path to take me there.
May I joyfully take up this task
To reach the core of me,
And there to find all beings
Residing in my heart.

seasonal focus
Outer darkness calls for nourishment within.

Tuesday, December 10, 2024

morning focus
The angel of Joy

opening
Surrender to the joy hidden within you
through a song or chant that sings you.
Just open your mouth and let it out.

meditation
This morning gives a song to me,
A lovely melody for me to play
Within my heart,
To give my spirit wings.
And I must close my eyes
To let the music come.
Unhurried, without force,
It yields its gift to me.
And just as gently I share this gift,
I hum this melody.
The air accepts, the world is nourished,
And I become my song.
*(Allow some song or chant to come
to you in meditation and give it wings.)*

today I will bring the spirit of Joyful Music to my _____

feelings _____

_____
_____
_____
_____
_____

the blessing
Within my being lives a silent power,
A firm, sound frame of wise and compassionate strength.
How often do I deny this gift,
This blessing from my Source?
Perhaps as the outward power of the sun recedes in winter,
I will learn to own the strength within.

evening focus
The angel of Power

Wednesday, December 11, 2024

seasonal focus
Outer darkness calls for nourishment within.

morning focus
The angel of the Sun

deepening
Focus intently on a candle flame
until you sense a merging of you and flame.

meditation
You run from me,
You who have showered me with light and warmth.
In summer's fullness was I nourished by your glow,
But now I must provide this warmth myself.
The glow must be found within my heart,
The light within my spirit.
When next we meet in summer's glory,
I will wiser be.
Till then I take your light inwardly with me.

today I will bring the spirit of Inner Glow to my _____
_____

✱ feelings _____
_____
_____
_____
_____
_____

the blessing
(On this evening, we use the form of a love song, in the higher sense of Love.)

Love is the o-cean, Love is the o-cean, I am one with thee

Once a tiny lake, Now a mighty sea, Love, I am one with thee

Repeat, substituting the name of each person present for the word Love. If you sing the Blessing alone, use your name, and repeat the verse until you can allow it to be true for you.

evening focus
The angel of Love

♈ → ♉

seasonal focus

Outer darkness calls for nourishment within.

Thursday, December 12, 2024

morning focus

The angel of Water

deepening

Hold water in your cupped hand as you read.
Drink it in a sacred manner.

meditation

As I enter the sacred temple of inner knowing,
I purify my being to prepare myself for the initiation
That I have longed to find.
I cleanse my mind and heart
As I strip away
Whatever stands between my spirit and the source of All.
I make myself ready.
And I wait.
And it will come to me.

today I will bring the spirit of Purification to my _____

feelings _____

the blessing

Ancient is the one in me
That the spirit of this season,
With its quiet murmur,
Calls.
Beyond, beneath the outer me,
My wise old seer
Looks out upon the dance with compassion,
With a smile.
And the ancient one waits
For the young one to knock upon the door.
And both of them
Are me.

evening focus

The angel of Wisdom

383

Friday, December 13, 2024

seasonal focus
Outer darkness calls for nourishment within.

morning focus
The angel of Air

opening
Do alternate nasal breathing slowly.
Allow yourself to die after each outbreath and
to be born anew at each inbreath.

meditation
Each life upon this earthly plane
Knows beginning and knows ending.
Each turn of the yearly wheel as well
Brings birth and death.
Each breath I take reminds me, too,
That I must die each moment
So as to bring a blessed newness
To the next breath that I take.
For if each outbreath ends in death,
Each inbreath sees me born anew,
And present to that moment.

today I will bring the spirit of Clarity to my _____

feelings _____

evening focus
Our Heavenly Father

♉ → ♊

the blessing
Throughout the flow of passing seasons,
You have shared your Light with me.
No middle-person have I required
To walk the path with you.
For in my heart
You dwell forever,
Not in some mansion high,
And the blessings that you give to me
Come from deep inside.

seasonal focus
Outer darkness calls for nourishment within.

Saturday, December 14, 2024

morning focus
Our Earthly Mother

deepening
Hold a bare twig as you meditate. Empty yourself.

meditation
The morning calls to me
To slow my pace and be,
To ease my crowded schedule
And perhaps just sit and stare.
To focus on a burning log,
On a raindrop on a leaf,
Or to find my own image
In a flickering candle flame.
The Mother's weather urges me
To let it go, let go.
A deep primal inner voice
Is whispering…within.

today I will bring the spirit of Focused Awareness to my _____

feelings _____

the blessing
I have seen the maple tree;
The leaves have left its limbs.
It stands bare and brittle now, its spirit gone within.
And in my mind I know that deep within the earth
Its lifeblood pulses in its roots, rejuvenating strength.
How like that maple tree am I, as I go within my core,
Experiencing outer death
And inner depth once more.

evening focus
The angel of Eternal Life

385

Sunday, December 15, 2024

seasonal focus
Outer darkness calls for nourishment within.

morning focus
The angel of Earth

deepening
Hold moist earth in your hand as you read,
for your own new seed to grow in — alone.

meditation
The seed within the earth
Lies alone, awaiting.
It knows not loneliness,
But strength of purpose.
Throughout the year
I have known loneliness in crowds,
But aloneness is quite different.
I must pass through the gate
To the inner temple
Alone.

today I will bring the spirit of Aloneness to my _____
_____

feelings _____
_____
_____
_____
_____
_____
_____
_____

evening focus
The angel of Creative Work

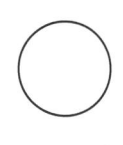

♊ → ♋

the blessing
My inner wellspring bubbles over,
And the more I share the more I have.
Help me to be of valued service,
Yet not attached to being a server.
For the tools of service are compassion and humility,
And these are born in a loving heart,
Which is open enough to take as well as give.
From you I receive, to you I give,
Together we share, from this we live.

seasonal focus
Outer darkness calls for nourishment within.

Monday, December 16, 2024

morning focus
The angel of Life

deepening
Do nothing. Simply *be*.

meditation
As leaves fall to the earth
And surrender to the soil,
So I, too, move my attention
From my outward stance
To my inner Buddha nature.
The life in me flows back and forth
From exerting my will
To flowing with the Will of All.
And in this season of stillness,
My direction is clear
As I return unto my source.
The stillness calls to me.

today I will bring the spirit of New Beginnings to my _____

feelings _____

_____

_____

_____

_____

_____

_____

the blessing
The whispering of the candle flame
Invokes the peace within,
Reminding me of the quiet journey that I seem to be on.
I have been given a peaceful heart and a path to take me there.
May I joyfully take up this task
To reach the core of me,
And there to find all beings
Residing in my heart.

evening focus
The angel of Peace

Tuesday, December 17, 2024

seasonal focus
Outer darkness calls for nourishment within.

morning focus
The angel of Joy

opening
Surrender to the joy hidden within you
through a song or chant that sings you.
Just open your mouth and let it out.

meditation
This morning gives a song to me,
A lovely melody for me to play
Within my heart,
To give my spirit wings.
And I must close my eyes
To let the music come.
Unhurried, without force,
It yields its gift to me.
And just as gently I share this gift,
I hum this melody.
The air accepts, the world is nourished,
And I become my song.
*(Allow some song or chant to come
to you in meditation and give it wings.)*

today I will bring the spirit of Joyful Music to my
_____

feelings _____
_____
_____
_____
_____
_____

evening focus
The angel of Power

the blessing
Within my being lives a silent power,
A firm, sound frame of wise and compassionate strength.
How often do I deny this gift,
This blessing from my Source?
Perhaps as the outward power of the sun recedes in winter,
I will learn to own the strength within.

seasonal focus
Outer darkness calls for nourishment within.

Wednesday, December 18, 2024

morning focus
The angel of the Sun

deepening
Focus intently on a candle flame
until you sense a merging of you and flame.

meditation
You run from me,
You who have showered me with light and warmth.
In summer's fullness was I nourished by your glow,
But now I must provide this warmth myself.
The glow must be found within my heart,
The light within my spirit.
When next we meet in summer's glory,
I will wiser be.
Till then I take your light inwardly with me.

today I will bring the spirit of Inner Glow to my _____

feelings _____

the blessing
(On this evening, we use the form of a love song, in the higher sense of Love.)

Love is the o-cean, Love is the o-cean, I am one with thee

Once a tiny lake, Now a mighty sea, Love, I am one with thee

Repeat, substituting the name of each person present for the word Love. If you sing the Blessing alone, use your name, and repeat the verse until you can allow it to be true for you.

evening focus
The angel of Love

Thursday, December 19, 2024

seasonal focus
Outer darkness calls for nourishment within.

morning focus
The angel of Water

deepening
Hold water in your cupped hand as you read.
Drink it in a sacred manner.

meditation
As I enter the sacred temple of inner knowing,
I purify my being to prepare myself for the initiation
That I have longed to find.
I cleanse my mind and heart
As I strip away
Whatever stands between my spirit and the source of All.
I make myself ready.
And I wait.
And it will come to me.

today I will bring the spirit of Purification to my _____
_____

✦ feelings _____
_____
_____
_____
_____
_____

evening focus
The angel of Wisdom

the blessing
Ancient is the one in me
That the spirit of this season,
With its quiet murmur,
Calls.
Beyond, beneath the outer me,
My wise old seer
Looks out upon the dance with compassion,
With a smile.
And the ancient one waits
For the young one to knock upon the door.
And both of them
Are me.

seasonal focus
Outer darkness calls for nourishment within.

Friday, December 20, 2024

morning focus
The angel of Air

opening
Do alternate nasal breathing slowly.
Allow yourself to die after each outbreath
and to be born anew at each inbreath.

meditation
Each life upon this earthly plane
Knows beginning and knows ending.
Each turn of the yearly wheel as well
Brings birth and death.
Each breath I take reminds me, too,
That I must die each moment
So as to bring a blessed newness
To the next breath that I take.
For if each outbreath ends in death,
Each inbreath sees me born anew,
And present to that moment.

today I will bring the spirit of Clarity to my _____

feelings _____

the blessing
Throughout the flow of passing seasons,
You have shared your Light with me.
No middle-person have I required
To walk the path with you.
For in my heart
You dwell forever,
Not in some mansion high,
And the blessings that you give to me
Come from deep inside.

evening focus
Our Heavenly Father

♌ → ♍

winter solstice

We have arrived at the longest night, when the power of the sun is at its lowest point. From this point of Solstice onward, the sun will experience a "rebirth"; that is, each day will see more and more sunlight from this Solstice until Summer Solstice when solar influence will be at its peak.

The ancient peoples used this time of "longest night" to focus on the power of darkness. Not the negative image of darkness, but the richness of that unknown, dark, fertile, deep part in each of us wherein our intuitive, creative forces abide. In modern terms, it is a time for owning one's shadow, so as to transform any negative energy associated with it into the energy of creation and psychic ability. We must accept and know our Darkness before we can fully know our Light.

The Christ energy enters the earth at this time in our yearly cycle, infusing our world with the ideal of perfection and the desire for a re-merging with the One. As the Essenes prepared for this infusion at the beginning of the Piscean Age, so do we prepare for this entry of Christ energy at this season. On the morning following Solstice, the Yule log is lighted, signifying the return of the sun (Son) after our long night of inner preparation.

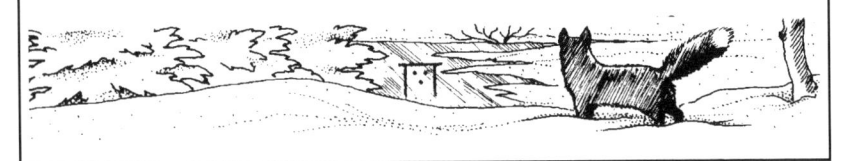

seasonal focus
The seed stirs in the earth.

morning focus
Our Earthly Mother

deepening
Hold a seed in your hand as you read the meditation.

meditation
I am bathed in an ocean
Of love and guidance
As I begin my journey
Out from the center.
All the earth nourishes me
And I return this nourishment
As love.
As the wisdom of the Mother
Slowly urges me to new awareness,
I joyfully surrender
The safety of the womb
So as to experience my part
In the unfolding plan of Light.

today I will bring the spirit of Giving to my _____
_____

feelings _____
_____
_____
_____

Saturday, December 21, 2024

This is the Winter Solstice, the longest night of the year.

the blessing
As the long night slowly yields to day,
Even as the old millennium surrenders to the new,
I, too, surrender to my next step
Which carries me toward
My natural state of limitlessness.
The winter teaches me of inner abundance,
Inner completeness,
As I now prepare for the outer learning
That this new year brings.

evening focus
The angel of Eternal Life

Sunday, December 22, 2024

seasonal focus
The seed stirs in the earth.

morning focus
The angel of Earth

deepening
Hold earth, dirt, in your hand as you read. Feel it.

meditation
From the calm place
At my spiritual center
I have touched the wisdom
Of the earth in winter.
Regeneration streams
From the holy earth to me,
And I am full.
I now gather to me the lessons
Which will empower me
To channel this life-giving earth force
For the good of all beings.

today I will bring the spirit of Calmness to my _____

feelings _____

evening focus
The angel of Creative Work

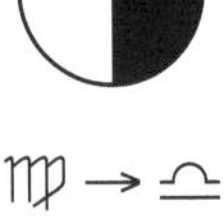

♍ → ♎

the blessing
The winter's journey
To the source of inner creativity
Now turns and guides me slowly
Toward outward manifestation.
Depth will be fulfilled in expansion
As I contemplate
My dharmic path of service.
I give thanks for the Mother's gifts
Which have brought me to this.

seasonal focus
The seed stirs in the earth.

Monday, December 23, 2024

morning focus
The angel of Life

opening
Study your face in a mirror; what do you really see? Take this awareness to your meditation.

meditation
Slowly the balance shifts from inner creativity
To outer manifestation.
Slowly my core of inner strength streams outward
Along my nervous system,
Bringing health and vitality to the whole of my being.
The life in me prepares itself,
Strengthens itself for the moment in the cycle
When it will overflow its bounds,
Surging toward a oneness with all of life.

today I will bring the spirit of Honesty to my _____

feelings _____

the blessing
I evoke the forces of peace and harmony
And ask these forces
To prepare me as a channel
For their overlighting guidance.
My heart swells with thanksgiving
For a winter of inner preparation
Which will lead me to the first step
In becoming a channel for peace:
That of finding peace within my own being.

evening focus
The angel of Peace

Tuesday, December 24, 2024

seasonal focus
The seed stirs in the earth.

morning focus
The angel of Joy

opening
Loosen all clothing. As you read,
cause your belly to hang out and relax.

meditation
Wherein lies the source of joy?
The inner peace of winter prepares me for the answer;
It shouts quietly to me,
"Do not seek happiness; seek rather
Your true nature, your true reason for being;
Seek your dharma.
Joy is the child of completeness,
Of living your dharma."
At this time of new, small beginnings,
I feel the clarity of vision growing in me,
And I am pregnant with joy.

today I will bring the spirit of Joy to my _____
_____

feelings _____
_____
_____
_____
_____

evening focus
The angel of Power

the blessing
The silent stirring of the new life in me
Fills me with an inner strength.
The strength is good;
And it comes from a place deep inside my being
That has only been reached
In the depth of ego-death.
This power I trust;
This is the power of love and compassion
The world cries out for.
The veil of illusion lifts slowly and reveals
The direction of my path.

seasonal focus
The seed stirs in the earth.

morning focus
The angel of the Sun

deepening
Focus on a candle flame before and after the reading.

meditation
The promise, the prophecy, is within me.
That which I have waited for is now present.
No longer need I fear.
Within me shines
The first glimmering of the Light,
And I am filled with the awareness
That the fulfilling of the prophecy
Is not a thing apart from me;
It *is* me.
As the first small rays of the sun
Return to my world,
I, too, return slowly to the world of form.
I humbly accept the mantle of that which I AM.
As I merge my light
With the light of all the beings of Light,
I surrender to my own divinity.

today I will bring the spirit of Courage to my _____

feelings _____

Wednesday, December 25, 2024

♑

the blessing
Life, you are a profound expression of Love.
The gentle, quiet expansion
Of the winter-mother's love
Fills me with inner joy.
I bow before the purity of this love
Which nourishes without attachment.

evening focus
The angel of Love

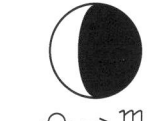

♎ → ♏
Hanukkah   Christmas

397

Thursday, December 26, 2024

seasonal focus
The seed stirs in the earth.

morning focus
The angel of Water

deepening
Hold water in your cupped hand as you read.
After, drink it as a sacred act.

meditation
As the clear winter water
Nourishes the seed within the earth,
I am nourished by new-found awareness
Of who I truly am.
This awareness has not yet fully matured,
And I rest content
In the arms of the unfolding universe,
Which will reveal all wisdom
In its time.
The Power of the unmanifest
Even now works within my spiritual heart,
And I am at peace.

today I will bring the spirit of Contentment to my _____

feelings _____
_____
_____
_____
_____
_____

evening focus
The angel of Wisdom

the blessing
I call upon my own internal voice,
Which is ever linked with the universal voice
Of inner knowing.
I ask, as I slowly move
From winter's inner development
To the first stirrings of outer work,
That I be given the strength
To trust my own still small voice,
Whose guidance is never faulty.
For this blessing I give thanks.

seasonal focus
The seed stirs in the earth.

morning focus
The angel of Air

opening
Before reading meditation, take three very deep breaths, exhaling fully so your lungs empty of air.

meditation
There is a force in me,
Pushing, pushing,
Beginning its outbreath
After a long sleep.
Sacred darkness slowly yields
To newborn light.
As I move outward
From the stillpoint of outer death
To share my new-found breath of life with all,
I shall never forget
The inbreath of the Mother
That nurtured me
Through the winter's night.

today I will bring the spirit of Newness to my _____

feelings _____

Friday, December 27, 2024

the blessing
I ask that the Light,
The Creative Force of the universe,
Breathe the cleansing outbreath of spirit
Into my heart and my deeds.
I rejoice in this time of promise,
Of new stirrings, of the rebirth of the lotus
Which will one day open fully to God.

evening focus
Our Heavenly Father

Saturday, December 28, 2024

seasonal focus
The seed stirs in the earth.

morning focus
Our Earthly Mother

deepening
Hold a seed in your hand as you read the meditation.

meditation
I am bathed in an ocean
Of love and guidance
As I begin my journey
Out from the center.
All the earth nourishes me
And I return this nourishment
As love.
As the wisdom of the Mother
Slowly urges me to new awareness,
I joyfully surrender
The safety of the womb
So as to experience my part
In the unfolding plan of Light.

today I will bring the spirit of Giving to my _____

feelings _____

evening focus
The angel of Eternal Life

the blessing
As the long night slowly yields to day,
Even as the old millennium surrenders to the new,
I, too, surrender to my next step
Which carries me toward
My natural state of limitlessness.
The winter teaches me of inner abundance,
Inner completeness,
As I now prepare for the outer learning
That this new year brings.

seasonal focus
The seed stirs in the earth.

morning focus
The angel of Earth

deepening
Hold earth, dirt, in your hand as you read. Feel it.

meditation
From the calm place
At my spiritual center
I have touched the wisdom
Of the earth in winter.
Regeneration streams
From the holy earth to me,
And I am full.
I now gather to me the lessons
Which will empower me
To channel this life-giving earth force
For the good of all beings.

today I will bring the spirit of Calmness to my _____

feelings _____

the blessing
The winter's journey
To the source of inner creativity
Now turns and guides me slowly
Toward outward manifestation.
Depth will be fulfilled in expansion
As I contemplate
My dharmic path of service.
I give thanks for the Mother's gifts
Which have brought me to this.

Sunday, December 29, 2024

evening focus
The angel of Creative Work

Monday, December 30, 2024

seasonal focus
The seed stirs in the earth.

morning focus
The angel of Life

opening
Study your face in a mirror; what do you really see? Take this awareness to your meditation.

meditation
Slowly the balance shifts from inner creativity
To outer manifestation.
Slowly my core of inner strength streams outward
Along my nervous system,
Bringing health and vitality to the whole of my being.
The life in me prepares itself,
Strengthens itself for the moment in the cycle
When it will overflow its bounds,
Surging toward a oneness with all of life.

today I will bring the spirit of Honesty to my _____
_____

feelings_____
_____
_____
_____
_____
_____
_____
_____
_____

evening focus
The angel of Peace

the blessing
I evoke the forces of peace and harmony
And ask these forces
To prepare me as a channel
For their overlighting guidance.
My heart swells with thanksgiving
For a winter of inner preparation
Which will lead me to the first step
In becoming a channel for peace:
That of finding peace within my own being.

seasonal focus
The seed stirs in the earth.

Tuesday, December 31, 2024

morning focus
The angel of Joy

opening
Loosen all clothing. As you read,
cause your belly to hang out and relax.

meditation
Wherein lies the source of joy?
The inner peace of winter prepares me for the answer;
It shouts quietly to me,
"Do not seek happiness; seek rather
Your true nature, your true reason for being;
Seek your dharma.
Joy is the child of completeness,
Of living your dharma."
At this time of new, small beginnings,
I feel the clarity of vision growing in me,
And I am pregnant with joy.

today I will bring the spirit of Joy to my _____
_____

feelings _____
_____
_____
_____
_____

the blessing
The silent stirring of the new life in me
Fills me with an inner strength.
The strength is good;
And it comes from a place deep inside my being
That has only been reached
In the depth of ego-death.
This power I trust;
This is the power of love and compassion
The world cries out for.
The veil of illusion lifts slowly and reveals
The direction of my path.

evening focus
The angel of Power

New Year's Eve

notes

MORE ON THE ESSENES

While on a smuggling expedition from Jordan to Palestine in 1947, a group of Ta'amire Bedouins paused at the only place for many miles where fresh water could be found, a spring close to the Wadi Qumran, the site of an ancient settlement. A Bedouin boy threw a rock into a cave, heard something smash, and that was the beginning of the fantastic discovery of dozens of clay jars containing the Dead Sea Scrolls, written on leather and copper. These scrolls have unraveled the mystery of an ancient network of spiritual communities that lived in this desert from about 250 B.C. to 100 A.D.

Other sources have linked many Biblical figures to the Essene tradition; John the Baptist was the teacher of Jesus in one of these communities. Mary and her cousin Elizabeth were Essene initiates, and early Christianity took much of its moral code from these simple-living communes that lived in attunement with natural and cosmic forces. In addition to the scrolls, the contemporaries of the Essenes give us a glimpse of their lives. In 20 A.D., Philo of Alexandria wrote: *They were a sect of Jews, and lived in Syria, Palestine, more than 4,000 in number, and called Essaie, because of their saintliness, for* hosio — *saintly* — *is the same word as Essaeus. Worshippers of God, they yet did not sacrifice animals, regarding a reverent mind as the only true sacrifice. At first they lived in villages and avoided cities, in order to escape the contagion of evils rife therein.*

> *They pursued agriculture and other peaceful arts, but accumulated not gold or silver, nor owned mines. No maker of warlike weapons, no huckster or trader by land or sea was to be found among them. Least of all were any slaves found among them; for they saw in slavery a violation of the law of nature, which made all people free.*
>
> *Their lifelong purity, their avoiding of oaths or falsehood, their recognition of a good providence alone showed their love of God. Their love of virtue revealed itself in their indifference to money, worldly position and pleasure. Their love of man in their kindliness, their equality, their fellowship, passing all words. For no one had a private house, but shared his dwelling with all; and, living as they did in colonies, they threw open their doors to any of their sect who came their way. They had a storehouse, common expenditure, common raiments, common food eaten in Syssitia or common meals. This was made possible by their practice of putting whatever they each earned day by day into a common fund, out of which also the sick were supported when they could not work. The aged among them were objects of reverence and honor, and treated by the rest as parents by real children.*

Josephus, who lived with the Essenes, wrote in about 75 A.D.:

> *None are to be found among them who hath more than another; for it is a law among them that those who come to them must let what they have be common to the whole order — inasmuch that among them all there is no appearance of poverty or excess of riches, but every one's possessions are intermingled with every other's possessions and so there is, as it were, one patrimony among all. They think to be sweaty is a good thing, as they do also to be clothed in white garments. They also have*

stewards appointed to take care of their common affairs, who every one of them have no separate business for any, but what is for the use of them all.

They have no certain city, but many of them dwell in every city; and if any of their sect comes from other places, what they have lies open for them, just as if it were their own; and they go into such as they never knew before as if they had been ever so long acquainted with them. For which reason they carry nothing with them when they travel into remote parts. Accordingly there is, in every city where they live, one appointed particularly to take care of strangers and to provide garments and other necessaries for them. Nor do they allow of the change of garments or of shoes till they be first entirely torn to pieces or worn out by time. Nor do they either buy or sell anything to one another, but every one of them gives what he hath to him that wanteth it and receives from him again in lieu of it what may be convenient for himself; and although there be no requital made, they are fully allowed to take what they want of whomsoever they please.

And as for their piety toward God, it is very extraordinary; for before sun-rising they speak not a word about profane matters, but put up certain prayers which they have received from their forefathers, as if they made a supplication for its rising. After this, every one of them are sent away by their curators to exercise some of those arts wherein they are skilled, in which they labor with great diligence till the fifth hour. After which they assemble themselves together again into one place; and when they have clothed themselves in white veils, they then bathe their bodies in cold water. And after this purification is over, they, every one, meet together in an apartment of their own, into which it is not permitted to any of another sect to enter; while they go, after a pure manner, into the dining room, as into a holy temple, and quietly set themselves down; upon which the baker lays them loaves in order; the cook also brings a single plate of one sort of food and set it before every one of them; and it is unlawful for any one to taste of the food before grace be said.

They dispense their anger after a just manner and restrain their passion. They are eminent for fidelity and are the ministers of peace; whatsoever they say also is firmer than an oath; but swearing is avoided by them and they esteem it worse than perjury; for they say that he who cannot be believed without swearing by God is already condemned. They also take great pains in studying the writings of the ancients and choose out of them what is most for the advantage of their soul and body; and they inquire after such roots and medicinal stones as may cure their distempers.

But now, if any one hath in mind to come over to their sect, he is not immediately admitted but he is prescribed the same method of living which they use, for a year, while he continues excluded; and they give him* a small hatchet and the aforementioned girdle and the white garment. And when he hath given evidence, during that time, that he can observe their continence, he approaches nearer to their way of living and is made a partaker of the waters of purification; yet he is not even now admitted to live with them for after this demonstration of his fortitude, his temper is tried two more years, and if he appears worthy they then admit him into their society.

*or her, for women were equal to men

The ancient documents continue on to describe a people who were masters of an even older wisdom of cosmology, astrology, herbal healing and numerology, and who could be used as models of holistic living for today's disconnected society. Their love of one another and of the Spirit, their harmony with all living things, and their understanding of universal Law stand as timeless teachings for anyone seeking to re-attune to the subtle, natural spirituality that lies behind the fragmented theology of present religion. In the bibliography are given several readily-available references which will allow you to investigate the Essene lifestyle in depth.

Jesus and the Essenes

The first small groups of Jews who retreated to the desert in approximately 250 B.C. were followers of the ancient tradition of Melkesedek. This tradition told of a being who had appeared thousands of years prior in a ball of fire, without mother or father. He was Melkesedek, the Teacher of Righteousness. He had come to tell the world that our birthright gave us a direct connection to the Godhead; that God lived in our hearts, not in some high place available only to priests and kings. In those times, this was quite radical to say or believe.

Over the centuries people forgot and a class of priests/politicians had inserted themselves between God and the people. If they wanted to communicate with their God, they had to pay a priest to sacrifice an animal, and then maybe, just maybe, the priest could intercede for them with God. The followers of Melkesedek tradition left the corruption of these cities and established communities in the desert where they could reestablish their direct God-communication. They called themselves Essaie and prepared themselves for the return of Missiayah (see "From Age to Age" on the page following January 6), which would manifest through the next Teacher of Righteousness.

As the first Essenes grew old, they realized that Missiayah was not going to return in their lifetimes and therefore, they would have to reorganize their communities so that their lineage could continue the preparations for as long as it took. The Essene desert communities then became true villages of families raising their young in the consciousness of "preparing the way" for newness, for the change that was to come. The Dead Sea Scrolls tell us that each succeeding generation became more attuned and that finally babies were being born who already were conscious of their role in the bringing of this energy of the Missiayah. One such lineage was that of Elizabeth and her kinswoman Mary, in the community of Qumran, near Mount Carmel. The scrolls indicate that Elizabeth gave birth to a conscious being who became known as the Daystar and who went to the wilderness to prepare for the imminent arrival of the Teacher of Righteousness. Was this Daystar John the Baptist?

And then Mary gave birth to a son at Qumran who grew to become the Teacher of Righteousness. (The name Jesus is not mentioned in the scrolls. However, with reference to the term Jesus of Nazareth, it seems the "Nazarine" referred not so much to a place 2000 years ago as it did to a spiritual belief, a particular way of living, and it appears that the term Nazarini and the term Essene meant the same thing. It also seems that six of the apostles were raised in the Essene tradition; Peter and his brother Andrew, Phillip, Bartholomew, James and his brother John, as well as the Nazarini, the Teacher of Righteousness.)

It is perhaps more than a coincidence that during the same years that our Bible tells us that Jesus was "in the Desert" and says no more, the scrolls tell that the Teacher of Righteousness was involved in a comprehensive educational process. He was first taken to every Essene community to learn from all the wise teachers therein. Then he was taken to India to learn the wisdom of the ancient Vedic tradition and then to Persia. After this he was led to Egypt to study with the White Brotherhood. During the last few years of his training, the scrolls fall silent about his whereabouts. The thread is perhaps picked up by another ancient tradition, in the Celtic lands now known as southern England. Glastonbury, the mystical site of the Druid Chalice Well and the spiral Tor mountain, was not always landlocked. Two thousand years ago it was the island of Avalon. Celtic legend tells of two beings from the holy land, Joseph of Arimathea and his nephew Jesus, sailing up the river to Avalon teaching, learning and bringing great joy. They left a gift, a white rose bush, that would only bloom in the midst of winter. (A cutting from a cutting of that bush still blooms through the Glastonbury snow each winter.) It was only after these far-flung teachings and initiations that the son of the Essene Mary became the receptacle of the energy of Missiayah, allowing the love of Agape to flow in the world, changing our human destiny forever.

Bibliography

Gaster, Theodore. *The Dead Sea Scriptures*. Anchor/Doubleday 1976.

Gribbin and Plagemann. *The Jupiter Effect,* Vintage 1976. (For an update, see article by Gribbin in "Omni" magazine, June 1980.)

Jackson, F. J. *Josephus and the Jews,* Baker Books 1976.

Kitter, Glenn. *Edgar Cayce on the Dead Sea Scrolls,* Warner 1973.

Lawrence, R. *The Book of Enoch,* Artisan 1980.

Levi. *The Aquarian Gospel of Jesus the Christ,* DeVorss and Co. 1976.

Spears, Ralph. "Jesus, the Essenes, and the Dead Sea Scrolls" (cassette tape), Assn. for Research and Enlightenment, Virginia, VA.

Szekely, E.B. *From Enoch to the Dead Sea Scrolls,* International Biogenic Society 1978.

_____. *The Essene Gospel of Peace, Books 1, 2, & 3.* 1978.

_____. *The Essene Jesus* 1977.

Vermes, Geza. *The Dead Sea Scrolls in English,* Pelican 1962.

About Danaan Parry

On November 14, 1996, the world lost one of its finest citizens. Danaan Parry suffered a massive heart attack and passed away on Bainbridge Island, Washington. Despite this immense loss, Danaan's gifts as a global visionary will continue to bless the human family for generations to come. His commitment to positive change through the expansion of human consciousness was relentless; he never stopped dreaming up ways to awaken ourselves to our full potential.

Danaan John Raymond Parry, born in Orange, New Jersey, spent his childhood on the Jersey shore. Later he became a helicopter pilot in the U.S. Coast Guard and spent a year at the North Pole, a year at the South Pole, then served as skipper of a search-and-rescue vessel in New York Harbor.

After working as a research physicist with the United States Atomic Energy Commission, he became a clinical psychologist and served on the faculty of the Graduate Theological Union in Berkeley, California.

A harrowing near-death experience on a deserted Kauai beach led him to a year of isolation. After meeting Mother Teresa in Bombay, he realized the need to bring spirituality down off the mountain and created the Holy Earth Foundation in 1980. Through this foundation—now known as the Earthstewards Network—Danaan's work in conflict resolution developed around the world.

He worked in Northern Ireland, bringing together people from the Catholic and Protestant sides. He brought teenagers from conflicted cultures together to reforest the earth and to become friends in the process. In 1983, he helped create the spirit of Citizen Diplomacy by bringing groups of Soviet citizens to the USA and by taking American citizens to the former Soviet Union, to melt the fear and prejudice that had often divided the people of these cultures.

Danaan's ability to help people touch the humanity behind the image of the "enemy" brought him international recognition and endeared him to thousands of friends around the world. He was as comfortable with kings and queens and heads of state as with families and shopkeepers in the most remote villages.

Through his *Warriors of the Heart* trainings, thousands of people in many countries were inspired to tap their own natural ability to resolve conflict and lead more effective lives. Danaan believed deeply in the necessity of creating collaborative models of global leadership for women and men, and co-created the *Essential Peacemaking Women and Men* program with his wife, Jerilyn Brusseau.

Danaan's most recent gift to the world was his vision of reconciling the aftermath of war by calling forth the cooperation of former enemies to remove landmines left from the Vietnam war. Once cleared, the land is then revitalized through tree planting by international citizens working with Vietnamese citizens.

This bold program and the work of the Earthstewards Network symbolize Danaan's commitment to practical mysticism: inspiring individuals to take action in circumstances which seem hopeless and out of reach.

Earthstewards Network

The Earthstewards Network (ESN) began in 1979, envisioned initially as a network of those who care for the earth and its inhabitants, and a support group for peaceful, positive earth-stewardship. The ESN expanded greatly over the next 17 years, including projects and programs in conflict resolution, citizen diplomacy, and global communication. In 1996, the sudden death of Danaan Parry, co-founder, impacted world-wide membership and reduced many of the ongoing programs. Danaan's legacy continues to inspire, connecting us at the heart and assuring us that we are not alone in our individual efforts to co-create a more human, sustainable future for each and every one of us. There are still members worldwide, each making changes locally and globally, creating positive alternatives, and finding ways to say YES to a better future for all of us.

Being an Earthsteward is a state of consciousness, a state of mind that increases awareness and stirs compassion, driving one to action. ESN is alive and well in the hearts and minds of those who were mentored and inspired by Danaan, and by one another. There is a tremendous wealth of compassion and wisdom at work in the world today that was seeded, influenced, and nurtured by ESN.

All over the world, women and men are waking up to the importance of creating new models of leadership. The Earthstewards Network has created precedents in people-to-people exchanges throughout the world. We have arranged for Soviet and American families to visit the homes of each other. We have lived in Northern Ireland homes, and hosted Northern Irish in the U.S. We have traveled to Europe, Central America, the Middle East, India, Nepal and Tibet (China). We have brought together war veterans from both sides to share their pain and to look for new alternatives.

Since 1987, the PeaceTrees program has empowered people throughout the world to learn how to work together and to discover how they can make positive changes in their own neighborhoods and communities. Whether they are ripping up 20 tons of concrete in Washington, D.C., planting 80,000 seedlings along an eroded river bank in Costa Rica, or reclaiming desert in Southern India, participants learn communication and conflict resolution skills needed to create lasting trust.

PeaceTrees Vietnam—the 20th International PeaceTrees program and Danaan's final legacy—pioneered a bold effort to reconcile the aftermath of war. Since 1996, the project has provided a model for humanitarian landmine clearance through cooperation of former adversaries, and for ordinary citizens from around the world to plant indigenous trees on the cleared land. Today, PeaceTrees Vietnam's work continues in Quang Tri Province, providing ongoing clearance of landmines and unexploded ordnance, and sustaining families living with these threats daily. PeaceTrees Vietnam has established its own 501(C)(3) tax exempt organization (www.peacetreesvietnam.org) and has built the Danaan Parry Landmines Education Center for Children in Quang Tri Province, where more than 32,500 trees have been planted.

Several other projects that were part of the Earthstewards Network have gone on to become their own 501(C)(3) tax exempt organizations. If you have access to the internet, you can find out more about Earthstewards Network and our past projects by going to our website: www.earthstewards.org. You may also email publishing@earthstewards.org for more information.

Earthstewards Network is a 501(C)(3) tax exempt organization. Donations are tax deductible.

You are invited to become a part of

The Earthstewards Network

When you become an Earthsteward, you get connected to a group of people who still feel drawn to, and carry on, the concepts and philosophy of the Earthstewards Network as conceived and developed by Danaan Parry. You may participate in any trainings, trips and gatherings. For many years after Danaan's death, gatherings continued in Europe, where people came together to joyfully learn and laugh and connect. There is currently little going on in the Earthstewards Network. Our web site has information about projects that grew out of Earthstewards Network, although not all of the information is current. http://earthstewards.org/ESN-ProjProg.asp

We gladly accept donations. Through your donations and the publication of Danaan's books, we make every attempt to keep the work and the spirit of the Earthstewards Network alive and viable. Please make checks payable to the Earthstewards Network.

· to contact us ·

Our mailing address is :
Earthstewards
1425 Cowgill Ave
Bellingham, WA 98225-8016

Contact us or visit the Earthstewards Network web site for more information.
www.earthstewards.org   publishing@earthstewards.org   800-561-2909

notes

notes

notes

peace
be with
you

Printed in Great Britain
by Amazon